RELIGIOUS THOUGHTS IN PERSPECTIVE

AN INTRODUCTION TO CONCEPTS, APPROACHES, AND TRADITIONS

Ibigbolade Simon Aderibigbe

The University of Georgia

cognella

San Diego, CA

Bassim Hamadeh, CEO and Publisher
Christopher Foster, General Vice President
Michael Simpson, Vice President of Acquisitions
Jessica Knott, Managing Editor
Kevin Fahey, Cognella Marketing Manager
Jess Busch, Senior Graphic Designer
Zina Craft, Acquisitions Editor
Jamie Giganti, Project Editor
Brian Fahey, Licensing Associate

First published in the United States of America in 2012 by Cognella, Inc.

Trademark Notice: Product or corporate names may be trademarks or registered trademarks, and are used only for identification and explanation without intent to infringe.

Images of Star of David, Pendant Mask, Makonde Carving, Queen's Mother Stool, Five Elements, Wall Painting, Baba in Kathmandu, Dharma Wheel, and Kopan Monastery cleared via Creative Commons CC0 1.0 Universal Public Domain Dedication, Attribution 2.0 Generic License, Attribution 2.5 Generic License, and Creative Commons Attribution-Share Alike 3.0 Unported License. Queen's Mother Stool used courtesy of The Children's Museum of Indianapolis.

All other images copyright in the public domain.

16 15 14 13 12   1 2 3 4 5

Printed in the United States of America

ISBN: 978-1-60927-203-6

www.cognella.com 800.200.3908

CONTENTS

PART III: RELIGIOUS TRADITIONS

DEDICATION

To

My late parents,
Omoparusi and Folashade Aderibigbe;

My wife,
Moradeke Abimbola;

My children,
Moronkeji,
Oluwaninyo,
and Ifedolapo;

My students, past, present, and future;

and

All from whom I obtained knowledge, to make it available to others.

Preface & Acknowledgments

RELIGIOUS THOUGHTS IN PERSPECTIVE: *An Introduction to Concepts, Approaches, and Traditions* is a product of over three decades of research and teaching of courses in the Phenomenology of religion, Philosophy of Religion, Comparative Study of Religion, Sociology of Religion, Ethics, and Religious Traditions comprising Judaism, Christianity, Islam, African indigenous religion and Asian religions. The book also has "progenitors" in my earlier published books. The first was titled *Introduction to Religion* and was published in 1988; the second, an edited volume, titled *Religion: Study and Practice*, was published in 1988 and reprinted in 2001.

This book is divided into three unique parts in a continuum. The first part covers concepts in religion such as its definition, origin, its study, and religious symbols. The second part focuses on different approaches in the study of religion such as philosophical, sociological, ethical, and comparative. The focus of the third part is on world religious traditions. Those discussed are indigenous religion, Judeo-Christianity, Islam, and some Asiatic religions. Thus, the book covers issues that are not only current, but relevant and important to students, scholars, and others interested in an in-depth academic study of religion in all its perspectives.

Overall, the objective of the book is to present an anthology, with a rear insight into the study of religion, both from the theoretical, methodical, and practical perspectives, strategically objective without the overbearing burden of injecting personal preferences. Thus, the contents are "scholarly without being pedantic."

I am eternally indebted to a number of people without whose intellectual, moral, and filial contributions and support, the completion of this book would have been a mirage. My acknowledgment and gratitude start from the "home front." My wife, Moradeke, and children, Moronkeji, Oluwaninyo, and Ifedolapo, have showered loving support which has been a "lamp unto my feet" in over three decades of my teaching and research career. I must also give honorable mention to Dr. A. O. Olukunle. He was not only my supervisor for both my Masters and PhD projects, but more importantly, he is my mentor and friend—always. As I usually state in all my publications, Dr. A. O. Olukunle is the "cup" from which I tasted and drank philosophical waters to nourishing and productive fullness. I am also most indebted to Dr. Alloy S. Ihuah (Professor of Philosophy) of the Department of Religion and Philosophy, Benue State University, Makurdi, Nigeria. Apart from being a friend and distinguished colleague, he also graciously agreed to write the foreword of this book.

A colleague, who is also my close friend—Rev. Fr. Dejo Faniran, PhD, the Director, Center for the Study of African Culture and Communication, Catholic Institute of West Africa (CIWA), Port Harcourt, Nigeria, deserves my singular gratitude for his intellectual contributions in reading through and providing the much needed peer reviews that have significantly improved the scholarly standard of the book. Also, I am greatly indebted to the faculty and students of the Department of Religion and African Studies Institute of the University of Georgia, Athens, United States. I have enjoyed the necessary conducive and stimulating environment to teach and research since I joined the university in August 2008. I owe the completion of this work ultimately to that "luxury."

This acknowledgment would be incomplete without paying tribute to my late parents—my father, Joseph Omoparusi Aderibigbe, and my mother, Elizabeth Folasade Aderibigbe. They were the "vessels" of my existence, upbringing, and education, by virtue of which I have become useful in my own "limited" ways to humanity.

Finally and above all else, I pay homage to the *Almighty God*—the *Beginner* and *Finisher* of all things. Without Him, *NOTHING* would have "come to pass in *time* and in *space*."

It is my hope and prayer that all those who read this book will find it useful to humanity and to the glory of God.

Ibigbolade Aderibigbe, PhD
Department of Religion/African Studies Institute
The University of Georgia, Athens, USA
March 2012

FOREWORD

In recent years, African scholars have made tremendous intellectual contributions to world scholarship traversing the fields of science and the humanities. The likes of Placid Tempels, Jahn Edward Taylor, John Mbiti, Awolalu, Bolaji Idowu, Akpenpuun Dzurgba, and now, Simon Ibigbolade Aderibigbe among many others, have in particular, left impressive intellectual footprints in the field of Religion and Philosophy. This is so because Africans are notoriously religious, and each people has its own religious systems with a set of beliefs and practices. Such strong dogma is most obviously the grounding thesis of this book, *RELIGIOUS THOUGHTS IN PERSPECTIVE: An Introduction to Concepts, Approaches, and Traditions.*

The book anticipates Mbiti's chronic conviction that religion permeates into all the departments of life so fully that it is not easy or possible always to isolate it. In one fell swoop, the book ambitiously prompts the thesis that religion (but all religious traditions) is the strongest element in human affairs, and exerts the greatest influence upon the thinking and living of the peoples of the world. Written in three parts covering twelve chapters, the book traverses the subject matter of a standard text on comparative religion, i.e., conceptual issues dealing with such matters as definition, origin and development of religion, the study of religion, and religious symbols. Part Two encapsulates the varied approaches in the study of religion detailing the philosophical, sociological, ethical, and comparative approaches. Part Three, the last section, devotes itself to an evaluation of a number of living faiths (a discourse on religious traditions) which includes African, Judeo-Christian, Arabico/Islamic, and Asiatic religious traditions. As the title implies, the book gives its readers full and authoritative knowledge on the entire cycle of world religion, thus ranking it as one of the leading authorities in the field of comparative religion.

Bursting with intellectual energy and ambition, the book distinguishes itself and ranks among the first category of informative studies, combining three typologies (methods) of a standard book on comparative religion—namely, the informative, whose purpose is to review in detail the beliefs and practices of various religious systems; the analytic, which presumes on information and goes on to evaluate a number of living (archaic) faiths according to certain normative principles; and the projective, where an author combines factual data and personal theory to anticipate what the future of man's religion may (or should) be like. A combination of these strategies earns this book the title of a phenomenological study of religion. In addition, the book strives to unmask the nothingness in religious bigotry. It thus sees every benefit in the unity of the different religious traditions and cultural groups to reach out of their "ghetto" mentality of isolationism, exclusivism, and denominationalism. With this, the book opines that the morality of the society is enhanced, peace, harmony, prosperity, and discipline are promoted, and universal blessings are assured. After all, our humanity and our gateway to the humanity of others lie in believing in the uniqueness of ourselves and in accepting ourselves as the mouthpiece of true understanding and inclusive acceptance.

Well researched, written and presented in lucid and straightforward language, the book treats the traditions, beliefs, and practices of the major contemporary religions of the world from both the within and without perspectives, and with thoroughness and objectivity. Each chapter is written in clear and penetrating style. Having taught African and Asian philosophy myself for the past twenty years, I can vouch that the author has succeeded brilliantly in making the religions (philosophies) of the West, Africa, and Asia not only sufficiently comprehensible, but he has done so in an intelligent and sympathetic appreciation.

Undoubtedly, Dr. Aderibigbe has made a rationally persuasive and ultimately convincing point that differences between peoples in beliefs and values, political, and social systems are assets rather than liabilities. Like Radhakrisnon, a Hindu philosopher, Aderibigbe eventuates that believers with different opinions and convictions are necessary to each other and should not waver in their determination that the whole human community shall remain a united people, where indigenous worshipers, Muslims, Christians, Buddhists, Hindus, and others shall stand together, bound by a common devotion—not to something behind, but to something ahead, not to a radical past or a geographic unit, but to a great dream of a world society with a universal religion of which the historical faiths are but branches.

The author's broadmindedness, objectivity, comprehensiveness, and scholarship are evidenced throughout the work. These are achieved by his painstaking recourse to primary as well as the most important secondary material sources, with a demonstration of a rear capability of impartial and tolerant critical appraisal. This book should invigorate contemporary scholarship in Religion and Philosophy. It is, therefore, highly recommended to all serious students, scholars, and the general reader.

Alloy S. Ihuah, PhD
Professor of Philosophy
Benue State University,
Makurdi, Nigeria
March 2012

PART I

CONCEPTUAL ISSUES

CHAPTER ONE

DEFINING RELIGION

INTRODUCTION

D efining religion has never been a straightforward and uncomplicated "task." In fact, and strangely enough, it might be said that attempts to define religion have thrived on more controversies than those of the so-called "worldly" subjects. By any means, the problems associated with defining religion are not a result of lack of attempted definitions. Indeed, there are hundreds of these (a situation which in itself constitutes a considerable problem). Rather, and most probably, the real puzzle here has to do with ambiguity as well as the triviality that the multiplicity of definitions has brought to bear on the subject. This has led to the raising of salient questions on whether it is necessary to engage in the task of defining religion at all; whether there is a need for it; and whether something of value is even likely to accrue from the exercise.

Even when it has been accepted that the task is desirable, further debates suffice on the following pertinent questions:

- What are the constraints that have prevented a "breakthrough" to a largely objective and acceptable definition(s) of religion?
- What can one say to have constituted the assets and limitations of definitions that have been attempted in the past?
- Are there guidelines to be followed so that we could at least have acceptable standards for defining religion?
- Is an operational definition or explanation of religion possible in such a way that what may be aptly referred to as "religious experience" may be adequately expressed?

These are the primary issues that inform this chapter.

POSSIBILITY AND NECESSITY OF DEFINING RELIGION

The problem here is ultimately involved in the question of the significance of defining religion, to determine why the attempt to define religion and subject the need for such an exercise to preconceived skepticism. This line of reasoning may have been largely informed by the anthropologists' conception of religion as a universal phenomenon, indeed a common one. Is there, then, strictly speaking, a need for a definition of such a phenomenon?

It is in answering this question that opinions and standpoints become divergent. Some have insisted that the definition of religion is neither needed nor, in fact, possible. For example, C. C. J. Webb is a typical apostle of scholars in this school of thought. He uses Durkheim's definition of religion to make his point. Durkheim's definition stipulates that religion is in the realm of the "sacred" and the "profane" (Durkheim, 1971). If this is true then, in Webb's view, definitions of religion are not needed. This is because what religion means would be quite obvious, in that everyone would know what it means to hold a thing to be sacred better than any definition can tell us, as in the case of what it means to designate things beautiful, which is better than any definition of beauty can provide (Webb, 1916). In addition, Webb is even prepared to submit that, in the particular case of religion, a definition is not possible, in that religion is "something" that can only be felt; therefore, to describe it in words is to distort its very nature (Webb, 1916).

Richard Gombrich also holds a similar view. In his own case, he opines that defining religion is essentially trivial and even futile. To him, it is possible, as he has often done, to discuss religion in general terms without attempting to define it, as everyone knows what is being talked about. He then concludes that in any case, the problems of definitions are essentialist problems, thus essentially trivial (Gombrich, 1971).

The two views above, to our mind, vividly represent how people may hold (though often erroneously) that simply because everyone knows what is meant by religion, there is no need to define it. We say "erroneously" because if we critically examine the postulations of Webb and Gombrich, they may be disposed of as mere smoke screens. For example, in the case of Webb, his submission for the impossibility of defining religion in itself, paradoxically, constitutes a form of definition of religion. But unfortunately, a definition that makes an academic study of religion as a unique phenomenon impossible. For it allows religion to remain open only for the "true believer," thus stressing only the esoteric character of religion to the negligence of the esoteric nature of religion, which, we believe, is equally important.

In the case of Gombrich, it is gratifying to note that it actually became impossible for him to sustain his stand as he eventually succumbed to the sociological understanding of religion. Our contention, therefore, is that the kind of understanding provided by Webb, Gombrich, and their ilk is neither sufficient nor in fact desirable in tackling the problem of defining religion. Thus, their positions on the problem are unacceptable even on the common-sense level of discussion.

We therefore wish to subscribe to the view that a definition of religion is not only possible but absolutely necessary, and may be approached from two basic angles. First, from the normative or substantive perception, whereby an attempt is made to reveal the very essence of religion or religions. This may generally come at the conclusion of research into or discussions about religion.

Secondly, there are the operational definitions, which are more used at the beginning of the work of any researcher or discussant in religion as guides to intentions and delimitations.

However, there is the question as to whether this kind of distinction is, in fact, desirable or as clear-cut as is often asserted. We must accept that there are attendant problems and implications for approaching the definition of religion through either of these two ways. In any case, whatever objections are raised and responses made to them can only further constitute the very need or significance, rather than the impossibility or triviality of defining religion. For as Spiro (1966) succinctly points out:

> Unless we already know by definition what religion is, how can we know which "concrete reality" we are to consider? Only if religion has already been defined can we perform this initial operation or the subsequent one disengaging those elements which are shared by all religions (p. 91).

Thus, following the position of Spiro, it may be impossible to engage in any study of religion without undertaking some preliminary definition of religion. Where this is not done, there is the danger of everything being open to inquiry, which may ultimately lead to a lack of specification in the study of religion. Thus, if for nothing else, a definition of religion is necessary to "point out" the phenomena to be investigated.

We may at this stage point out that the assertion of the possibility and necessity for defining religion does not, strictly speaking, call for distinguishing in an absolute or arbitrary way between what has been earlier referred to as essential or normative definitions from operational ones. Even if it is agreed that this kind of distinction may be useful in a pragmatic procedure, a purely operational definition that is separated from the normative or essential type may ultimately become unnecessary, arbitrary, and consequently of no use in delimiting the subject matter for investigation.

In fact, there is the danger of such a definition becoming enumerative or denotative in seeing "such" as all and only those things included in the following listed systems are to be regarded as "religious things," e.g., Christianity, Islam, Judaism, Hinduism, Buddhism, etc. With this kind of stipulation, a definition cannot escape the indictment of arbitrariness and even irrationality. For it may be called upon to justify, if not explicit, then the implicit reasons for including the stipulated and excluding the non-stipulated.

Robert Baird (1971), in criticizing this form of definition, refers to it as the "essential-intuitional method" of defining religion, which tends to proceed as if the word "religion" corresponds to something that has unequivocal status, in which case the word could be regarded as unambiguous and that the reality and the essence which it deals with is intuitively identifiable.

The only means by which this pitfall could be avoided is to regard a definition of religion as being essential in "taking off" in the study or discussion of religion and not necessarily ascribing to such a definition the task of locating and stipulating once and for all the rigid essence of religion. This is done usually by making stratified and exclusive assumptions of the possible inclusive types of phenomena that may be "acceptably" counted as religious.

Spiro and Ferre provide some directions here. In the case of Spiro, he suggests two criteria for such a definition, namely, that it must first be cross-cultural applicative and second, intercultural intuitive. Ferre adds a third complementary criterion to the two offered by Spiro. To him, if a definition is to be useful, it must depict a responsibility of cruciality—in which case the definition must be able to "slice the universe at what, for our purpose, are its natural joints," so that even if it is stipulative and arbitrary it must be informed by the fact that:

… there are discoverable uniformities or resemblances in our experiences, with various degrees of pervasiveness, obviousness or importance for shared human interests. These are the uniformities which have been applied to them, and it is at the major intersections of such uniformities that we are likely to find our most crucial interests delineated (F. Ferre, 1987).

CONSTRAINTS OR CONFORMITY IN DEFINING RELIGION

Having attempted to set out submissions that defining religion is possible and is indeed needed and desirable, if we are not to wander off course when we undertake the study or discussion of religion, it may be very unlikely that we shall ever attain uniformity or objectivity in defining the phenomenon known as "religion." This is why there have been, and will continue to be, numerous and almost irreconcilable definitions of religion in terms of being varied and "apart" in content, usage, and approach.

As Yinger (1970) points out, if one is given an hour in a library worth its salt, he is likely to easily list over one hundred definitions, resembling themselves only in relation to the subject matter, but definitely neither in verbal expression nor contents of thought. Also, J. B. Pratt, in reporting Prof. Leuba, said that the professor failed to convince himself of any persuasive definition of religion, after he had listed forty-eight definitions of prominent scholars and added two of his own (Aderibigbe, Gbola, 1988).

These two views aptly demonstrate the difficulty that a search for conformity in defining religion is likely to entail. That is, if this is at all attainable. We are by no means claiming that this kind of difficulty is limited to defining religion, as most subjects, if not all, suffer the same fate when it comes to the question of definition and interpretation. There has been hardly any form of consensus on what these should be or how they could be approached.

When it comes to the constraints responsible for this state of affairs, as far as religion is concerned, the first line of constraints that may be held responsible for this is the diverse interests and standpoints from which the definitions are offered. A significant convincing argument that may be advanced is that since religion is multifaceted and is a phenomenon that is approached from varying points and "stations," the definitions propounded in the processes must of necessity be divergent in approaches and applications.

However, we believe that the problem is more fundamental than this. It needs to be addressed more dispassionately and seriously rather than conceding to the superficial persuasion the above states. Consequently, we identify the following reasons (among others) that may be available to the reader, as being responsible for the exclusive multiplicity of definitions of religion.

+ As we earlier pointed out, the attempt to distinguish normative or essential definitions from operational or functional ones definitely constitutes one of the fundamental reasons for divergence in defining religion. For while the former are seen generally coming at the beginning to guide the researcher, the latter are provided as conclusions at the end of such researches or studies. If this distinction is then sustained, it would be indeed farfetched to expect resemblances in the definitions that are likely to emerge from these two opposing "stations." Invariably, the formulation and stipulations contained in the definitions of the propagators of the first type are bound to be largely unacceptable to propagators of the second type, while the propagators of the first type are certain to regard the second type as inadequate.

+ In line with the above is the fact that the majority of those who had concerned themselves with the task of defining religion have done so from the theoretical perspective. In which case most of such definitions have failed to take cognizance of the overriding emotional and spiritual involvement that should characterize such definitions. The main factor that has been identified as responsible for this is the fact that proponents of definitions concern themselves with engaging in the theoretical or expressive explanation of what religion is. This is unlike practitioners of religion, who are more concerned with "living" the religious experience and seem to be immured from the kind of academic curiosity that spurs the scholars to provide definitions for religion.

+ A further obstacle to conformity in defining religion may derive basically from the fact that scholars who have propagated definitions have hardly made their positions clear when doing so. As a result, it has always been very difficult to assert if the definition offered is from the viewpoint of acceptance of and sympathy toward religion or that of rejection or even antagonism toward religion.

+ A more basic problem may have to do with the nature of religion itself. Essentially, a genuine religion should contain a reciprocal relationship between the secular and the supernatural, between the human and the divine. Granted, the definitions could take care of the human aspect (and this is even doubtful), the grasping of the divine initiative in religion posits bewildering difficulties of aspiring to define the unknown, which at best could only be classified as "mysterious."

CRITICAL APPRAISAL OF SOME EXISTING DEFINITIONS OF RELIGION

In spite of the constraints enumerated above, many definitions of religion have been formulated by scholars. Thus it was possible, as we earlier indicated, for J. B. Pratt to report the complication of Leuba. This depicts that both normative and operational formulations have been approached, mainly from various perspectives or disciplines of their propagators. These include etymological, sociological, psychological, moral, acculturalistic, divine, and mysterious definitions. Our critical appraisal of various authors' definitions of religion here, under the categories enumerated above, is with the primary objective of determining their search for a definition(s) that could, to some objective measure, provide an essential representation of what we mean when the phenomenon of religion comes up for discussion.

MORAL PERSPECTIVE—DEFINITIONS

When approached from the moral point of view, two definitions of religion readily come to mind. These are the explications offered by Immanuel Kant and F. H. Bradley. First that of Kant (Idowu, 1979), who saw religion as the recognition of duties arising from divine commands. He said:

Religion is the belief which sets what is essential in all adoration of God in human morality. … Religion is the law in us, insofar as it obtains emphasis from lawgiver and judge over us. It is a morality directed to the recognition of God (p. 71).

It is not surprising that Kant paraphrased religion in this way. This is because he had always postulated that the idea of the Supreme Being arose from man's awareness of the moral law. In this regard, the basic asset of the definition may be said to be largely contained in the well-known truism that religion essentially depends on a relationship that is based on mutual agreement between the devotees and their objects of devotion. The conventional natures of Judaism in the Old Testament and Christianity in the New Testament underline this position. This has made the moral element crucial in conforming to the conventional arrangement in most religions.

However, Kant's definition becomes faulty in his attempt to equate morality with religion. Even if we accept that the source of morality is divine, since it is derived from God, morality could only be an offspring of religion. To ascribe more to it is to put the cart before the horse in stressing the law before accepting the lawgiver. Put in the proper perspective, the lawgiver must first be recognized and accepted. It is only after this that the law, when accepted, would have meaning and relevance, consequently leading to genuine fulfillment of the moral duty.

Secondly, there is the definition of F. H. Bradley (1969), who explained religion as "the attempt to express the complete reality of goodness through every aspect of our being" (p. 405).

Just as in the case of Kant, Bradley has only succeeded in equating religion with morality. However, this effort of syncretizing has not met with the favorable dispositions of thinkers. Karl Marx, for example, against the background of his doubt of the usefulness of religion, viewed Bradley's attempt as one of those supporting the moral norms of the privileged and the ruling class. To him, the very reason why religion should be rejected is that it restricts human freedom and moral responsibility, which should form the fundamental basis of religion. If Bradley's definition were to be accepted, to Marx this would not be so, in that, as he claims, "individuals or groups whose only reason for being morally upright is the fear of supernatural punishment cannot be counted upon to respect other persons once their fears lose hold of them."

SOCIOLOGICAL APPROACH

Emile Durkheim's (1981) definition of religion is predominantly and aptly representative of definitions of religion that are sociologically based. He defines religion as, "A unified system of beliefs and practices which unite into one moral community called a church, all those adhere to them" (p. 560).

The only positive thing that could be said about Durkheim's definition is the sociological tendency it gives to religion and its practice. However, the problem with this definition is its potentiality of admitting into the religious phenomenon all matters that constitute an obligation to a society. This may unwittingly open the door for secular concepts such as communism, capitalism, and nationalism to adorn the garb of religiosity.

Apart from these, the definition seems to restrict religions to the so-called revealed institutionalized or organized religions, to the detriment of other religions, such as primal religions and orient religions.

PSYCHOLOGICAL APPROACH DEFINITIONS

The definition by J. B. Pratt is clearly drawn from the psychological approach. Having cautioned that religion should not be seen as a law, a hypothesis, or a doctrine, he went on to define religion as "a service and social attitude of individuals in a community towards a power which they regard as having control over their interests and destiny." With this definition, Pratt may be said to have designated religion a phenomenon that involves the whole of man.

The strong points in favor of the definition consist in its provision for the attitude of the self toward an object in love, in which the whole personality of the believer is fully involved and devoid of mechanical manipulations.

However, the definition is found defective in its wideness or generalization, without any conscious attempt to clearly pinpoint specifics. Thus, it is rendered too obscure. This, of course, understandably stems from Pratt's psychological bias in attempting to define religion in a manner that all those who claim or project religious behaviors and attitudes maybe adequately embraced.

Another definition with psychological traits is that of Schleiermacher (Idowu, 1979). It states:

> ... universe is an uninterrupted activity and at the very moment reveals itself to us ... it is religion to take up into our life and to allow ourselves to be moved in these influences. ... The one thing and everything in religion is to face all that moves us our feeling (p. 71).

This definition clearly depicts religion as ultimately constituting a feeling of absolute dependence on God. This, of course, shows God as indispensable and thus accepts and confirms man's limitations as a creature of God. The problem with the definition, however, is that it absolutely restricts religion to the realm of one element in man and that is his psychic composition. Thus, all that is religious in man is bonded up in his feelings.

Some have seen this position taken by Schleiermacher as a reaction or protest against defining religion from the intellectualist perspective. However, in doing this, he has gone to the other extreme; thus falling victim to the same weakness sought to be rectified in others.

Also, the definition is—to say the least—very confusing in that it is very difficult to grasp the actual object of the religion defined here by Schleiermacher. Is it the universe, as a self-directing force, or is it God? In which case, the universe, as a created order, only offers man the creative and redemptive activities of God.

MYSTICAL-CUM-DIVINE-ORIENTED DEFINITIONS

Three definitions from the mystical and divine perspective are clearly noticeable among the definitions of religion so far offered. These are the definitions offered by Rudolf Otto, A. C. Bouquet, and Max Müller.

In his book *The Idea of the Holy*, Rudolf Otto defines religion as the awareness of an "awe" that instills a unique blend of fear and fascination of the divine. This consists in what he calls the *Mysterium Tremendum*—which is the wholly otherness of the divine. The Old Testament prophets *such* as Isaiah, Jeremiah, Amos, and others must have encountered this "awe" of God and were thus unable to escape from the compelling otherness of Yahweh, about whom they prophesied against their own wish. This awe—*numinus*, meaning mighty—is the supernatural reality which is mysterious and at the same time infinite and completely different from all other human experience. A contact with this reality evokes two contradicting yet blending reactions, a paralyzing feeling of fear and a compelling attraction.

Otto's (1958) definition is certainly significant in that it not only identifies the object of man's religion, but actually goes further to set out the qualities of the object. However, the definition has been objected to on a number of grounds. First, Otto seems to delight in portraying the supernatural reality as a fearful and unapproachable Supreme Being. While this conception of the Supreme Being might have been more at home in the Old Testament, the father figure, loving, and benevolent nature of the Christian God and God as conceived by some other religions render Otto's definition an uncomfortable one to accept. Further, the definition would be hard put to take care of all religious persuasions. Indeed, there are universally recognized religions (for example, Buddhism) which lack a concept of the nature of the Supreme Being as portrayed by Otto. These oriental religions are more preoccupied with the thoughts of stressing man's oneness with the encompassing universe.

In his own case, A. C. Bouquet (1945) defines religion as:

> The relationship between the human-self and the non-human entity—which is the sacred, the supernatural, the self-existent; or simply—God (p. 17).

This relationship, as far as Bouquet is concerned, is the "way." This definition, no doubt, represents by and large what religion meant to many Jewish religious leaders. For example, Judaism was seen and called the "way of the Pharisees." Also, Christianity is often referred to as the "way" in the Acts of the Apostles. The conception of religion as the "way" constitutes the strong point of Bouquet's definition, in that in showing religion as the "way," there is implication of direction. Thus, there is the indication that there is a goal or a purpose for religion. In which case, anyone who practices it knows what he is out for and the proper way to go about achieving it.

In Max Müller's definition, one finds a strong stressing of the divine, when he renders religion as "The perception of the infinite on its face value." Thus, the definition may be taken to have provided for the two major parts in religion: namely the subject (man) who perceives and the object (infinite Being) that is perceived. The definition further shows that the perception should be an all-involving one, demanding positive activities from the subject.

However, upon closer examination of the definition, a number of shortcomings raise some objections against it. First, Müller has not been able to identify clearly what he means by "infinite." This may lead to confusion and possible misrepresentation. The "infinite," taken as presented here, could be anything: probably man or one of the numerous gods? Or whatever being anyone examining the definition wishes to identify with. This is certainly not good enough and leaves much to be desired in such an important subject as religion.

Second, the word "perception" is by itself ambiguous and could be employed for a number of notions. The difficulty that arises as a result of this is to determine which one Müller is referring to in his definition. There is a sense in which the word could also be misleading—and, in fact, deceiving. There is a sense in which the word could suggest perceiving something when indeed nothing is perceived. For example, if one is driving on a tarred, smooth road on a sunny afternoon, at a distance he may think that he "perceives" a pool of water, but upon getting to the spot, he finds no water and discovers that he has been deceived. This is referred to as seeing "a mirage."

At other times when we think we "perceive" a particular object, we may eventually discover on closer observation that it is another object entirely. Religion is a very important phenomenon and its definition should not be approached from positions of ambiguity, misconceptions, and misleading that seem to characterize the definition of Müller.

OTHER FORMS OF DEFINITIONS

Other propagators' definitions of religion have avoided a reductionist approach and have rather attempted to define religion either by identifying characteristics that are common to religions or providing the etymological explanation of the word religion. In the first category, the effort of Wittgenstein is worthy of consideration. Avoiding a particularized definition of religion, Wittgenstein employed his "world game" in propounding the family resemblances of all religious concepts. He thus identified characteristics that are common to all of them. He then opined, for example, that all religions promise their adherents salvation whereby they can escape from a state of unsatisfactory desires and expectations to one of infinite bliss and perfect satisfaction in the future. Thus, to Wittgenstein, religion is ultimately a game played by different people for different reasons.

In spite of all the attractiveness that Wittgenstein's conception of religion in this way may entail, the comparison of religion to a game played has tended to trivialize religion, making it a not-too-serious phenomenon. But we do know that religion has too much significance to be treated in this kind of fashion. Accepting the definition of Wittgenstein would only constitute a kind of apologetic to defend religion from the antagonism of the positivists. In the final analysis, the triviality with which the matter is treated makes it more vulnerable to its opponents.

In the second category are some scholars who, even when they accepted that a functional definition of religion is necessary, have always insisted that a definition of religion reflecting the origin of the word religion is very much in place and could be very illuminating in grappling with the meaning of religion. In this regard, the term "religion" is taken to derive from the Latin word *religare*, meaning "to bind." This has been further designated to imply a bond of scruples within which its members share communion with one another. This kind of definition of religion ultimately depicts religion as a phenomenon that suggests separation from the larger societal groupings and tends towards fellowship among particular adherents.

While altogether this may not be a damaging characteristic in religion, in overall consideration, this kind of definition has come to be identified more for its liability rather than asset. That is because defining religion in this way stresses the negative rather than the positive aspects of religion. In which case religion may come to be seen as nothing more than a bond depicting a fellowship that in the long run may become fanatical as a result of being wedged together by rules, obligations, and responsibilities that are dogmatically essential to laws and observances of the religion

In addition, defining religion this way may expose religion to being contemptuously considered. This may—and indeed has—given room to some scholars being interested in only negative or even ridiculous interpretations of religion. For example, Salomon Reinach, using the etymological meaning of religion, defined it as "an assembly of scruples impeding the free exercise of our faculties." This cannot definitely be regarded as a complimentary definition of religion.

Standard toward Acceptable Definitions

The consideration of a number of definitions above has portrayed the difficulties to be encountered in the attempts to define religion. It has also highlighted the fact that it would be rather presumptuous to attempt a wedging together of these and many other definitions in the bid to draw a cord of compromise in the age-long disputations concerning an acceptable definition(s) of religion. However, the insistence must be made, even in the face of envisaged limited success that definitions of religion are desirable, and they must be made. However, such definitions must be able to address the issue at hand to the satisfaction of those who come across them. This then presupposes that there must be standards which such definitions must attain before they can be regarded as acceptable definitions of religion. On the other hand, attainment of standard necessarily calls for guidelines which have to be followed at least broadly by those who aspire to propagate definitions, if they intend to genuinely and sincerely attempt interpreting religion or even explaining it through their definitions.

Perhaps as a starting point, we should learn from the advice of J. B. Pratt in his identification of what religion is and should not be. As we have indicated elsewhere in this chapter, Pratt advocates that religion is not a doctrine or a law or a hypothesis or a thesis, and thus should not be seen as a matter of any one facet of man's psychic makeup.

The warnings of Prof. P. Tillich are also of immense service in any attempt to define religion. He is of the view that any statement made in religion should have God as its center. If this is not so, he fears that we may not be able to arrive at a plausible explication. We agree with Tillich that any definition of religion that fails to pay close attention to this warning would be greatly defective, since it would have omitted an essential aspect of religion which it sets out to explain.

Also, anyone attempting to define religion must realize that it is ultimately a fact of human nature. Thus, it is the totality of the human personality that should be involved in it. A worthwhile definition of religion must reflect this and should avoid, as much as possible, segregation or a reductionist mentality that have characterized many, if not all, the suggested definitions discussed in this chapter.

H. H. Farmer (1935) stresses the fact of the importance of the totality of man responding to religion and the need for being well represented in a good definition, when he states:

> Religion is … a response of the whole personality. It is the whole personality grasping, intuiting something, through its own profound interest in its own fullest realization (p. 42).

Farmer's words here should be seen as invaluable advice for any endeavor to define religion.

Another important ingredient of religion that cannot be ignored when it is being defined is its transcendent nature. In fact, most known religions have always claimed a transcendent origin. Consequently, no definition of religion should leave out the transcendence of religion. To do so is to have a body without a soul—providing tea without sugar.

Finally, we must also warn that in grappling with the task of defining religion, its universal nature and appeal must be given due recognition.

What perhaps is left to be determined at this stage (granted that the above discussed standards or guidelines are regarded as constituting the necessary and sufficient ingredients for a basically "above board" and widely receptive definition) is the possibility or indeed the practicability of integrating them for the task. The fear that this may eventually end up in an unrealistic ambition is not misplaced. However, without preempting others in providing definitions in line with our suggested guidelines above, we would like to propose the following definition as largely representing our idea of an all-embracing but concise definition, or interpretation, of religion.

> Religion, in its essence, is the means by which man discovers the "face" of God, and formulates a dependent relationship with Him in communication of practices as the infinite creator of the universe.

REVIEW QUESTIONS

1. Examine the main arguments of and responses to the protagonists of the impossibility of defining religion.
2. What factors would you consider to be the main obstacles to acceptable definitions of Religion?
3. Attempt a critique of definitions that have been propagated.
4. Identify various approaches in defining religion and explore the challenges they constitute for the exercise.
5. Identify and discuss the standards to be met so as to give an acceptable definition of religion.
6. Provide your own definition of religion and show how it aligns with the required standards.

Bibliography and Further Reading

Aderibigbe, G. 1988. *The Study of Religion*. Ibadan: Jola Publications.

Aderibigbe, Gbolade & Aiyegboyin, eds. 2001. *Religion, Study and Practice*. Ibadan: Olu-Akin Press.

Aliston, W. P. 2005. "Religion," in *Encyclopedia of Philosophy*, vol. 7, Paul Edwards, ed. New York: Macmillan and Free Press.

Baird, R. 1971. *Category Formation and the History of Religion*. London: Mouton.

Bianchi, U. 1972. *The Definition of Religion*. E. J. Brill.

Bowker, J., ed. 1977. *The Oxford Dictionary of World Religions*. London: Oxford University Press.

Bradley, F. H. 1969. *Appearance and Reality*. Oxford: Oxford University Press.

Byrne, Peter and Clarke, Peter, 1993. *Definition and Explanation in Religion*. England: Macmillan Press.

Deming, Will. 2005. *Rethinking Religion: A Concise Introduction*. New York: Oxford University Press.

Dewart, Leslie. 1970. *Religion, Language and Truth*. London: Herder & Herder.

Durkheim, E. 1971. "Elementary Forms of Religion," in *Introductory Sociology*. London: Macmillan Edu. Ltd.

Ferre, F. 1957. *Basic Modern Philosophy of Religion*. London: Oxford University Press.

Geertz, Clifford. 1973. "Religion as a Cultural System," in *The Interpretation of Cultures*. New York: Basic Books.

Gombrich, R. 1971. *Precept and Practice: Traditional Buddhism in Rural Highlands of Ceylon*. London: SMC Press.

Harding, J. S. & Rodrigues, H. 2009. *Introduction to the Study of Religion*. New York: Routledge.

Idowu, Bolaji. 1976. *African Traditional Religion: A Definition*. London: SMC Press.

Kristenson, W. B. 1966. *The Meaning of Religion*. London: Mouton Press.

Livingstone, James C. 2009. *Anatomy of the Sacred: An Introduction to Religion*, 6th ed. New Jersey: Prentice Hall.

Otto, Rudolf. 1950. *The Idea of the Holy*. London: Oxford University Press.

Spiro, M. E. 1968. *Religion: Problem of Definition and Explanation in Anthropological Approaches to the Study of Religion*. London: SMC Press.

Webb, C. C. J. 1976. *Group Theories of Religion and the Individual*. London: Allen & Unwin.

Webb, D. 1981. *Religion and Truth: Towards an Alternative Paradigm for the Study of Religion*. London: Mouton.

Yinger, J. M. 1970. *The Scientific Study of Religion*. London: Macmillan.

CHAPTER TWO

ORIGIN AND DEVELOPMENT OF RELIGION

INTRODUCTION

When the question about the origin and development of religion is asked, responses may be provided in varied forms. However, the basic responses are more likely to be expressed in relation to:

i.   How religion began;
ii. The form (earliest) in which religion began;
iii. The reason(s) for the religiousness of man.

The first two responses to the question of origin and development of religion are basically historical and sociological in nature. This is because they essentially focus their inquiry on the sources of religion in terms of personality, the form that took precedence, the time it all began, and the gradual development thereafter. The third response is psychological in nature, in that it inquires into the origin and development of religion in relation to why man as a rational being decided by choice (or otherwise) to become religious.

Along these two broad divisions, two schools of thought have been identified on the origin and development of religion. These are the sociological school of thought and the psychological school of thought. Personalities within these schools of thought have propounded theories on the origin and development of religion.

Before considering the theories from the two schools of thought, it is important to briefly address the issue of the earliest form of religion. As Smart (1976) contends, one must ask the fundamental question on the form in which religion began, because not only has religion been a vital and pervasive feature of human life, but also because this question has tasked the minds of scholars of the phenomenon of religion for quite some time. Three schools of thought have emerged on this issue. These are the evolutionary, the devolutionary, and the revolutionary.

The evolutionary school insists that the earliest form of religion was polytheistic. This is the theory that Charles Darwin propagated in his book, *The Origin of Species*, in 1859. His main argument in the book is that there is a sequence of stages in religion from lower to higher. The highest form of faith, according to Darwin's hypothesis, is usually thought to be monotheism. The main propagators of the evolution theory in religion were religious scholars and anthropologists like Herbert Spencer, James Frazer, and Edward Taylor.

However, David Hume gave vivid expression to the evolution theory which depicts that the earliest form of religion was polytheism. In his book, *The Natural History of Religion* (1756), Hume argued for this position by holding that the "One God" concept is a very late development. He further insisted that if the improvement of human society is considered from rude beginnings to a state of greater perfection, then polytheism should be seen as necessarily being the first and most ancient religion of mankind. To him, polytheism is more tolerant and less violent to reason.

On the other hand, the propagators of devolutionary theory have insisted that monotheism was the earliest form of religion. Scholars like Voltaire, Andrew Lang, and Wilhelm Schmidt have all argued for this position. Voltaire, for example, argued in his *Dictionnaire Philosophique* (1962) that man began by knowing a single God and that it was as a result of human weakness that mankind subsequently adopted many gods. In his own argument in support of monotheism, Andrew Lang insisted that among the primitive people there was a definite knowledge of God, an indigenous knowledge. Thus, Lang maintained the position that the so-called "savages" are as monotheistic as the Christians.

To Lang, the idea of one supreme God was not built up by a slow process of accretion. It was intuitively and vaguely grasped by primitive man from the start. He consequently concluded that the magical and polytheistic element in present-day "savage" religions is a mark of degeneration from the original purer religion.

The most substantial contribution on the primacy of monotheism was made by Father Wilhelm Schmidt in his works, *The Origin and Growth of Religion* and *The Origin of the Idea of God* (1935). In both works, he argued that the Supreme Deity is universal among all really primitive peoples and that the belief is not a late development or traceable to missionary influences. Thus, according to Schmidt, man began by worshipping one Supreme Being, who is the genuine monotheistic deity.

The third school of thought, the revolutionary school, seeks to dismiss the devolutionary position. Raffaele Pettazzoni, a leading proponent of this theory, cited four instances of religion whereby polytheism preceded monotheism. However, according to him, monotheism was brought about not by the evolution process but by sharply revolutionary figures who broke away from the polytheistic past. In these instances, Moses (Judaism), Jesus (Christianity), Muhammad (Islam), and Zarathustra (Zoroastrianism) did not evolve from polytheism but came from it by revolutionary means.

THEORIES OF THE ORIGIN OF RELIGION

As earlier indicated, theories of the origin and development of religion may be grouped under two broad schools of thought—the psychological and the sociological. We can only present brief highlights of these theories here.

I. The Psychological Theories

Generally, the psychological theories of the origin of religion are based on attempts by scholars to reconstruct the ways of thinking of early man in the world. The scholars claim that in the early days, primitive man found himself in a universe he could not understand. He was ignorant of the natural causes at work about him. Consequently, in his ignorance, man created gods or supernatural beings to assuage his fears and anxieties. It is significant to note that the psychological theories have been further divided in two: the intellectual and the emotional theories.

The Intellectual Theories

The intellectual theories of origin of religion suggest that early man became religious in an attempt to discover by "seasoning" the real explanations of things about him. In the main, these theories insist that man became religious in order to put the world into a shape that was comprehensive and satisfying. Thus, primitive man reasoned ultimately that if he could not control such strange things as thunder, lightning, seasons, birth and death, and so on they must be controlled by spirits more powerful than he. Man's activities in placating these spirits eventually became religion. A sample of such theories is discussed below.

The Theory of Animism

In his 1871 book *Primitive Culture*, E. B. Taylor advanced a theory of the origin of religion known as the "animism theory." The theory stipulated that the races of the rudimentary culture were conscious of the difference between the material and the spiritual. This consciousness was derived from the phenomena of dreams and visions. According to Taylor, primitive man took dreams as realities. Thus, when a man slept and dreamed, he found himself engaged in certain activities that he believed were real. However, when he woke up he discovered this was not so, and that his body had remained the whole time where he lay and the activities in his dreams had been carried out by something other than his body, which must have left his body. This notion made primitive man realize that the soul is different from the body, even though it existed in the body, and in addition, that it was responsible for the activities in his dream. This element that inhabited the body was called "spirit," and it could leave the body whenever it pleased.

Primitive man also extended this notion in distinguishing a living state from a dead state. This constituted the difference between a body and a corpse. In the body, there is a soul that has departed when we have a corpse.

From the above position, primitive man according to Taylor derived the belief in a material-cum-vaporous soul, detachable from the body. Consequently, primitive man established the practice of making sacrifices to the departed and burying material objects designed to help the soul on its way to placate the wrath of spirits. They equally developed the universal cult of the souls of the dead, which were believed to linger in or around the grave. These two forms of belief led to ancestor worship, which then became the original form of religion where the first altars were the tombs.

In addition to the belief in a body/soul dichotomy, Taylor also insisted that primitive man projected that everything in his environment had souls. Thus, rivers, trees, rocks, and so on had souls inhabiting them.

Primitive man did not stop at projecting souls for these natural objects, but in addition came to regard the souls as gods and consequently began to worship them. The souls, which inhabited all natural phenomena, became gods who ruled the rain, the sky, thunder, lightning, storms, and so on. These gods had to be placated in a polytheistic religious belief. However, in Taylor's view, the powers ascribed to these gods (which made the original form of religion polytheistic) were later transferred to a single deity, thus paving the way for monotheism.

Comments

There are both areas of strength and weakness in Taylor's animism theory. The major strength of Taylor's theory lies first in the fact that there is a sense in which it can be said that animism forms a major and vital element in some indigenous religions, particularly if animism is explained in relation to the existence of spirits. Second, in Africa, spirits are regarded to be distinct from material objects, even though they live in them or express themselves through the objects. Third, as highlighted by Herbert Spencer, animism could be regarded as the center of many beliefs and customs. These include ancestor worship, transmigration of the soul, and witchcraft.

However, in spite of these positive elements in Taylor's theory, it is not possible to conclude that the theory is impeccable. This is because there are a lot of limitations in the theory: (1) There is no historical evidence to back Taylor's theory. His hypothesis is, at best, an a priori speculation in which Taylor attempted to place himself in primitive man's world and thereafter postulated "his" own early man's thought. (2) Many scholars have disputed Taylor's claim that the so-called primitive man could draw a distinction between spirit and matters. They claim that this concept of dualism was a product of much later civilization, precisely that of the Greek civilization in the 6th century bc. (3) If the very premise of Taylor's theory has been found to be false, then his conclusion cannot be but false. This is so because, as pointed out in the first limitation, Taylor's theory seemed to have been based on speculative illusion rather than historical evidence. (4) Scholars such as R. R. Marett have postulated that animism was not the earliest phenomenon of primitive man. They claim there was an earlier stage known as the animistic age. (5) Animism as the origin of religion based on polytheism has been contested by both Lang (1891) and Schmidt (1935). Both scholars have claimed that the very first form of religion was monotheism, that the belief in and worship of the supreme deity was universal among all really primitive races of the world. (6) There is the argument that though animism may form the foundation on which religion may be based, it is not a religion itself. (7) Finally, the suggestion that the world of the spirits is the creation of man is curious. For if it were so then it would mean that man, with all his gifts of intelligence and purpose would have willingly created for himself those "things" that he would come not only to fear but also worship.

The Emotional Theories

On the other hand, the emotional theories of the origin of religion stipulate that religion emerged from human emotions. Thus, religion, strictly speaking, was not a "thought-out" process; rather, it was "danced out" (Aiyegboyin, 1997). The main purpose of religion was to forestall the mounting fear and anxiety in man. It was to ultimately rectify the emotional tensions experienced by man in situations of helplessness and unfulfillment. Man invariably created gods whom he believed could solve his problems. A sample of the emotional theories is discussed below.

The Theory of Animatism

The theory of animatism was proposed by the English anthropologist R. R. Marett. The theory, proposed in his *Threshold of Religion* (1909), claims that religion constitutes man's emotional response to the unknown. To begin with, he criticized Taylor's animism theory, dismissing it as improbable in that it was too intellectual and that early man, being neither a philosopher nor a scientist, could not develop such thoughts. Marett then proposed that religion actually originated not from primitive man having the notion of a personal soul, but from his belief that there existed a personal and powerful force which enlivened everything.

This force is believed to be a hidden strength and operates silently and invisibly in persons, as well as in living or moving things. It is this belief, according to Marett, which excites emotions of awe and fear in man. Later on, the belief was accompanied by magical practices and a cult of worship developed around the objects that possessed the impersonal forces as deified beings. Thus, primitive religion began. Marett's justification for his theory is based on the studies he carried out in communities such as the Melanesians, American Indians, the pygmies, the Bantu, and some aboriginal people in different parts of the world.

Comments

Marett's animatism found support in the work of Bishop Codrington. In his book *The Melanesians* (1891), Codrington submitted that religion originated prelogically as man's response to the existence of an impersonal power in the world. This notion, according to Codrington, was confirmed by his study among the Melanesians who had a word—*mana*—for the impersonal power. *Mana* is seen as the power in storms, in whirlwinds, in charismatic leaders, in warriors, in outstanding medicine men and prophets, as well as in all wonderful and dreadful things. However, *mana* is a not a living spirit, it is just power.

In spite of Codrington's support for the theory of animatism, the theory can still be faulted on four major grounds: (1) The theory simply reduces religion to mere emotional expressions. This certainly cannot fully represent (if it does at all) man's religious characteristics. Thus, Pritchard may be correct in being skeptical of emotional theories of origin of religion. To him, the idea of deriving any form of religion from feelings should be discarded. (2) The second problem with the theory is the methodology adopted by Marett. Just as in the case of the animism theory of Taylor, Marett has attempted to prescribe the origin of religion by projecting himself back to primitive man's mind and world. (3) It is not easy to really determine whether animatism was more primitive than the worship of spirits. This is because animism, animatism, magic, and ancestor worship were generally found side by side. (4) Finally, the fact that the impersonal force in animatism can be manipulated either for good or for evil makes the process magical rather than religious.

II. SOCIOLOGICAL THEORIES

Essentially, sociological theories of religion seek to explain religion in its functional role as a societal phenomenon. Consequently, they search for the origin of religion in the need and features of religion in the society. Sociological theories are concerned with explaining the widespread and pervasive nature of religion in all societies and in all ages. There are two prominent sociological theories of religion. These were propagated by Emile Durkheim and Karl Marx. Both are presented briefly below.

Religion as the Worship of the Society

Emile Durkheim, an eminent sociologist and anthropologist, stands out as the most influential propagator of the sociological origin of religion. His contributions to the debate on the origin of religion are presented in his work, *The Elementary Forms of Religion* (1935). Durkheim based his submission on the origin of religion on two basic questions. First, what is the origin of religion? Second, what are the functions of religion? In answering these questions, he claimed to have explained the origin of religion in regarding religion as a social phenomenon, and that all religious beliefs carry with them social obligations. Consequently, Durkheim said religion was a product of the society that has morality as its foundation. According to him, it was in the bid to protect itself that society originated religion. To do this, the society introduced certain codes of behavior which individuals in the society have to keep for orderliness, peace, and the smooth running of the society. Thus, individuals who wish to live in the society must abide by the society's stipulations. To buttress his argument, Durkheim opined that the social character of religion is vividly demonstrated in three ways. First, it is passed on from one generation to another, thereby transcending the life span of individuals. Second, it is accepted and believed by all in the society, and third, it is compulsory, based on the claim that almost everybody partakes in the collective religious rites of his society if he does not want to be ostracized.

Comments

Durkheim's sociological theory of the origin of religion is essentially based on three basic explanations. The first of these explanations points to some basic facts about human nature in relation to religion. These are that man everywhere has the awareness of being confronted with the absolute demands of sacred values and that these demands have to be obeyed by all, with the values having been always connected to religion in man's mind. Next, the theory has attempted to point out that man is always in need of support and refuge, which he tries to attain by all means. In doing this, however, man should avoid clinging to illusionary support; rather, he should identify himself with the society he lives in because all he seeks is present there. Third, the theory strongly advocates that this awareness is a product of man's own mind, as derived from societal arrangements.

Based on the explanations above, there is quite a number of points which give credit to the theory. Some of these points are:

i. It is indeed true that religion is a social phenomenon.
ii. It is also a fact that religious beliefs carry with them social obligations.

iii. There is no doubt that the stress of every religion is that there should be harmony and the well-being of the individual within the society.

iv. Any religion worth its salt also aims to make individuals in the society selfless and committed to the promotion of harmony, stability, and the well-being of such a society, desisting from anything that may disrupt or prevent the peace of the society.

v. It is also a fact that since religion claims a universal existence, it becomes an instrument of cohesion not only in a particular community, but it also strives to carry out the mission of bringing about peace and harmony to the whole world.

However, there are also some telling limitations in Durkheim's theory. To begin with, the theory completely negates the importance of the individual in the society. If the theory is to be taken seriously, the individual then becomes just a drop of water in the ocean of the society. That is, the individual is of no importance. He becomes at best a blind follower of the dictates of the society, which has no consideration for his interests. Moreover, the individual is robbed of his identity and also his personal freedom and responsibility.

Second, it is quite obvious that not all religions can be essentially accounted for through Durkheim's theory. For example, many of the Asiatic religions actually shun the social trappings of religion as enumerated by Durkheim.

Third, very many believers would certainly hold that their religious convictions cannot be mere derivation of human society. So also they would be hard put to see their goal of religious worship as terminating with societal "spirit" rather than the Supreme Being. Indeed, Durkheim's theory would make nonsense of men's experiences of the supernatural Being, experiences that have been well articulated and which provide the main characteristics of godly men in human history.

Finally, Durkheim's theory cannot account for the exemplary lives of religious figures such as Shadrach, Meshach, and Abednego in the biblical Old Testament scriptures, who, acting on the dictates of their consciences, defied outright societal persuasion and expectations to uphold their religious conviction and worship of the Supreme Being.

Religion as the Opium of the Masses

Karl Marx propagated the idea of religion as the opium of the people. This essentially denotes religion as a negative societal agent. As background, it must be realized that Karl Marx's opinion was largely influenced by his disdain for capitalism and his endorsement of a socialist economy, which was later called Marxism after him. On the origin of religion in particular, Marx argued that religion was made by man and there is nothing external or supernatural about it. Man, according to Karl Marx, endowed nature with supernatural possession and in the end made gods, spirits, devils, angels, and so on of them. In the resolve of man to pacify these supernatural beings, his intention was to avoid the harm and suffering that he perceived they could bring upon him. To secure the help of the gods, man began to placate and worship them. This, in Karl Marx's submission, actually brought about religious worship in prayers, sacrifices, and other rites. Personalities such as priests, sorcerers, pastors, and others became relevant to support the religious mechanism.

However, according to Marx, in spite of the falsity of religion, it still provides a societal function, though a negative one. To him, religion is antirevolutionary and is used by the rich and mighty in the society for economic gains in suppressing, oppressing, and exploiting the ordinary people.

Perhaps the greatest negative role of religion in the society, as far as Karl Marx was concerned, is that it is used by the exploiting class to maintain the status quo by using it to "convince" the poor in the society to be content with their position and consequently continue to assist the rich in getting richer.

Comments

We must accept that Karl Marx's position on religion in Marxism has greatly influenced human endeavors in different fields. For example, his insistence on suppression of religion in its role of sustaining societal status quo has revolutionized not only world economics, but has provided avenues for both technological and industrial sectors. Also as an ideology, Marxism has shown the inadequacies of the capitalist democracy in dealing with equality of opportunity for all citizens and providing for the suffering of the large proportion of these citizens.

However, some obvious defects appear in Karl Marx's view on religion, particularly if Marxism as an ideology is taken into consideration. In the first place, it cannot be totally true that man's desires for religion were derived from superstitious or illusionary tendencies. Marx's position on this issue is better explained as being a product of his imagination and contortions.

Next, it is not always the position that religion encourages and sustains inequality. If the Christian religion is taken as an example, the teachings of Jesus Christ are centered on the equality of man. In addition, contrary to Marx's position that religion is anti-revolution and progress, there have been glaring occasions when religion has been the catalyst of positive revolutions. Indeed, the teachings of Jesus in Christianity and Muhammad in Islam were, by all standards, revolutionary in the context of their contemporary worlds.

Also, it has become obvious that the Marxist ideology has not been able to give man the envisaged freedom and liberty from capitalism. Indeed, practical observations have shown that the economic, political, and social aspects of human freedom and liberty are more curtailed in Communist countries, where Marxist ideology has been adopted.

Finally—and most significantly—the prophecy of Marx that religion would disappear once the Marxist ideology was embraced, has been proved wrong. Religion has continued to wax stronger and stronger. Indeed, Parrinder's own prophecy on the side of religion has been the enduring one. He said, "as long as men are men, they will seek to discover the final meaning of life and the highest ideas of conduct which religion alone claims to offer" (1976). In consequence, world religions have continued to make converts in places where they did not originate (Christianity and Islam). On the other hand, the Marxist empires all over the world seem to be crumbling. Most formerly Communist countries of Eastern Europe have become capitalist nations. Significantly, even the Soviet Union, the symbol of communism, has collapsed.

REVIEW QUESTIONS

1. Identify and discuss the questions that come to mind when the issue of the origin of religion is raised.
2. Give detailed arguments and the responses available when considering the three schools of thought on the earliest form of religion.
3. What would you consider the merits and demerits of the sociological theory of the origin of religion?
4. How far can the theory of animism be justified as the origin of human religiosity?
5. How far can Marx's position that religion is a product and sustainer of oppression be justified?

BIBLIOGRAPHY AND FURTHER READING

Anderson, B. W. 1967. *Creation versus Chaos: The Reinterpretation of the Mythical Symbolism in the Bible*. New York: Association Press.

Ayala, Francisco J. 2006. *Darwin and Intelligent Design*. Minneapolis: Fortress Press.

Barbour, Ian G. 1997. *Religion and Science: Historical and Contemporary Issues*. San Francisco: Harper & Row.

Brandon, S. C. F. 1963. *Creation of Myths in the Ancient Near East*. London: Hodder and Stoughton.

Benedict, R. 1971. *Patterns of Culture*. London: Routledge & Kegan Paul.

Cogley, J. O. 1968. *Religion in A Secular Age*. London: Paul Mack.

Eastwood, C. C. 1964. *Life and Thoughts in the Ancient World*. London: Oxford University Press.

Eliade, M. 1974. *Gods, and Goddesses, and Myths of Creation*. New York: Harper & Row.

Evans-Pritchard, E. E. 1965. *Theories of Primitive Religion*. Oxford: Clarendon Press.

Gilkey, Langdon. 1985. *Creationism on Trial: Evolution and God at Little Rock*. New York and San Francisco: Harper.

Guthrie, W. K. C. 1957. *In the Beginning: Some Greek Views of the Origin of Life and the Early State of Man*. New York: Cornell University Press.

Hume, D. 1956. *The Natural History of Religions*. London: Oxford Press.

Leach, E. R., ed. 1968. *Dialects in Practical Religion*. Cambridge: Cambridge Press.

Lincoln, B. 1986. *Myths, Cosmos, and Society: Indo-European Themes of Creation and Destruction*. Cambridge, MA: Harvard University Press.

Long, Charles. 1983. *Alpha: Myths of Creation*. New York: Scholars Press.

Lovin, R. and Frank E. Reynolds, eds. 1985. *Cosmogony and Ethical Order*. Chicago: Chicago University Press.

Marett, R. R. 1909. *Threshold of Religion*. London: Methuen and Co.

Parrinder, E. G. 1976. *A Book of World Religions*. London: Houlton Pub.

Philip, H. L. 1956. *Freud and Religious Belief*. London: Rockliff.

Pratt, J. B. 1924. *The Religious Consciousness*. New York: Macmillan.

Smart, N. 1976. *The Religious Experience of Mankind*. London: Collins & Co.

_____. *The Phenomenon of Religion*. New York: Scribners.

Smith, H. 1976. *Forgotten Truth: The Primordial Tradition*. New York: Harper & Row.

Taylor, E. B. 1929. *Primitive Culture*. London: John Murray Pub.

CHAPTER THREE

THE STUDY OF RELIGION

INTRODUCTION

The practice of religion is usually accepted as essential to the life of man. In fact, it is considered to be an inescapable phenomenon dominating the whole strata of human existence. The same cannot be said when the issue of studying religion is raised. It seems justification for this cannot be taken for granted. In which case, explanations have to be provided for indulging in such a task.

The skepticism toward the study of religion may not only come from ardent practitioners of religion, who understandably insist that religion—a subjective, emotional, and direct relationship between a subject and his object of worship—calls for no more than expressions of feelings and activities of veneration that are born out of faith, which needs neither questioning nor objective studying to be authentic. This skeptical grab is usually also put out by atheists and agnostics who, in seeing no relevance in religion, consider studying it a waste of time and of no significance.

Positions such as these, in essence, have given rise to and justification for asking the question: Why study religion? Answers to this question, to our mind, are derivable from the very premises that justify and give authenticity to the practice of religion. However, the premises or grounds which make the study of religion imperative cannot be considered in isolation. They have to be examined in relation to issues such as:

- Why the study of religion?
- How to study, and who is best suited to engage in the study of religion.
- How the task of studying religion could profitably and adequately be approached.
- What is (are) to be studied in religion?

WHY RELIGION SHOULD BE STUDIED

Perhaps the all-embracing reason why religion should be studied is its importance and undeniable significance and hold on human life. If this is accepted, the simple but important task subsequent to this conviction is to enumerate why and the ways in which religion is important to man. These, we believe, are essentially contained in the following reasons, among many others.

First, there is the currency of religion as a human phenomenon. We mean by this that religion is ever present in every moment of human life, so much so that it would not be anything out of place to conclude that religion is inescapable. In that it dominates the thoughts and actions of all men, either positively for those who believe and take their faith seriously, or negatively for the unbelievers who despise religion.

Secondly, and as an offshoot of the first premise, the presence of religion is so dominating that its existence and functions in society have come to be so accepted that no apology is deemed necessary for both its acceptance and its practice. In consequence, it has become virtually impossible to ignore or neglect the multi-involvements toward it. A. C. Bouquet (1945) drives this point home by pointing out the gravity of relegating religion and the necessity to have it in one form or another because of its significance. He asserts:

> Religion cannot wisely be ignored or neglected as it is by so many frivolous persons today, even a defective or obsolete scheme of religion will serve the individual better than nothing at all (p. 15).

We grant that Bouquet is making very useful and cogent points here, as long as one is prepared to overlook his overenthusiasm for religion in recommending a defective or obsolete religion over nothing at all. There is no doubt that the message he wishes to impart—and which is, in any case, discernible—is the undeniable fact that individuals need religious stabilization in their lives. Religion has always, to a large measure, served as the bedrock of lives of men irrespective of age, tribe, sex, or calling.

This universal relevance of religion leads to the third reason why religion must be studied. Religion has a universal application that transcends human acclaimed demarcations of place, race, color and time. In consequence, religion and its practices in diverse forms are observed universally by people who believe and worship a sacred and supernatural power who transcends the profane world. Thus, many human beings could be said to be inescapably religious. The reason for this universal urge of involvement that makes religion an ultimate concern is well put by H. G. Wells (1971), when he opined that:

> Nearly all of us want something to hold us together, something to dominate our swarming confusion and save us from blackmail and exploded pride of thwarted desire, of futile conclusions. We want oneness some steadying thing which could afford an escape from fluctuations. It seems me that this desire to get the complex of life simplified is essentially what has been called religious motive, and the manner in which a man achieves that simplification, if he does achieve it and impresses an order upon his life, is his religion (p. 79).

Another reason, in our belief that essentially makes religion important and significant, is the fear that it may be impossible to find a replacing value that could satisfactorily fill the vacuum that an absence of religion is most likely to create. Bouquet (1945) once again stresses the indispensability of religion for man and the danger of its absence, when he states:

Anyone who is inside a working scheme of religion is well aware that to deprive him of that scheme is, to a large extent, so to say; disembodies his life.

Julian Huxley (1914) is also of the same view if we are to go by his statement that:

If you are going to take people's religion from them, you must provide them with a reasonable or acceptable substitute (p. 6).

OTHER REASONS FOR STUDYING RELIGION

Apart from the importance of religion as discussed above being the major reason for the study of religion, other factors are equally crucial for undertaking the study of religion, particularly from the angle of the benefits that are derivable from such a study.

Ronald R. Cavanagh (1978) identifies three of these in:

- Emancipation from ignorance;
- Information and skill;
- Appreciation.

It will be proper to give brief consideration to each of these as expectations from the study of religion.

Emancipation from Ignorance

The study of religion as part of a liberal education can fulfill the role of saving man from ignorance and also the kind of dogmatism that blinds the critical disposition of man. Students of religion, through courses they undertake in the field of religion, should achieve the goal of freedom. This is expected to be so in that they would be adequately exposed to various data that bring into focus the diverse expressions of people's religious values. In addition, the method of critically examining these values and beliefs are provided in such a way that violence would not be done to the unique and legitimate claims of the beliefs concerned. In fact, the discriminating opportunity is provided to segregate among what should be authentically appreciated and those to be discarded among the religious values, beliefs, and practices.

Information and Skill

Those who undertake the study of religion in the process and at the end of the study would certainly come to the realization of the benefits of such an engagement. For the task in any course in the field of religion always attempts to identify particular areas of interest, it provides examples of religious data for the student, and also indicates the method or methods for carrying out the study. Thus, at the end there is bound to be a lot of information on these aspects. So it would be quite easy to understand and interpret for those who desire to do so.

Appreciation

It must be understood that the study of religion is not necessary to make its students religious. Rather, the basic preoccupation of the study (which of course should be a critical evaluation of the religious expression of people in religious contexts of restricted valuation) is to develop the students' interpretative skills so that they can then be able to discriminate the crucial elements that are involved in their own religious values, as well as in or against other people's values. With these, students are likely to appreciate not only their own but other people's religious expressions and determine how crucial and immediate they are as unrestricted and/or unconditional valuation in the quest for the ultimate value of mankind.

Problems Facing the Study of Religion

It cannot be denied that the study of religion as a phenomenon is beset with immense difficulties. This is even more so if such a study is interested in the serious consideration of questions such as the truth or falsehood of religions, the practice of religion in terms of the behavioral patterns of leaders and followers of religions, as well as the competitive instances depicted by most religions, in particular, claims. This is why there is the need for anyone involved in the delicate task of studying religion to be very cautious so as not to run afoul of not only acceptable standards but also not to inadvertently take the shadow for reality, as well as unwittingly getting embroiled in intrigues of subjective evaluation as analysis of religious claims, practices, and values.

One such difficulty, particularly having to do with the truth of religion as raised by W. Contwell Smith (1959), is the problem of the complexity of religion, not only in definitive terms, but also—and most importantly—in its practices in vast varieties. There are many religions in the world, all of them with a considerable number of adherents. They also lay claim to religious truth and authenticity. Students of religion cannot but be in a dilemma in reconciling sometimes conflicting assertions and claims of these religions. More often than not, the student may also be bothered about what William Christian (1972) refers to as the questions of coherence and adequacy of various religious claims and doctrinal ramifications, which are almost endless. How far are these religious systems coherent and free from self-contradiction or contribute significantly to human experience? Can they, in fact, satisfy the needs and reasons for religion?

The changing nature of religion may also constitute some obstacle to the study. This has to do particularly with organized religions. Religions often change devastatingly, as they develop and migrate culturally from generation to generation and from one place to another. Thus, it is often difficult, if it is even possible, to get at the unique original form of a religion in later studies, as it would have assumed a wide variety of interpretations and significance and would also have become so elastic that, not only would the judgment of its truth and values have to change constantly, but also judgment about its opposition to or compatibility between theistic Christianity (which is becoming more existential in theology) and the nontheistic and fundamentally existential Buddhism.

Wilken (1971) also raises the same point with particular reference to Christianity in pointing out that, though one may eventually get at what could be regarded as an original Christian faith, the changes that have occurred over the centuries have made the existing traditions within Christianity at any given point in time and place largely a remembrance of the Christian past that is unique to that experience. This has no doubt placed the study of the Christian past at the mercy of controversy and apologists.

The difficulty associated with the practice of religion is multidimensional. There are the problems derivable from the universal practice of religion. There are also those that are a direct consequence of the attitude and utilization of religion by the leaders of religion and their followers. The universal practice of religion may become an obstacle to its study in a number of ways. First, appearances may be taken for reality, in the sense that when everybody claims to be practicing religion it is usually asserted without the necessary clarification as to what is meant by "practicing religion" or "being religious." Is it by going to church regularly, or by being pious? But experience has shown that these two activities do not necessarily make a religious person out of a man as they are mere external manifestations that may neither have impact on nor be a true reflection of the spiritual quality of the person.

The prophecy of Amos vividly drives this point home in his condemnation of the external religious observances of the Jews when there was complete religious and moral bankruptcy (Amos 5. 18–27). Christ himself alluded to the distinction between the external manifestation of religion and the pure spiritual being of the person when he said in the Gospels:

> Not everyone who says to me, "Lord, Lord", shall enter the kingdom of heaven but he who does the will of my father in heaven …" (Matt. 7:21).

Consequently, a clear distinction must be made between "having a religion" and actually living a life that is spiritual and motivated by a dynamic faith. The problem then arises when we say we are studying religion. Which one are we studying? If we are not careful, we may fall prey to studying religion in a manner of studying the kind of religion which Contwell Smith (1959) denounces thusly:

> Objective study of religion (which does not make classification) leaves out the very part of religion that counts, it analyzes the externals but misses out the core of the matter, studying the only aspect of religious history that is available for study; namely, the mundane manifestations, but either neglecting or misunderstanding and at least unable to deal with the only part that essentially signifies.

Secondly, there is usually the tendency to confuse religion with culture. This confusion is usually inadvertent because the practice of religion is carved out within a given culture and when religion migrates from one culture to the other in its passage of development and spread, there is the interplay of religion and culture whereby there is mutual assimilation of one another for acceptability. The historical development of Islam spreading more rapidly than Christianity lends a lot of weight to this occurrence, with the result that in time, it may in fact become difficult, if not impossible, to separate the cultural values and practices from the religious ones. Things like mores and types of dress, marriage, and so on come to mind here.

It is essential that the faulty conclusion that religion and culture are the same—and the confusion that usually ensues—must be avoided with a clear-cut definition of what is culture, which is different from religion, and vice versa. In real terms, culture should be seen as a total scheme of life as different from religion which is more appropriately an important part of that scheme, and to a large extent, gives direction to and reflects it.

Another problem making the study of religion difficult is the comparison of religions. A study of religion that is approached from this perspective has, more often than not, ended up in sinister motives of slighting, condemning, and seeking for the total eradication of the other religions. This is because the comparison is done from the competitive sense or the desire to claim superiority for one's own religion over and above others. Thus, the negative aspects of the other religions are unduly highlighted, or at best the good ones are misinterpreted and presented out of context and sometimes with deliberate "lies." What—and what not—to believe and separating the grains from the chaff become a knotty problem for the student of religion.

When it comes to the problems constituted for the study of religion by practitioners of religion, the first point must be the group referred to by Bolaji Idowu (1976) as constituting the "priestcraft." Members of this group are made up of leaders of religious organizations, Christians, Muslims, African Traditional Religionists, and all other world religions. They are supposed to be the custodians of religion in its purest form. Thus, they are expected not only to instruct their followers on parts to, and lives of the highest of values, but also to lives that depict that they themselves are practical examples of these values. However, it is most unfortunate that, rather than enhancing the chances of religion and people's acceptance of and participation in it, by upholding the best of values, most of them have constituted embarrassing offenders in abusing their exalted offices. It is not uncommon to witness not a few of them indulging in horrible shortcomings of inhumanity, even in the name of religion. Invariably, theirs have become more or less "do what I say, but not what I do."

While these "sins" may be regarded as debasing religion on the personal level, a more serious debasing of religion is done by leaders of religion employing it and its organization to enslave man physically and morally, to apply the most inhuman and indecent cruelty, to steal and to subject humanity to one oppression or another. For example, history has vividly recorded the world's wicked acts sanctified in the name of the Crusades and the Inquisition on the part of Christianity, jihads on the part of Islam, and human sacrifices on the part of African Traditional Religion.

Since it is always difficult, if not impossible, to distinguish between religion per se (pure religion) and religion as practiced, it has become ultimately fashionable not to be able to come to terms with what is to be studied in relation to leadership in religion, and thus identify what actually is being protested against when people revolt against religion. Is it religion itself or religion as it is wrongly practiced and applied by those who matter in it? This unfortunate sequence has been symbolically put by Idowu as "throwing the baby away with the bath water." That is, throwing away the basis of religion and the bad practices together.

However, there is no doubt that the incompetence or outright irresponsibility of authorities in religion has gone a long way to make people ignore religion, or in fact become atheists and agnostics, thus denouncing religion as irrelevant. In this case, they have championed the secularism of states and individuals. The examples of formerly Communist Russia and the Eastern bloc nations are still vivid as resulting from positions of being fed up with, and thus revolting against, the excesses of priests and other custodians of religion, who have employed religion as an instrument of oppression, keeping people subservient and ignorant. All these have inadvertently degenerated religion into "an opium of the people" to protect and sustain the status quo.

PERSONALITIES IN THE STUDY OF RELIGION

The consideration of personalities involved in the study of religion may be approached in a variety of ways, depending on what areas of interest are to be stressed. For example, the consideration may be mainly, if not only, in past and present scholars who have had, or are still having, one thing or the other to do with the study of religion. On the other hand, what are of interest may be the students studying religion with a view to determining who and what should qualify them to study religion.

For our purpose here, we intend to consider the two categories. Thus, the classes of personalities who have had to contribute to the study of religion in the past will be identified and their roles will be critically analyzed to determine how far they have served the course of religion, whether positively or negatively.

Four classes of such scholars have been identified. These are made up of the traveler and the armchair scholar in the first, the sociologist and the anthropologist in the second, the humanist in the third, and the theologian in the fourth.

The Traveler Scholar

The first important thing about this scholar is that, most times, his travels have little or nothing to do with religion. However, in the course of his journey, he would have come across religious components. He inevitably brings home stories which, for effectiveness and ego-boosting sake, are exaggeratedly narrated. In most cases, the ultimate motive of the traveler scholar is to entertain rather than educate. Thus, the more weird, mysterious, strange, and larger-than-life the stories are, the better. Another significant point is that this scholar is never particularly interested in the methods adopted to collect the information. As he must satisfy the stay-at-home writers, he sees no reason to ensure that his methods are authentic and scientific. In fact, more often than not, his methods are bundles of confusion, which are unclear even to him.

It is also worth noting that as ill equipped as the traveler scholar is in dealing with the religions of the lands he visits, and that the information he brings back is widely exaggerated, the "thesis" he propounds is held in high esteem and becomes a "work" classified as scholarly and as factual. Consequently, it is regarded as authentic on the religious lives of the places where the stories are said to have originated.

The Armchair Scholar

This scholar, though he calls himself an investigator, never leaves home or his desk. Thus he undertakes no travels. This is why he is designated an "armchair investigator or writer." The primary and "authentic" source of his "data" is the traveler. This he complements with materials from literature in libraries in his vicinity. Strangely enough, this scholar is satisfied that the materials at his disposal through these two means are accurate. In any case, he has no "fail-safe" method of determining otherwise, since he has made no effort to cross check what the traveler provides him; the materials from the libraries may, in fact, be the thesis of one traveler or another. He may, of course, make no effort to venture into the lands where the data, in the form of stories, came from.

These inadequacies in no way prevent the armchair scholar from considering himself a competent authority on the religions of the lands he knows next to nothing about. Invariably, he is likely to be invited in his locality as an authority to give lectures. He will also probably turn out books, chapters of books, and articles in journals as a specialist on these religions.

From the above discussion, it would be very difficult to consider scholars in this class as being an asset to the study of religion. Rather, they constitute a kind of menace in the study, in that they indulge in perpetuating half-truths and exaggerations, turning mere opinions and conjectures into facts, and arrogating to themselves authoritative claims they least qualify to make. In these regards, they constitute avenues of misinformation and distortions that have done—and may continue to do—untold harm to the study of the religions of those concerned. It must also be stressed that the unfortunate cooperation between the traveler and the stay-at-home scholars has produced a "bank" of "facts," which are no facts at all. However, these have been unwittingly "swallowed" by a largely gullible public for a very long time.

Sociologists and Anthropologists

These scholars belong to the second class. By their "calling" and method of conducting their researches, they are scientific in approach and usually very serious, dedicated, and painstaking in their work. All this makes them specialists in their fields. While the sociologist is devoted to the study of the society in the inter-relationships at different levels of the human components of it, the anthropologist is ultimately concerned with the study of man in matters of his nature, having to do with the development of the body, the man, and the society. Religion is not the actual preoccupation of these scholars. However, since they deal with man and the society he lives in, they cannot but pay some attention to the encounter with religion in their studies. As would be expected, their treatment of religion has to be limited to the bearing it has on their studies. Thus, their concern with it seems an inevitable one, sometimes a nuisance, that must be quickly gotten rid of. This is attested to by the fact that there is no way the anthropologist would talk about man, and the sociologist about society, where religion could be avoided. As Evans-Pritchard (1962) says:

> When a sociologist studies man, he thinks that man's study is incomplete if he does not study his religion, but religion is just an item of the many items considered in sociology, he is not studying religion as theological but as sociological.

From the above, it could be easily predicted that scholars in this class must suffer some uncontrollable inadequacies. These, in the main, have to do with their qualifications and the tools they employ, which may not get at the very basics of religion but only deal with it superficially. This is why Smith points out that the psychologist or the sociologist has only been able to prove the aberrations of faith, thus missing out the heart of the essentials of the norms of religion. In any case, this class of scholars, though, must be respected for the seriousness and competence in their fields; the limitations they suffer cannot but lead to dismissing them as serious and profitable contenders as scholars of religion.

The Humanists

Humanist scholars have always advocated a humanistic view of religion. This view is dominated by an overbearing consideration of religion as mainly a function of the human organism. A very prominent representative of this class of scholars is Julian Huxley (1930). He, for example, sees religion as a natural product of human behavior and attitudes. The result of this position is to ascribe to man the major role in religion, and invariably to relegate the divine aspect to a secondary position. This is considered a serious weakness, for the divine and the human have to strike a balance where religion is concerned. With this, humanists can hardly be regarded as well suited to adequately study religion.

The Theologians

So far, the scholars discussed could not be said to be concerned directly with religion. All of them have come across religion as "side effect(s)" of their adventures or specialized fields. However, with theologians we come to a class of scholars that has direct dealings with religion. By their profession, theologians are supposed to be on the "home ground" as far as religion is concerned. If all other things were to be equal, theologians should ordinarily possess the qualification, the tools, and the methods to do justice to the study of religion. But all other things are hardly ever equal—particularly in this case—for theologians. The problem with theologians, as far as the study of religion is concerned, seems to start with what definition to give to theology that would be accepted as all-embracing for the study of religion. The word "theology" has been generally defined as "the science of the concept of God" or "the study in regard to Him."

This definition raises a fundamental question of acceptability and application. Over the decades, it has become glaringly evident that theologians have not demonstrated enough commitment and enthusiasm to strictly apply the term in a manner that would encompass what it is to study religion. This major deficiency is traceable to a number of factors. The first of such originates from the theologians themselves. This has to do with the interpretation they give to the word "theology," particularly in their usage of it. The word, unfortunately, has come to be identified with particular religions—the so-called revealed religions. In this regard, it is, in fact, so much associated with the Christian religion that the notion that it belongs to it exclusively has come to be generally accepted. A number of implications attend this claim. To start with, there is a subjectivity that becomes fundamental with the study of religion right from the very beginning of the task. This cannot help but create a deep-seated bias in the study.

Also, carried to its logical conclusion, this kind of claim can only lead to the localization of God, as witnessed in the conception of the Israelites in the Old Testament. Whereby Yahweh was the possessive God of Israel, who protected and cared for them at the expense of other races such as the Egyptians and the Canaanites. God thus became the monopolized God of a people or religion. A carryover into the Christian consciousness has led, for example, to the agents of Christianity who first came in contact with Africans and their religion ignorantly believing that there was no God on the continent. To them, God, who had revealed Himself to the Christians, could not be conceived to do the same to a primitive group of people like the Africans were.

Another factor of note is the method usually adopted by theologians in their task. It has become fashionable for them to be scientific. In this case, they attempt to rival the scientists in their employment of empirical and hard, impersonal experimentation in the study of religion and faith-related issues. This is done in the search for recognition and acceptance by the scientific-minded contemporary society. This, of course, leads to no other consequence than the suppression of, or, in fact, the eradication of crucial elements, such as personal emotions, feelings of awe and faith, thus leaving out illuminating instincts that defy explanation, which are the bedrock of true religion. With this, the study of religion becomes nothing more than a thoroughly theoretical exercise, devoid of the participating, personal, and emotionally involved practices of man that religion, which is being studied, should be.

From above discussions, it would seem that the theologian has fallen short of being properly suited to provide a profitable study of religion. Superficially, this may seem so, but it must be pointed out that theologians stand the very bright chance of studying religion as it should be better than anybody else. Consequently, solutions must be sought, so that the inadequacies in the path of theologians could be overcome. This, we believe, could be achieved by application of proper methods and certain procedural guidelines, among other things in the study of religion. However, before attempting to discuss these, we should end this section by briefly considering the second poser raised at the beginning: Who, as a student, is qualified to study religion?

STUDENTS OF RELIGION

The question to be addressed here is, who is studying religion? This question could be framed differently as, who are the students of religion? Or who should be students of religion? Or even, what qualifies a student to study religion? We may even ask, is there any particular kind of student who is best suited to participate in the study of religion? More questions may even follow: Do students of religion need some special kind of insight, knowledge, attitude, and belief that are different from those required by students in other disciplines?

These questions have arisen as a result of the "mute" yet salient controversy that has developed in connection with who should be students of religion. Positions have been taken along the following lines. First, a student who aspires to study religion must belong to one religion or the other. The argument here is that only such a student could properly recognize religious data, appreciate their values, and consequently treat them with adequate relevance and meaning. There is the second position that is opposed to the first that insists there is no need for any special attitude, insight, or belief requested from the student of religion that are different from the ones demanded from students in other academic fields.

There is no doubt that a lot may be said to justify each of these two positions. However, we shall not belabor the issue here. Rather, we would like to submit that our position is more in agreement with the second position. There is, to our mind, no need for any special insight, knowledge, attitude, or belief for a student of religion that singles him out from students of other subjects. Also, the student need not be religious, for this makes little or no contribution whatsoever to either the student's understanding or application of a functional definition of religion, nor does it in any data. What is important for any student of religion is the capability of carefully recognizing and applying relevant definitions of religion, appreciating the data that are crucial to religion, and handling them in such a way that a meaningful and cogent study of religion could be carried out. The ability to do all these requires a degree of intellectuality, insight, independence of thought, and the critical-mindedness that would apply in any academic discipline.

On the whole, it is our conviction that all kinds of students can pursue the study of religion, as long as there is the commitment, seriousness, interest in, and dedication to the study of religion, just as in other fields of study. We see no need for special qualifications, participation, or attitude.

Methods and Guidelines for the Study of Religion

Having discussed why religion should be studied and having also considered questions of scholars of religion and which students should study religion, we may now examine the methods available for the study of religion. Also, we shall delve into the guidelines that necessarily go along with the methods.

When the issue of methods is addressed, what really comes to mind is the question of how religion is to be studied. By how, we mean what procedure(s) are to be taken when one undertakes the study of religion. It is important, however, to point out that what makes the adopted procedure methodical is the systematic manner in which the study is carried out. Also, it must be realized from the onset that methods of studying religion are as varied as there are various data in religion, as well as varied approaches. Consequently, the method that is adopted depends on the interest and the envisaged appropriateness of the procedure in attaining the goal of the study.

Over the years, certain methods of studying religion have emerged. Principal among these include: historical, philosophical, comparative, sociological, and psychological. These methods have developed basically from the points of interest of their propagators. For example, if one's interest is in the developmental process of religion—particularly in the area of how world religions came about, their founders and growth—the historical method would serve adequately. If it is the truth and falsity of religion and its claims that constitute the scope of interest, the method to be adopted should be the philosophical one. When the researcher is faced with the task of examining how the forms and values of one religion can be compared to another, either in their definitive forms or as practiced by communities who own the religions, the comparative method comes into play. On the other hand, if the realm of investigation has to do with the study of the nature and interactional tendencies of religious communities, then the sociological method should be embraced. The psychological method would be indispensable when the study has to do with the influence of religion, particularly religious myths, on individuals.

On the whole, what is important is the realization that there is no one method for the study of religion. The researcher must make his own choice from the available variety of methods. However, he must bear in mind that the method he chooses must be determined by the kind of questions he is out to answer, as well as what data in religion he is dealing with. However, a more important point must be recognized and be applied. This stipulates that certain guidelines should be brought into play if any meaningful and tangible results are to be attained. We now proceed to enumerate and discuss some of these briefly.

Openness and Sympathy

Whatever method one adopts for the study of religion, it is of utmost importance that the researcher display a large measure of openness and sympathy in the process. This is indispensable if a profitable study of religion is to be attained. It is only when there is openness of mind that the truth can be revealed. This means that there must be avoidance of a biased conclusion and preconceived notions concerning the religion to speak for it. The student should not depend on what he himself thinks or what others outside the religion say of it. The sympathy that the scholar has for the religion is very vital in providing him with the openness of mind to realize that without prejudice, he must assume a position of ignorance and humility and be prepared to learn step by step.

Reverence

The level of sympathy that the scholar applies to his study is derived mainly from the amount of reverence he has for religion in general or, as the case may be, the particular religion he is studying. However, reverence can only be a product of the realization that religion is a thing of supreme concern for man. It therefore deals with man's aspirations and dreams. For these reasons, the scholar must approach his task with the preparedness to acknowledge what the religion holds holy or sacred. His treatment of that must be in accordance with the beliefs of the religion and its propagators. It is only then that he would be able to see the real values that are manifested in religion.

Caution

The scholar's attitude of openness, sympathy, and observance of reverence can only be realized in a situation of cautiousness. Each step of the study must be taken with deliberate care and painstaking thoroughness. By being cautious, the scholar will soon realize that there must be tact and honesty.

These would, in turn, lead to the realization that no one has all the knowledge needed to claim authority in any field. If this is accepted, the scholar would be able to free himself from forming the impression that he has the last say on the subject under study. This is because, after all, research in any given field goes on and on, and as this happens new facts are discovered that may change what was earlier held to be certain. This is even more so when the subject of study is religion, dealing with the Deity, who is divine and mysterious. It would be self-deception to think that one could know everything about Him. If we take a cue from the fact that there is no way we can ever have full knowledge about persons we live with every day and events that we are always part of, we would come to appreciate our limitations about our knowledge of the Divine and His worship. In fact, we can only claim to meet the Divine "mystically," and this very sparingly. As Paul says: "For we see him in a mirror dimly." This is a warning to scholars of religion(s) that religion is a very delicate subject to deal with. As such, their approach to it must be well grounded in cautious disposition if they are not to go astray, treating the shadow rather than the reality.

Participation

All the guidelines discussed so far can bring fulfillment to a large extent (this may apply more when studying particular religions, rather than religion in general), if not exclusively, when there is participation. What we mean by this is that if one is to study a religion and get to the root of it, no other functional way could be found than being part of that religion, at least to a reasonable extent. The scholar may have to practically experience the religion. With this there would be identification with the religion, its beliefs, practices, and its followers. When the confidence of the followers is secured, the path to inside knowledge about the religion would certainly become easier.

In the absence of the above, the scholar would probably come to conclusions that are products of guesswork or hearsay. This situation can be avoided when he has become one with the followers of the religion—working with them, living with them, sharing as much as possible every aspect of their lives, in meals, conversations, dreams, and aspirations. At the end of the day, the scholar is sure to have his "prize"—the in-depth knowledge of the true values of the religion he is studying. It is only when this has been attained that a profitable study may be said to have been done.

WHAT SHOULD BE STUDIED IN RELIGION?

When we speak of the study of religion, perhaps the most important question to ask is what actually in religion is studied? We may say that this is the most important issue because, in the real sense of it, the why, the personalities who study, and the method by which religion is studied, depend on what is or are contained in it, making it an object of study.

As in all other fields of study, what constitute objects of investigations are generally referred to as "data." In essence, data may be defined as "the things that can be denoted or specified by some perspective of thought or speech." In this sense, data can include things such as ideas, individuals, feelings, man-made objects, and natural and social phenomena.

When this notion is applied to religion, the data that are studied need not be restricted, as long as they can be classified as religious by implication. What this amounts to is that there is no way that one could arbitrarily fix a specific or exclusive number of religious data, or in fact determine what religious data are. This is because an item would be or not be a religious datum to be studied only when certain factors have been critically considered. At times, a datum may be religious when approached from the religious dimension, while at other times it loses such a status because it is employed in situations that have nothing to do with religion. Ronald Cavanagh (1978) gives the example of the cross, which could be a religious datum from the Christian usage, where it represents the crucifix. However, this same cross represents a crossroads for a driver and a hated object of the Ku Klux Klan's hatred for a black person.

On the other hand, things or ideas regarded ordinarily far from being religious may become religious data by definitions, implications, or interpretations. This is why, in the study of religion, it may become imperative to include areas of human concern such as drugs, voting, patterns, politics, corruption, justice, fair play, humanism, medicine, abortion, suicide, and so on.

On the whole, one may proffer two broad categories of religious data. The first would consist of ideas, personalities, and objects which are primarily or exclusively religious data. Examples of these are religious beliefs, origins and developments of various religions, scriptures of these religions, doctrines, dogma, and practices of religions, as well as religious figures. All these are to be studied in religion. The second category is made up of general items in different human valuations that are primarily secular in nature and consideration. These can, however, secondarily become religious data to be studied in religion, when by implication they assume bearing either on religion directly or on humanity in its religious ramifications.

REVIEW QUESTIONS

1. From your own perspective, why should religion be studied at all?
2. Identify and discuss the obstacles facing a profitable study of religion.
3. Explain the steps to be taken if religion is to be gainfully studied.
4. Attempt a critique of different scholars who have studied religion in the past.

5. Based on your own experience and study, who do you think is qualified to be a student or a scholar of religion?

6. Overall, what benefits would you ascribe to the study of religion?

BIBLIOGRAPHY AND FURTHER READING

Bouquet, A. C. 1945. *Comparative Religion*. London: Pelican.

_____. 1933. *Man and Deity: An Outline of the Origin and Development of Religion*. Cambridge: W. Heffer.

Capps, W. H. 1995. *Religious Studies: The making of a Discipline*. Minneapolis: Fortress Press.

_____. 1972. *Ways of Understanding Religion*. London: Macmillan.

Cavanagh, Ronald. 1978. In T. M. Hall, ed. *Introduction to the Study of Religion*. London: Harper & Row.

Christian, W. A. 1964. *Meaning and Truth in Religion*. Princeton, NJ: Princeton University Press.

Evans-Pritchard, E. E. 1962. *Essays in Social Anthropology*. London: Faber & Faber.

_____. 1965. *Theories of Primitive Religion*. London: Oxford University Press.

Fenton, J. Y. 1970. *Reductionism in the Study of Religion*. Soundings: Macmillan.

Flew, A. and A. McIntyre, eds. 1955. *New Essays in Philosophical Theology*. London: SCM.

Hick, John. 1989. *An Interpretation of Religion*. London: New Haven.

Hultkrantz, A. 1970. *The Phenomenology of Religions: Aims and Method*. Temenos: Kluwer Academic Publication.

Huxley, J. 1930. *Science, Religion and Human Nature*. Oxford: Watts & Co.

McDermott, E. A. 1968. *Religion as an Academic Discipline*.

Proudfoot, Wayne. 1985. *Religious Experience*. California: Oxford University Press.

Sharma, A., ed. 2002. *Methodology in Religious Studies: The Interface with Woman Studies*. Albany: State University of New York Press.

Sharpe, E. J. 1971. "Some Problems of Methods in the Study of Religion," Religion I.

Smith, W. C. 1959. *Comparative Religion: Whither and Why?* UK: Oriel Press Ltd.

Stark, Werner. 1970. *Humanistic and Scientific Knowledge of Religion: Their Social Context and Contrast*. NJ: Transaction Publishers.

Streng, F. J. 1970. "The Objective of Religion and Unique Quality of Religiousness," *Religious Studies*, 6.

Tambiah, S. J. 1990. *Magic, Science, Religion, and the Scope of Rationality*. Cambridge: Cambridge University Press.

Toynbee, A. 1956. *A Historian's Approach to Religion*. London: Oxford University Press.

de Vries, Jan. 1967. *The Study of Religion: A Historical Approach*. Harcourt, Brace & World.

Waardenburg, J. 1983. *Classical Approaches to the Study of Religion: Aims, Methods, and Theories of Research*. London: Mouton.

Webie, Donald. 1985. "Explanation and the Scientific Study of Religion." *Religion* 5.

Wilken, R. L. 1971. *The Myth of Christian Teachings: History, Impact on Belief*. Doubleday.

Wilson, B., ed. 1970. *Rationality*. Oxford: Oxford University Press.

CHAPTER FOUR

SYMBOLS AND RELIGION(S)

INTRODUCTION

General Concepts and Definitions and Functional Characteristics

In defining the word *symbol*, Carl Jung (1964) distinguishes it from the term *sign*. According to him, while a sign stands for something known, a symbol, on the other hand, represents the unknown; it is unclear and imprecise. Thus, a symbol should be regarded as an indication of different layers of meaning. Consequently, a symbol depicts a deeper meaning than the superficial or literary connotation of a sign. In essence, a symbol should be taken as a sign that demands deeper levels of meaning. Within this context, a symbol means more than what it literally says.

Some scholars have categorized symbols into three types of representation. These are: personal, cultural, and universal.

In the personal category are symbols with the dynamics of how every human being relates to objects in their different realities. The cultural classification depicts how different objects may change in meaning, depending on cultural particularities. The third type, which is the universal, is indicative of symbols with universal meanings. This category of symbols underlines the possibility of the objective understanding of humanity in general. Based on these categories of symbols, humanity has the advantage of understanding the complex and sometimes intriguing natures of not just one's own individual and cultural sensibilities, but also those of others and their cultures. In order to fully grasp and appreciate the meaning and significance of symbols, it is important to give some basic definitions of symbols here.

For example, Namy (2005) defines a symbol as:

> The ability to use a signal to represent and refer to some object, action, or event in the world—is fundamental to everyday cognitive functioning … Symbols give a person the ability to communicate with others effectively and efficiently … The effectiveness of symbols can be represented by the use of a traffic stop sign.

The meanings of symbols are clearly demonstrated in their everyday usage. Within this context, symbols become part of everyday life for humans. For instance, if a symbol is defined in the form of a stop sign, it then indicates what a person must do when he or she comes to an intersection, for instance. This gives the driver, without the need for an actual person, an understanding and the line of action to take at an intersection—to stop or to go.

This exercise becomes a communication strategy, sometimes deployed either verbally or through gestures. Using the example of a child, who is learning different human abilities, symbols both verbal and in the form of gestures play a large and decisive role. As Goldin-Meadow (2005) indicates, a child can learn the word "dog" by its barking as a symbol, for example. Through this process, the child comes to the knowledge of what that dog sounds like and is able to differentiate it from other sounds. In this case, symbols function as strategies through which a person learns how to differentiate word sounds and meanings from one and other. Also, this statement shows that symbols play a large role from the beginning of a person's life.

In the case of gestures as symbols, they can be used without verbal components to describe a state of being. For instance, if one is hungry, he or she could illustrate this state by jabbing a fist toward the mouth, pretending to chew (Goldin-Meadow, 2005). The gestures of the movement of the hand toward the mouth and the chewing clearly symbolize the state of being hungry and the desire for food.

RELIGIOUS SYMBOLS

Symbols have become significantly functional in the practice of religion. This stems essentially from the dual nature of religion. The negotiating dynamics between the sacred and profane natures (objects and subjects) of religion make the use of symbols as communication linkages imperative. Within this context, it is the fundamental function of symbols to not only address the distinctive characteristics of both sides, but more importantly to bridge the "gulf" between the two "spaces."

In achieving these objectives, symbols in religion discharge two unique roles, signifying what they mean in religion and its practice. The first is functioning as something that "represents," "stands for," or "signifies" something else. The second is functioning as "the means by which people orient themselves to the symbol's referent" (Deming, 2005:16). In combining these two inclusive functions, religious symbols provide religious followers the pathway to understanding and negotiating the meeting points between the mundane world and the ultimate reality—thus encompassing both corporate and individualistic connotations in relation to the two spaces. In summing up the role of symbols in religion, Goldammer (1995) identifies a religious symbol as a major tool which helps the individual religious follower to understand the divine, and his or her own identity as a follower.

The significant functions of symbols in religion and its practices definitely warrants asking questions such as: How can religious symbols be described in terms of meaning? What is the standard to observe so as to determine the truthfulness and/or correctness of such symbols? How may the followers of religions identify with and make spiritual meaning of the symbols? Are those symbols true or correct? How do adherents of a religion recognize those symbols? To what extent can the symbols lead to recognizing the difficulty of understanding religion and the function of religious symbols in making it easy for the religious to summon this difficulty?

Perhaps the starting point of addressing these question is to agree with Goldammer (1995) that religious symbols come in many shapes and sizes, but that their meaning is universally accepted by a given community or followers of particular religions. Within these contexts, a religious symbol is any object, word, or gesture that serves to convey the meaning of a religious ideal. This is why it is fundamental that a religious symbol have a universally accepted meaning to the followers of a particular religion. This ensures easy recognition and constitutes the basic level of understanding for such religious followers.

It is also worth noting that the concept, process, and functions of a symbol can vary from one religion to the other. Consequently, in some religions, symbols are a reminder of sacrifice or of a savior figure, while in others they are the physical representation of the divine, and in still others they constitute important lessons to help facilitate and sustain goodness.

With all this at the back of our minds, it is not very difficult to subscribe to the conclusion that religious symbols are crucial to the understanding of what a religion is. In addition to the symbols defining a person's identity as a follower of a religion, and that without the symbols religion would become for all intents and purposes mere individual subjective worship of the divine. Another very important function of religious symbols is that they fundamentally assist followers of a particular religion in understanding their religion, and in addition, through the symbols others outside the particular religion are able to recognize it. Invariably, it becomes imperative that in order to understand a particular religion, its attendant symbols must be understood through knowing what they are.

Over and above the meaning and functions of religious symbols discussed above, some scholars of the 20th and 21st centuries have viewed the significance of religious symbols within the connotations of the symbolic dynamics of religion rather than its rationality. Such scholars have therefore stressed the importance of religious symbols from their psychological and mythological perspectives. Other scholars have explored the comparative significance of religious symbols as basic components of religious expression. Yet other scholars have approached the content and process of religious symbols as theological strategies (for example in Christianity). Here, the emphasis centers on themes of religion such as redemption, salvation, forgiveness, grace, atonement, and sacrifice.

Whatever the "bent" of perspectives on religious symbols, they can all be summed up as fundamental expressions of the significance of religious ideals and practices. In achieving this basic objective, there are, of course, varieties of religious symbols. Thus, while some of the symbols signify life and death, others serve to represent the life of a religious figure, etc. Consequently, no matter the symbol's exact function, it ultimately indicates a deeper meaning and understanding of a particular religion as processes of effective communication.

RELIGIOUS SYMBOLS IN SELECTED RELIGIOUS TRADITIONS

Religious symbols have evolved over time in different religious traditions. These symbols have typified the fundamental beliefs, doctrines, and theologies of these religions. It is definitely impossible to discuss either the multitudes of available religious symbols or all the religions in which they are found. Consequently, only two or three major religious symbols of the religions discussed in this book—Judaism, Christianity, Islam, African Traditional Religion, and Asiatic religious traditions in Hinduism, Buddhism, and Confucianism are examined.

1. JUDAISM

In Judaism, the *menorah* is one of the earliest and most prevalent symbols. This religious symbol essentially represents Hanukkah. The symbol has seven arms and is commonly found in synagogues. At other times it is used in many funerary contexts, such as on tomb walls and sarcophagi. This Judaic religious symbol is principally regarded as a priestly symbol rather than representing the totality of Judaism (Hachili, 2001). The *menorah* stands for the concept of "light." This is why it is called the "lamp" and the "light of God" in the Bible (1 Samuel 3:3).

Another major religious symbol in Judaism is the Magen David. Translated into English, this means the "Shield of David." The most significant thing about this figure is that it is recognized as the overall symbol of Judaism. Most times it is called the Star of David. The symbol is a six-pointed star that is made up of two interlocking, equilateral triangles. As described by the Jewish Encyclopedia, the *Magen David* has actually been used as a non-Jewish motif and was found in Christian churches during the Middle Ages. It is also very interesting that the symbol is absent from contemporary Jewish decoration and rabbinic literature. In tracing the origin of the name, the same Jewish Encyclopedia indicates that it is derived from the 13th century in the "practical Kabbalah," where it was used as a magical symbol; it became associated with the pentagram or the Star of Solomon. Overall, the symbol is seen as the hexagram formed by the star in symbolic representation of the creation of the Earth. Here, each of the points represents a different day and a different aspect of the

creation story (Leet, 2004). Today, this religious symbol has become the official symbol of the State of Israel and can be found on the flag.

A third religious symbol in Judaism is the *mezuzah*. The symbol consists of two parchments with different verses from the Torah written on them. They are handwritten by a scribe and in the same language that is found in the Torah (Chill, 2000). The two verses are known as the *Shema* and the *Vehayah*, and both contain the phrase "And it shall be written on the doorposts." The parchment is encased and nailed to every doorpost in the home except for bathrooms and rooms which are smaller than 16 cubits, which is just less than 2 square feet (Chill, 2000). The word *Shaddai*, one of God's names, is written on the back of the parchment. The symbol on the front of the mezuzah is Shin, which is the first letter of *Shaddai*. The top must be slanted in toward the middle of the room in order to be considered a genuine *mezuzah*.

2. Christianity

The cross, which is the most significant and widely accepted symbol of Christianity, signifies the reality (historical) of the belief that Jesus in human nature as the Son of God was crucified, died, and then was resurrected to life (John 19:17–33; 20:1–29). When Emperor Constantine was converted to Christianity in the early 4th century, he made Christianity the state religion of the Roman Empire. The cross then became a symbol for Christianity. Over the decades, the cross has evolved in different shapes. For example, evolving over time, the Roman cross, which was actually used for the crucifixion of Jesus, was more likely T-shaped. Thus, it was possible for the Roman authority to write the charge out and placed it on top of the cross for everyone to see. Though the appearance of the cross has been altered over time, its meaning runs

deep and remains the same. It signifies and brings back the memory of the moment where Jesus was crucified as the ultimate sacrifice for human original sin with the prize of universal redemption. The symbol is now prominently found:

+ On church buildings;
+ On clothing, tattoos, jewelry (necklaces, earrings, rings, etc.);
+ In people's homes, on people's cars;
+ In movies, television, billboards, advertising;
+ In organizations such as the American Red Cross;
+ On world flags such as those of the United Kingdom, Sweden, Switzerland, Finland, Greece, and Norway.

Two other religious symbols in Christianity which are usually combined are the fish and the Chi Rho. These symbols, in fact, constituted the earliest symbols in Christianity. They were used as a sign of identification, orienting fellow believers to one another and to Jesus. The need for such derived from the fact that in the first three centuries, Christianity was persecuted and prohibited by Roman law. Thus, the Christians had to meet in secret. In addition, one could not speak openly as a Christian. It therefore became imperative for Christians to use covert symbols to identify one another without the authorities knowing what they meant. The symbols consisted of drawing one half of the fish, "∩" and others would indicate their Christian status by completing the fish with the other half, "∪." Also, a Christian

might draw the chi, "X," while another would follow with a "P" to declare the Christian identification. The

origin of the fish as a Christian symbol usually has been traced back to the Gospels, where Jesus declared he would make the disciples "fishers of men" (Mark 1:14; Matthew 4:17). Another such origination could be derived from the multiplication of the five loaves and two fish (in all Gospels). Yet another origin might have been the Greek word for "fish" (*ichthys*, or ΙΧΘΥΣ), "an acronym for the claim that 'Jesus is the Christ, the Son of God and Savior'" (Deming, 2005). In the case of the Chi and Rho monogram, both words are said to come from the first two letters in the Greek word for *Christ* (Χριστός). Though these do not technically represent a cross, they still invoke the crucifixion of Jesus and orient fellow believers to one another as well as to Jesus. These symbols have been represented in different shapes.

3. ISLAM

In Islam, "[t]he Rub el Hizb is a Muslim symbol, shaped as two overlapping squares. This is found on a number of emblems and flags. In Arabic, *Rub* means 'one fourth, quarter', while *Hizb* means a group or party. The symbol was initially used in the Quran, which is divided into 60 *Hizb* (60 groups of roughly equal length); the symbol determines every quarter of *Hizb*, while the *Hizb* is one half of *a juz'*. The main purpose of the division is to facilitate recitation of the Quran" (*Rub el Hizb*).

Usually the symbol is also used in Arabic writings, representing the end of a chapter. The origin of the *Rub el Hizb* is believed to be during the eight centuries when Islamic dynasties based in Andalusia used *Rub el Hizb* as a representation of *Tartessos*—the ancient civilization of Atlantis.

Today, the *Rub el Hizb* can be seen on:

+ The current coat of arms of Turkmenistan;
+ The current coat of arms of Uzbekistan;
+ Azat party flag;
+ The unofficial flag of Kazakhstan in the 1990s, the basis of the modern state flag, light blue with a hollow yellow *rub el hizb*;
+ The fictional flag of Hatay in the movie *Indiana Jones and the Last Crusade*;
+ Modified on the flag of Azerbaijan;
+ The emblem of the Organization of the Scout Movement of Kazakhstan;
+ The previous emblem of the Iraqi Boy Scouts and Girl Guides Council;
+ The logo of the Cairo Metro;
+ The logo of the musical group Faith No More (Rub el Hizb).

The star and crescent is the best-known symbol in Islam. The symbol was adopted by the Ottomans from the Byzantines. The star and crescent appeared on Byzantine coins.

The symbol is found on the Ottoman Empire's flag and also on the flags of other successor states. During the 20th century, the star and crescent were placed on many countries' flags, and it gained popularity among Muslim nations. "By the 1970s, this symbolism was embraced by movements of Arab nationalism or Islamism even though it was not originally an Arab symbol" (Curtis, 2006).

4. AFRICAN TRADITIONAL RELIGION

As a religion very much embedded in practicalities, religious symbols constitute a fundamental part of the religion as visual components of its rituals of devotions, especially to the divinities and ancestors. There are indeed numerous symbols characterizing different communities of devotees of the religion. Only three of such are presented here.

The first symbol is the mask, probably the most recognized religious symbols of African Traditional Religion. In African traditional societies, the art has always been an essential part of religion. Masks represent divine spirits of the dead or spirits of nature. The masks as figures are regarded as strong presences in ceremonies of change, such as rites, ceremonies, funerals, and memorials. In order to protect the community from free rein of the powerful spirits, the members restrain them by assuming the appearance of the higher power. For example, among the Yoruba people of Nigeria, the *epa* mask is considered the most ornate and is worn during rites, ceremonies, and funerals. Today, masks have continued to be part of Yoruba traditional religious ceremonies, and in addition, they have tremendously inspired and influenced modern art in Western civilizations of the world through the global popularity of Yoruba art.

Another common religious symbol in the practice of African Traditional Religion is the carving of images, which are then regarded as the embodiment of spirits with magical potency. A representation of these could

be found among the Benin society of West Africa. Here the carved objects stand for manifestations of divine forces, under which the people can place themselves for protection through rituals. Indeed, by so doing, they can "lend" their body to the deity during rituals.

Other carved objects which have become renowned religious symbols can be found among the Asante community of Ghana. These are chairs and stools, which are essential to the community. The stools vary in design and adornment and are given to a member of the Asante during a ceremonial entrance into society. A member's attachment to their stool lasts even after death, as the stool is then blackened to show that it now belongs to an ancestor. It continues to be venerated as a form of honoring the ancestor. Indeed, the tradition of stools can be traced back to the reign of the first Asantehene, Osei Tutu. Each of his successors has received personal stools since his rule. The stools are decorated based on

one's status in the community. Those stools belonging to high-ranking members have greater embellishments on them.

5. CONFUCIANISM

Confucianism has many religious symbols. However, there are two principal ones, which still remind people of Chinese philosophy, both religious and nonreligious alike. One of these symbols is the *yin-yang* symbol. The other one, also very famous, is the Five Elements symbol, closely linked with the Five Virtues (Berthrong, 2000). Both symbols have practically become the embodiment of Confucianism, through decades of its existence even till today.

The yin and yang symbol has embodied Confucius's philosophy that existence is a duality (Werner, 1986). This duality of nature indicates that opposites are everywhere in the natural world—representing male and female, living and dead, young and old. While yin is associated with darkness, femininity, and weakness, yang, on the other hand, is associated with light, masculinity, and strength (Berthrong, 2000). Through these opposites, one may view one side as better than the other, though they cannot exist without each other. This is why humans must always be aware of the inner harmony between these two forces as containing a "vital force" (or *qi*) that fluctuates between yin and yang, which is never completely yin nor completely yang (Berthrong, 2000). For Confucius, this was an attempt to create a harmonious society (Hoobler, 1997). To achieve this, he postulated that every member of the society must understand the dual nature of themselves as well as the dual nature of everything around them.

The harmony that Confucius strove to establish is also demonstrated in the Five Elements, examples of the dual nature of existence, thus becoming another prominent symbol of Confucianism. The five elements are called the *huhsing*, and they include: wood, water, metal, fire, and air (Werner, 1986). Each element is affected and shaped by the others, so that one cannot be useful without the assistance of the other elements. These elements are also connected with *qi* and must be monitored to make sure that not too much of one element is present, since it was the belief of Confucius that inner harmony among the elements sustains the outer harmony (Berthrong, 2000; Hoobler, 1993). These elements are intimately connected with the Five Virtues, which are: *Ren* (humaneness), *I* (righteousness), *Li* (ritual and civility), *Zhi* (wisdom), and *Xin* (faithfulness in thought, word, and deed) (Berthrong, 2000).

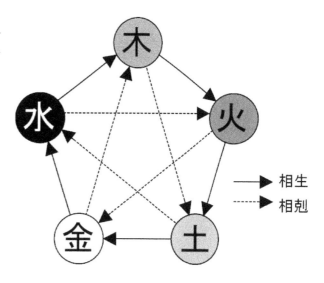

A proper understanding of the Five Virtues, the Five Elements, and the yin-yang as symbols demonstrates the basic premise of Confucianism, which is to achieve harmony in society as a continuation of achieving it within oneself. In Confucianism, a harmonious society is considered to be the ultimate achievement. However, this inner harmony is consequent upon the opposites in life, the ups and downs that come along, which must be balanced out (Hoobler, 1993).

6. HINDUISM

The *Aum/Om* is one of the most important Hindu symbols. The sound *Aum* is made up by the combination of three Sanskrit letters: *aa, au, ma* (*Religion Facts: Hinduism*, 2009). The symbol itself represents the

Brahman, who is referred to as the absolute. Thus, the symbol represents the universe and the ultimate reality, or essence, of the entire universe. The meaning of this symbol is even deeper because of the belief that God created sound first, from which the universe then rose (Pattanaik, 2003). This symbol plays an important role in everyday life, as it is used as the sound at the beginning and end of all Hindu prayers (*Religion Facts: Hinduism*, 2009).

Another symbol of Hinduism is the *swastika*. It is a symbol that has not only been identified with India, but also with other cultures and religions. The symbol originates from the word *svasti*, which means fortune, luck, and well-

being. The meaning derived from it is usually based on the way the arms are bent. If bent clockwise, then they are meant to bring good fortune. The symbol also represents the sun and the sun god. The clockwise orientation represents how the sun starts in the northern hemisphere, passes east, then south, and then west. If the swastikas are bent counterclockwise, they represent the goddess Kali. The swastika has been around for over 3000 years and has been used by many religions. Interestingly, it is most often associated with the Nazis. In spite of this, it is still considered an important religious symbol in Hinduism (*Religion Facts: Hinduism*, 2009).

Another symbol of Hinduism is the *tilak*. This is a mark made on the forehead of either a Hindu man or woman. For males, the line or lines identifies the sect to which they belong. For females, the *tilak*—usually a dot on the forehead—is referred to as *bindi*, which symbolizes that the Hindu woman is married. The *bindi* is believed to protect the woman and her husband. The *tilaks* are worn every day by Hindu practitioners and on special occasions such as weddings and other religious rituals. They are also applied to people when they visit a temple. The marks are usually applied by hand and can be made of ash, paste, turmeric, cow dung, clay, and some other items (Pattanaik, 2003).

7. BUDDHISM

There are many symbols in Buddhism. Among these, one of the most prominent ones is the *Dharmachakra*. This symbol represents the basic teachings of Buddha. The name of the symbol derives from the act of  Buddha turning the wheel of *dharma*. The wheel stands for many different things. Among them are the wheel's motion, representing the metaphor of rapid spiritual change caused by Buddha's teachings; the spokes of the wheel, of which there are eight, symbolizing the eightfold path of Buddhism (*Religion Facts: Buddhism*, 2009). Sometimes it is also used as a representation of the endless cycle of rebirth that people are caught in with the belief that they can only escape it if they follow Buddha's teachings. Today, the symbol is found in the art of every Buddhist culture (Dagyab, 1995).

Another very important symbol in Buddhism is the Tibetan Wheel of Life. This symbol represents the perspective of Buddhists on life. Yama, the lord of death, is designated with the responsibility of turning the wheel (*Religion Facts: Buddhism*, 2009). The inner circle of the wheel symbolizes the three root delusions: hatred, ignorance, and greed. Karma is represented by the ring around the center. The ring in the middle of the wheel symbolizes the six realms of existence. This is split into groups of three; the top half represents humans, gods, and demigods, while the lower half represents animals, beings from hell, and hungry ghosts. The outermost ring represents the 12 links of dependent origination (Dagyab, 1977).

The *Buddhapada* as a symbol of Buddhism actually represents the footprints of Buddha. The footprints usually have toes of equal length and a *Dharmachakra* in the center of the foot. The footprints symbolize the presence of Buddha (Dagyab, 1995). It is believed that the footprints are where Buddha actually touched the ground. Just as it represents Buddha's presence, it also represents his absence, symbolizing his entrance into *Nirvana*. The footprints serve as a reminder of the idea of nonattachment. This is why the *Buddhapada* are revered greatly by all Buddhists (*Religion Facts: Buddhism*, 2009).

REVIEW QUESTIONS

1. How can the concept of symbols be universally defined?
2. What are the dynamics that separate religious symbols from symbols in general?
3. What are the main characteristics and functions of religious symbols?
4. Which symbols are central to Christianity?

5. African Traditional Religion is essentially a practical religion. How does the use of symbols substantiate this notion?
6. Many symbols are used in different Asiatic religions to enhance their followers' understanding of the relationship between the mundane and the spiritual realms. Identify at least two of such symbols from Hinduism, Buddhism, and Confucianism and discuss their religious content and relevance.
7. How far is it justifiable to claim that the cross is the most important symbol in Christianity?

BIBLIOGRAPHY AND FURTHER READING

Barbour, Ian. 1974. *Myths, Models and Paradigms: A Comparative Study in Science and Religion.* New York: Harper & Row.

Bewkes, Eugene. 1937. *The Nature of Religious Experience.* N Y: Oxford University Press.

Chadwick, C. 1971. *Symbolism.* London: Methuen.

Deming, Will. 2005. *Rethinking Religion: A Concise Introduction.* New York: Oxford University Press.

Ejizu, C. I. 2002. *Ofo Igbo Ritual and Symbol.* Enugu: Fourth Dimension Publishers.

Goldammer, Kurt Moritz Arthur. (1995). "Religious Symbolism and Iconography." *Encyclopedia Britannica.*

Hick, John. 1992. *An Interpretation of Religion.* New Haven: Yale University Press.

Johnson, F. E. 1955. *Religious Symbolism.* New York: Doubleday Publications.

Jung, C. G. 1964. *Man and His Symbols.* New York: Doubleday Publications.

_____. 1938. *Psychology of Religion.* New Haven: Yale University Press.

MacFague, Sallie. 1982. *Metaphorical Theology.* Philadelphia: Fortress Press.

May, Rollo, ed. 1960. *Symbolism in Religion and Literature.* NY: Oxford University Press.

Namy, L. L. 2005. *Symbol Use and Symbolic Representation: Developmental and Comparative Perspectives.* Mahwah, NJ: Lawrence Erlbaum Associates.

Soskice, J. M. 1985. *Metaphor and Religious Language.* Oxford: Oxford University Press.

Teselle, Sallie. 1975. *Speaking in Parables.* Philadelphia: Fortress Press.

PART II

APPROACHES TO THE
STUDY OF RELIGION

CHAPTER FIVE

PHILOSOPHICAL APPROACH

INTRODUCTION

Over the centuries, the place of philosophy in religion has become guaranteed, though not without some measure of spirited antagonism, resulting from suspicion and skepticism from both ends, but principally from not a few religionists who, regarding philosophy as a "spoiler," would want to keep it at arm's length from religion. This kind of attitude notwithstanding, and with adequate considerations of the kinds of relations in conflicts and complementation that are envisaged obtainable between philosophy and religion, there has been the development and acceptance of a separate discipline of philosophy of religion as a positive amalgamation of the two fields of human endeavor.

PHILOSOPHY: WHAT IS IT?

"A definition of philosophy is notoriously difficult." This is how W. J. Abraham (1985) sums up the futility one may encounter in the attempt to define philosophy. The difficulty is further aggravated when it is realized that philosophers themselves are not unanimous in their opinions concerning the precise definition philosophy should be given. This is not to say that attempts have not been made, though they may not be acceptable to all.

Two main approaches may be adopted in this task. First, the etymological meaning of philosophy, actually a derivation of two ancient Greek words (*philo* and *sophia*), which, when combined, become *philosophia*, meaning "love of wisdom" or "love of knowledge." No wonder philosophers have come to be referred to as wise men. Second, from the "sort of things" that philosophy does: A definition from this perspective may be more appropriate, particularly if we want to free ourselves from the limitations that may be imposed by the layman and mundane conceptions of the etymological definition.

The principal preoccupation of philosophy is that of reflection, and this is done in three major areas of interest, as stated by W. J. Abraham (1985):

There has been interest in the analysis of the key concept in everyday language, e.g., what is justice, being and causality. There has been interest in arguments, e.g., what constitutes a good, as opposed, to a bad, argument? There has been the articulation of a worldview, e.g., what can be believed about life as a whole? What is the place of human beings in the scheme of things? What is the good life?

To critically engage in the task of finding answers to these questions, not only in a comprehensive but in an organized fashion, is to engage in philosophy with the objective of producing a body of natural knowledge that has been methodically obtained and ordered, whose main preoccupation is to give fundamental explanations of all things.

In summary, a working definition of philosophy from our perspective is:

The science which searches for the truth about reality as a whole and trusts reason to coordinate in a coherent and logical unity those things that seem strange to man in the natural order, and in doing so to also determine man's relation to this natural order.

Religion

Defining religion is a complicated task, and at the same time an interestingly rich experience. This is because the definitions of religion that have been offered have not only run into the hundreds, but have also reflected diverse subjects that religion is related to and the overriding interests of the authors offering them. Thus, to ask, What is religion? is not only to ask an ambiguous question, but to irresistibly indulge in ambiguities.

An attempt to get around this problem may consist of changing a restricting definition of religion to an etymological one, whereby the term "religion" has been originally linked with the Latin verb *religare*, meaning "to bind." However, defining religion in this way must be jettisoned because it has stressed the negative aspects of religion rather than its positive ones. Also, it has exposed religion to being contemptuously regarded. On the negative side, if religion is seen as a factor that binds, it may depict a rubric that becomes unreasonably fanatical as a result of being wedged together by rules, obligations, and responsibilities that are dogmatically essential to the laws and observances of the demands of their religion. Some scholars who are only interested in negatively or even ridiculously interpreting religion may join in on this meaning of religion, as indeed Salomon Beinaeh has done in defining religion as "an assembly at scruples impeding the free exercise of our faculties"(Aderibigbe and Aiyegboyin, eds., 1987).

If we must then seek to define religion from its operational sense, we must be prepared to be confronted with quite a number of divergent definitions that reflect various disciplines such as sociology, psychology, history, philosophy, theology, etc. All these are part of the human phenomenon. However, definitions of religion can be categorized to portray their areas of interest; for example, the phenomenological nature of religion that highlights the universal interest in it may support a definition found in the *Concise Oxford Dictionary* as:

Human recognition of a superhuman controlling power and especially of a personal God or gods entitled to obedience and worship.

Religion may also be defined from the sociological perspective when it is seen as comprising a set of beliefs, practices, and institutions that have been evolved by humans in various societies. Also, a psychological definition of religion essentially sees religion as the aggregate of the feelings, acts, and experiences of individuals in their solitude, while considering themselves to be in relation to that which they consider to be divine.

Whichever definition of religion is offered, certain key concepts are always of concern. There is the recognition of the object of worship, which is the divine. There is the presence of the subject of worship, which is man. And perhaps most importantly, there is the concern for in most, if not all, religions—salvation—which actually is the main reason for man being religious. Thus, any worthwhile definition of religion must adequately cater to a process of transition from the unsatisfactory and finite nature of the world and man to the perfect and infinite one. Such a definition, in addition, must portray the attainment of the ultimate in the object of man's religious worship. For our purpose in this book and without any pretentious claim of its adequacy or comprehensiveness, we adopt Emile Durkheim's definition: "Religion is that which deals with the sacred things set apart and forbidden. ..." (Durkheim, 1981). This definition becomes instructive when one considers the tensions that have characterized the relations between religion and philosophy and which mostly have been responsible for the position of demanding wholesale segregation of the two disciplines. For religion as a sacred thing set apart and forbidden would indeed be a strange bedfellow with such an open, critical, analytical, and rational subject as philosophy. Thus, they cannot but be embedded in a constant and deep-rooted suspicion, if not outright rejection, of each other's position, religion being the more aggrieved partner.

PHILOSOPHY AND RELIGION

The relationship between religion and philosophy has not always been cordial. In fact, the two spheres are more or less seen as rivals. Factors responsible for this state of affairs principally have to do with the nature of the two disciplines. Not only are they by themselves complex, but the corresponding attitude of one to the other has been subjected to so much fluctuation that it is almost impossible at any given time to precisely determine their stands. Matters are not helped by the controversial lack of consensus of religionists on the one hand and philosophers on the other on how the two disciplines should relate. While some on each side favor and insist on complementation, others of the same calling argue for and are vehemently disposed to upholding the complete segregation of the two.

On the side of religion, the negative attitudes of religious believers toward philosophy consist at times of suspicion and at other times outright hostility. Ironically, those who are suspicious of philosophy are not unconscious of its worth. All they argue for is its noninvolvement in what they claim is "divine." Martin Luther vividly represented this school of thought when he said:

Philosophy understands naught of divine matters. I do not say man may not teach and learn philosophy, I approve thereof so that it may be within reason and moderation let philosophy remain within her grounds, as God has appointed and let us make use of her as a character in a comedy, but to mix her with divinity may not be endured (Hugh, 1958).

At most times, the religious believer's suspicion is born out of fear—the fear of losing one's faith. For when too many questions are asked, doubts begin to make inroads and no one is quite sure where he may end up—might one not become agnostic or an outright atheist? The believer's fear, then, seems justified on the ground of protecting his faith from criticism, which may eventually lead to his losing it.

On the whole, the believer's suspicion is an end-product of the conception of the fundamentally opposing natures of philosophy and religion. By its very nature, philosophy is built on skepticism, and this skepticism is neither ordinary nor superficial in the sense that the philosopher's skepticism is deliberate and studied. For example, modern philosophy is taken to have developed from the philosophy of Descartes, who made doubt the center of his philosophical discourse. He asserts:

> Because I wished to give myself entirely to search after the truth, I thought it was necessary for me to adopt an apparently opposite course and to reject as absolutely false everything which I could imagine the least ground of doubt in order to see whether afterwards there remained anything in my beliefs which was entirely certain (Descartes, p. 14).

The problem posed by philosophical skepticism for religion is not limited to the above. There is also the disturbing fact that the skepticism is usually directed at concepts, beliefs, and practices held by many people, and which are considered to be guaranteed by common sense. The skepticism of philosophy leads philosophers to ask difficult, abstract, and sometimes embarrassing questions about life, knowledge, and the world in general. When this is applied to religion, the believer cannot help but feel the eventual erosion of his most cherished convictions.

Second, philosophy is principally based on reflection, which is derived from self-consciousness and rational criticism, mostly directed at serious problems and the mechanics of a given system. Third, there is the abstract nature of philosophy in dealing with not only empirical problems but those that transcend the immediate consciousness. It examines the ultimate questions of life, which have to do with the natural knowledge of man, which, of course, the believer claims are not related to divinely revealed supernatural knowledge of religion.

Fourth, philosophy is essentially an intellectual exercise. The important tool here is logic, which depends exclusively on the utility of the mind. So what is important to the philosopher is the rational mind of the individual, and this is what is appealed to—not the believing hearts of people, as in the case of religion.

Invariably, these elements in the nature of philosophy tend to set it apart from religion, which in the main contains elements bordering on emotive and dogmatic dispositions. Consequently, the dividing line must be maintained in that in the final analysis, the religious believer, in seeing the nature of religion significantly opposed to that of philosophy, considers his religious faith as containing elements that are set apart from the things of the world (the sort of things that preoccupy philosophy and thus irrevocably are not submissive to the wisdom of the world). The religious message is more often than not believed, even by the theologians, to be far from the obvious and sensible. Thus, it could be seen at first sight as foolishness, if not madness. No wonder Paul opined:

> For the word of the cross is folly to those who are perishing, but to us who are being saved, it is the power of God, for it is written, "I will destroy the wisdom of the wise and the cleverness of the

clever I will thwart. Where is the wise man? Where is the scribe? Where is the debater of this age?"
Has God not made foolish the wisdom of the world? For since in the wisdom of God the world
does not know through wisdom. It pleased God through the folly of what we preach to save those
who believe it (1 Cor. 1:18–21).

In this light, philosophy may become not only valueless to religion, but more damagingly, a hindrance as
a distraction, or even a snare. This, more than mere suspicion, has led to religious believers being hostile to
philosophy and considering it as irreligious.

Tertullian is a leading advocate of this notion. He disposed of philosophy as being heretical. As far as
he was concerned, the heresies that became famous in the Church could be taken as the errors of the philosophers that were later raised to levels of faith. Left to him, to bring philosophy into religion is to become
disloyal to revelation, for "what indeed has Athens to do with Jerusalem?" (Gonzalez, 1970). The implication
of Tertullian's view and those of other theologians like him was to consider philosophy as a speculative exercise
that is all out to destroy—or at best ignore—the values and significance of divine revelation.

While it may be argued that positions such as that of Tertullian are themselves based on philosophical
argument (and thus it would amount to mere pretentiousness to dismiss the richness and vastness of philosophy in such an out-of-hand manner, particularly when the significance and involving values of philosophical
conclusions are realized), we should not lose sight of the benefits of the type of position taken by men like
Tertullian, Karl Barth, Pascal, et al., in the sense that they constitute valuable warnings as to the hyperintel-
lectualism that may come into religion. Apart from this, according to Abraham, there is the highlighting of
how crucial revelation is to showing off the importance of the personal and inward character of actual faith in
God, as well as safeguarding the mystery and transcendence of God (Abraham, 1985).

However, it is with the conception of religious commitment as above, coupled with some basic elements of
the nature of religion, that not a few philosophers distrust and consequently dismiss religion as superstitious,
inconsequential, and ultimately to be discarded if man were to progress intellectually and proffer realistic solutions to the basic problems of life, rather than taking refuge in sentimental, emotive, and cosmetic remedies.
Elements in the nature of religion detested by philosophers include, principally, its conservatism, which has
made it to play the role of a reactionary, opposing change and progress and irresistibly committed to preserving the status quo. In this mood, it does not encourage investigation and critical analysis of positions and the
proposition of realistic solutions to problems.

There is also the dogmatic nature of religion, which makes flexibility and the employment of independent
minds outlaws. The overdependence on authority and the persuasion to cling to uninquired faith cannot but
be impediments to the critical and highly skeptical mind of the philosopher. For example, religionists would
be hard put to allow philosophy to let loose its rational process on religious issues in the manner that Peter
Bodunrin would want to see philosophy undertake:

Letting loose our entire intellectual ability in the consideration of a problem and using our enquiry with the preparedness to abandon our most cherished beliefs if reason demands that we do
(Bodunrin, 1981).

This presupposes an absence of "no-go" areas for philosophical enquiry. This, no doubt, would be "suicidal" to religion, which is packed full of mysteries, dogma, and beliefs that would be easily and promptly jettisoned if subjected to the simplest rigor of rational deduction. If the Christian religion is taken as an example, one discovers that the existence of a supersensible Deity is understood to have been given, and no further evidence is required for his existence. Thus, the very basis of the Christian theology is regarded to be beyond any serious critical questioning, as this may amount to querying the fundamental dogma and invariably lead to undermining the very foundation of theology, which is the existence of God. Even when religion has been approached from a detached and subtle intellectual perspective, as Aquinas attempted to do, the effort has often been attacked vehemently by other religionists and counterbalanced with an overwhelming emotional and subjective disposition characterized by mystical and awe-inspiring language, as well as rationally incomprehensible practices and devotions to concepts and rituals that are not only intangible, but make nonsense of any belief that is not completely dependent on "uninquired faith."

Many philosophers are impatient with this kind of outlook, and not a few of them have taken the extreme position of rejecting any religious outlook to life. Rather, they prefer and insist on materialism as the best form of worldly living, whereby everything—will, feelings, thoughts, politics, and even morals—are explained from the perspective of matter. The only form of belief that is possible is one that is derivable from observable scientific facts. Anything outside this is, as the logical positivist would want to aver, speculative and ultimately nonsensical.

COMPLEMENTARY RELATION

All the above notwithstanding, some measure of complementation is discernible and desirable between philosophy and religion. For example, the scholastics recognized this in their rejection of the two extreme positions—namely, the extreme positive position that sees no distinction between the two, and the extreme negative position that sees no relation whatsoever and demands that they must be strictly kept separated. They seem to be conscious of the danger that each of the two positions is likely to perpetrate. In the first, the total amalgamation of philosophy with religion would deny each discipline the justice that should be done to their peculiarities. In particular, it would not allow for the kind of detached objectivity through logical reasoning, which is the hallmark of philosophy, so there also would be inadequate consideration or at best a watering down of the very fundamentals on which religion is based so as to fit into philosophical expectations.

The second, the strict separation of philosophy and religion is likely to deny religion the vital significance to be seen and taken more seriously and not just as purely and unimportant emotion-laden expressions. This certainly cannot be representative of the amount of speculation and rationality that have been known to be part of religion as a human phenomenon.

In resolving this rather delicate issue, the scholastics evolved a kind of synthesis between philosophy and religion in the medieval format of reason and faith. Apart from all these, it cannot be denied that many of the great philosophers the world has known were dedicated and committed religious believers. It is also of historical fact that monumental contributions have been made to religious thought by philosophers, believers, and nonbelievers. With this consciousness, philosophy cannot be seen as being intrinsically irreligious or antireligious for that matter; consequently, a more positive approach should be adopted in which the attitudes of believers on one hand and philosophers on the other concerning the involvement of philosophy in religion are changed to that of mutual recognition and acknowledgment of identifiable benefits to one another.

From the perspective of philosophy, Abraham enumerates some ways in which these can be obtained.

- Philosophy itself being seen as religion in its zeal to guide man to a quasireligious conception of the world and man's living in it. The attempt to make religion out of philosophy was largely evident in the philosophies of Plato, the Platonists, and the Neoplatonists. It is equally paramount in modern thinkers such as Hegel and Spinoza.
- Even when philosophy does not see itself as performing religious functions, it is essentially considered to be complementary to religion in its understanding of the provision of the metaphysical or the intellectual base for religious doctrines and concepts, without which religion could only be seen as incomplete and jelly-boned.
- Also, from a practically modest disposition, philosophy has come to regard itself as both "positive handmaid and negative servant of religion." As a positive handmaid, philosophy provides a sort of apologia in defense of religion, justifying the fundamental concepts of faith and striving to help uphold its details, though in a negative fashion in showing the negative possibilities of faith and portraying such details as not being self-contradictory. Maybe the greatest gain of this is the synthesis of faith and reason that have been developed, whose chief proponent was Thomas Aquinas. He had found fellowship in other great thinkers like Augustine, Locke, Abelard, Mitchell, Swinburne, et al. The "negative" service which philosophy provides is identifiable in the position held by Kant and others of the limitations of philosophy in which they held that there need not be a necessary synthesis of faith and reason, and that what is demanded of philosophy is to make room for religion in conceding to the possibility of religion (Abraham, 1985).

In summary, philosophy's analytical role in religion is not in doubt. It asks important and searching questions concerning religious faith, and it would be sheer pretense to look on these enquires as heretical or devilish. The questions raised are fundamental to religion in general and theology in particular. Indeed, it would amount to denying the obvious if we dismiss the caliber of questions raised by philosophy such as the contradictions inherent in the notion of the omnipotent God and the limitation of being considered from purely historical perceptive. The endeavors of philosophers as well as others with the belief that religion must, out of "necessity," be subjected to philosophical enquiry, have led to the subject now known as the philosophy of religion.

PHILOSOPHY OF RELIGION

As with philosophy proper, an easy and straightforward definition seems unattainable for philosophy of religion. If one is to be provided at all, it may have to be deducted from a painstaking consideration of what the subject entails, i.e., what are the sort of things it does and what it is distinct from? i.e., what are the things it does not engage in? For our purposes here, we may proceed from the negative dimension—i.e., what philosophy of religion is not or what it does not engage in. A fitting point of commencement is the consideration of the difference of the philosophy of religion from fields of enquiry that are seen to be related to it. These are apologetics, systematic theology, and phenomenology of religion.

As for apologetics, philosophy of religion is distinct from it, particularly in the nature of things they both do. Apologetics, if we take the Christian example, strives to defend the Christian faith and doctrine against external oppositions and at the same time presupposes the truth of religion—this time, Christianity. On the contrary, philosophy of religion is not interested in any of these two exercises strictly for their own sake and may be said to be broader in its scope of its relation with religion, as it cannot be limited to one particular religion.

The same may be said of its relationship with systemic theology, which is also primarily concerned with the articulation of faith in Christianity and how this may be applied for a worthwhile Christian life.

The distinction of the philosophy of religion from the phenomenology of religion is derived from what its objective in religion is as opposed to the main preoccupation of phenomenology. While philosophy of religion is more interested in questioning the truth of religion, and these questions are considered from all ramifications without any exceptions, phenomenology's main engagement in religion is to understand better what religion is or its claims.

It must not be assumed, however, that philosophy of religion has to be in conflict with any of these; rather, its considerations of religion serve a complementary, sometimes overlapping, function in its treatment of the common problems in broadening scopes. It asks general questions that transcend the restricted approaches offered by them. This becomes more discernible in the realization that there are differences in aims and objectives (Abraham, 1985).

From the foregoing and in cognizance with the fundamental preoccupation of the philosophy of religion it may be concisely defined as "philosophical thinking about religion."

TASK FOR PHILOSOPHY OF RELIGION

When it comes to the consideration of what may have been said and expected as tasks for the philosophy of religion—i.e., the sorts of things it is expected to engage in—they may be said to center around resolving questions having to do with man, the world, nature, and the human relation to these, particularly as these are seen from the religious perspective. The ingredients of these would include, among others, themes such as causality; What is good as opposed to evil? What is justice? What is believable about life? What place does man occupy in the world's scheme of the universe and existence? What is the good life and how is it to be lived? Is the hope for the afterlife justified? etc.

The fundamental tasks of the philosophy of religion in grappling with these, specifically in their constituting the very basis of religion and human practice of it, are undertaken in a number of ways that underlie the constructive roles of philosophy of religion. We identify six such basic tasks here.

+ The analysis and clarification of terms, words, and concepts used in religion. For there is no way of coming to terms with religion, its traditions and claims, without understanding what concepts like miracles, myths, revelation, a supreme being, etc., mean.

+ Formulation of terms for religion. After a detailed and initial scrutiny of the main and central questions of religion, with the resolving of the superficial contradictions that seem to debase them, the proper, adequate, and meaningful terms that would fully reflect the intended meaning of concepts may be made available to theology and religion in general by philosophy.

+ Freeing religion from dogmatism. Philosophy by nature objects to dogmatic positions and encourages the free use of man's process of reasoning, with room for independent thought. Thus, philosophy of religion would be able to examine religion and its beliefs with the intellectual groundings that need to be free from a state of authoritative and uninquired conceptions.

+ The three tasks above make religion become acceptable not only to the so-called "simple at heart," the illiterate and fanatic, but also to rationally minded men who may come to hold on to religious belief out of reasoned and intelligent conviction, and not as products of blind faith.

+ Another important task for the philosophy of religion is the explanation of the claims of religion to the believers so that they may become not only both enlightened and grounded in the faith, but also come to possess enough understanding to convince nonbelievers of the values and truths of religion.

+ To some extent, though by no means the limit of its tasks, philosophy of religion could play the role of an apologetic agent in defending religion from oppositions raised against it, its beliefs, doctrines, concepts, and practices. This is done by the examination of the arguments used for such defenses and when necessary, formulating such arguments itself.

LIMITS OF PHILOSOPHY OF RELIGION

The recognition and consequent belief in the values of philosophy of religion in the positive contributions that philosophy can make to religion must not in any way becloud the possible danger that philosophy may pose to religion. If philosophical involvement in matters of faith, indeed, religion at large is not limited, it should be realized that a wholesale, undemarcated and uncontrolled field day for philosophy in religion may, in the final analysis, do more harm than good, and thus provide justification for the suspicion and hostility of many religious believers toward philosophy, particularly its amalgamation with religion.

If philosophy is not to become "a bull in a china shop" as far as religion is concerned, its role must be clearly defined, as we have attempted to do earlier in this discourse. It should not be allowed to prescribe an overdose to the ailments of religion. This may very well happen if philosophy seeks to subject the claims of faith to the same kind of verification process in its own field, or attempts to bend religion's positions to meet with its own philosophical principles and rules. It must be stressed that the overall role of philosophical enquiry must be limited to metaphysical, epistemological, and biological investigations carried out in such a way that it would be capable of cleaning the incompetence of human reason in matters concerning the divine so as to check the pretensions of human thoughts. As Kant perfectly puts it: "Reason must be limited in order to make room for faith" (Smith, 1958).

FAITH AND REASON

The practicality of the connection between religion and philosophy is vividly demonstrated by the interplay of faith and reason. Indeed, this dynamic has been significantly located in the controversy surrounding the possibility or impossibility of demonstrating God's existence. The advocates of "faith" alone have always seen faith as inevitably opposed to reason or even contrary to it. They tend to see faith, as Mitchell points out:

> Involving effort, the effort required to believe things that are inherently difficult to believe (Mitchell, 1980).

Here, there is no appeal to evidence for what is believed and the common acceptance of the fact that the reasonable man has to base his beliefs upon evidence at his disposal is done away with. This is on the assumption that faith needs no rational justification for both itself and the various beliefs it wants accepted.

Various reasons have been proposed for this desire to separate faith from reason. For example, the pietists of the eighteenth century were of the view that:

> … the sentiment of God's being and presence in life was sufficient in itself and that rational reflection about faith was actually to be avoided as a danger to faith (Reardon, 1977).

In D'Arcy's opinion, Luther, against the background of his dislike for the nominalists he thought spent their time in logic-chopping and clever sophistries, coupled with his low opinion of human nature which is unaided by God, was of the opinion that:

> The only kind of genuine faith was what we called "justifying faith." This consists in a confidence or trusts that despite the depravity of human Nature, God will reckon the sinner as justified. It is this faith which alone justifies a man (D'Arcy, 1944).

This seems to suggest that since reason is from the unaided nature of man, it must be dispensed with; it is only with faith that man can find justification. Kant's reason for not giving any part to reason in faith is due to his philosophical system, and as D'Arcy (1944) further indicates, it consists in his belief that:

> Our thinking is limited to phenomenon and that we can know nothing of God or spiritual freedom or spiritual personality because these conceptions have no basis in sense. But though philosophically speaking, such conceptions are illegitimate and have no content, they are demanded as postulates in the practical order. We cannot live as free, moral men without them. Faith, then is a postulate of the moral or practical order.

The tendency of the positions so far mentioned could be seen as portraying faith as an experience of a unique kind which could be said to be analogous to artistic experience. Taken as this, faith and its doctrine are separated from reason and they need no longer be defended on rational grounds.

On the other hand, there have been those who find complements between faith and reason and that faith could only gain and not lose in the application of genuine reason. For example, Friedrich Hegel was of this view when he said:

> We are bound to reason about our faiths if only to ask whether and how far intuition itself is authentic and trustworthy (Hegel, 1962).

Even Jacobi, as Reardon points out:

> ... [f]inds it necessary to discuss faith in a rational way, to the extent, indeed, of seeking to build a religious philosophy upon it (Reardon, 1977).

Others, such as the Pelagians, have extolled reason and see no way in which faith could be free of it. This is on the ground that if faith were to be a virtue, a conversion to it must involve in some way a part played by man, who may have to depend on his rational capability.

Also, St. Bernard Abelard, for example, believed that faith could be seen as a belief which is formed from reason, varying in quality and cogency. In all, the position of the believers of "reason in faith" is centered on the notion that even if faith, and particularly its strength, is seen to be passed on by an intuitive process—which could be said to be self-justifying, and that in bypassing inferential reasoning, it could be said to carry truth directly into the mind—there is no denying the fact that the holder of whatever faith, when questioned, still feels it necessary to supply a reasoned answer. Additionally, even if it is accepted that emotional satisfaction is all that faith requires, it may still be necessary to demonstrate how this is so. Invariably, it may become obvious that faith, even if it can be, should not be divorced from reason.

REVIEW QUESTIONS

1. With background definitions for religion and philosophy, account for the grounds of opposition between the two.
2. From the definition of what the philosophy of religion is and is not, what are the tasks most visible for philosophy of religion in religious discourse?
3. If philosophy is not to play the role of "a bull in a china shop," how much of it should be involved in religion?
4. If reason is the tool of philosophy and faith the tool of religion, how far can the two relate to be of any benefit to each other?
5. From the seemingly opposing natures of philosophy and religion, how can a philosophical approach in religion be justified and useful?
6. For the religionist, philosophy is a ready tool of agnostics and/or atheism. Is this position justified?

BIBLIOGRAPHY AND BOOKS FOR FURTHER READING

Abernathy, G. L. and Longford, T. A., eds. 1968. *Philosophy of Religion*. London: Macmillan.

Abraham, W. J. 1985. *An Introduction to the Philosophy of Religion*. Englewood Cliffs, NJ: Prentice Hall, Inc.

Aderibigbe, Gbola and Ajayi, Olu. 1986. *Topics in Philosophy of Religion*. Ilesa: Olufemi Press.

Aderibigbe, Gbola and Deji Aiyegboyin, eds. 2001. *Religion: Study and Practice*. Ibadan: Olu-Akin Press.

Aderibigbe, Gbolade. 2005. *Thomas Aquinas' Demonstration of God's Existence: A Contemporary Perspective*. Ibadan: Olu-Akin Press.

_____.1988. *Fundamentals of Philosophy of Religion*. Ikeja: Free Enterprise Publishers.

Ayer, A. J. 1952. *Language, Truth and Logic*. New York: Dover Publications Inc.

Basinger, David. 2002. *Religious Diversity: A Philosophical Assessment*. Burlington: Ashgate Publishing Company.

Bodunrin, P. O. 1981. "Philosophy: Meaning and Method," *Ibadan Journal of Humanistic Studies* No. 1.

Braithwaite, R. B. 1955. *An Empiricist's View of the Nature of Religious Belief*. Cambridge: Cambridge University Press.

Burr, J. R. and Multon Goldinger, eds. 1976. *Philosophy and Contemporary Issues*. New York: Macmillan Publishing Company.

Cassiver, H. W. 1968. *Kant's First Critique*. New York: Humanities Press Inc.

Concise Oxford Dictionary. 1984. London: Oxford University Press.

Craig, William Lane and J. P. Moreland, eds. 1991. *The Blackwell Companion to Natural Theology*. Oxford: Blackwell Press.

Curtis, S. J. 1950. *A History of Western Philosophy in the Middle Ages*. London: McDonald & Co. Ltd.

D'Arcy, M. C. 1944. *Belief and Reason*. London: Burns Oaths and Washborne, Ltd.

Davis, B. 1993. *An Introduction to the Philosophy of Religion*. Oxford: Oxford University Press.

Descartes, René. 1637. *A Discourse on Method*. Lieden: Ian Marie.

Durkheim, E. 1981. "Elementary Forms of Religion," in *Introductory Sociology*. London: Macmillan Press, Ltd.

Evans, V. B. 1932. "The Acquinite Proof of Existence of God," *Philosophy Journal of the British Institute of Philosophy*. London: Macmillan & Co., Ltd., vol. vii.

Flew, A. and A. Macintyre. 1961. *New Essays in Philosophical Theology*. London: Scay Press Ltd.

Galloway, G. 1955. "Proofs of the Existence of God," in Burnstein, ed. *Basic Problems of Philosophy*. Englewood Cliffs, NJ: Prentice Hall Inc.

Gilby, T., ed. 1969. *Thomas Aquinas Summa Theologica*. New York: Doubleday & Co. Inc.

Gonzalez, Justo L. 1970. *A History of Christian Thought*. Nashville: Abingdon Press.

Griffiths, Paul. 2002. *Problems of Religious Diversity*. London: Blackwell.

Hegel, G. W. F. 1962. *Philosophy of Religion*. Spears and Sanderson, trans. London: Routledge & Kegan Paul Ltd.

Helm, Paul. 2000. *Faith and Reason*. Oxford: Oxford University Press.

Hick, J. and A.C. McGill, eds. 1968. *The Many-Faced Argument*. London: Macmillan Press Ltd.

Hick, John. 1989. *An Interpretation of Religion: Human Responses to the Transcendent*. New Haven: Yale University Press.

_____. 1985. *Problems of Religious Pluralism*. New York: St. Martin's Press.

_____, ed. 1964. *The Existence of God*. New York: Macmillan.

Hospers, John. 1976. *An Introduction to Philosophical Analysis*. London and Henley: Routledge & Kegan Paul Ltd.

Hume, David. 1948. *Dialogues Concerning Natural Religion*. New York: Hefrier.

Kant, Emanuel. 1958. *Critique of Pure Reason*. N. K. Smith (trans.). London: Macmillan Press.

Kerr, Hugh T. 1958. *A Compound of Luther's Theology*. Philadelphia: Westminster Press.

Lewis, H. D. 1947. *Philosophy of Religion*. London: The English University Press Ltd.

Mackie, J. L. 1971. "Evil and Omnipotence," in *Philosophy of Religion*, Basil Mitchell, ed. Oxford: Oxford University Press.

Mitchell, Basil. 1980. "Faith & Reason: A False Antithesis?" *Religious Studies*. Cambridge: Cambridge University Press, vol. 61.

Plantinga, Alvin. 2000. *Warranted Christian Belief*. Oxford: Oxford University Press.

_____. 1974. *God, Freedom and Evil*. London: George Allen & Unwin Press.

_____, ed. 1965. *The Ontological Argument*. New York: Doubleday.

Reardon, B. M. G. 1977. *Hegel's Philosophy of Religion*. London and Basingstoke: The Macmillan Press Ltd.

Russell, B. 1927. *Why I Am Not a Christian*. London: National Secular Society.

Stitch, Cox. 1963. *Form of Religion*. London: SCM Press Ltd.

Swinburne, Richard. 1983. *Faith and Reason*. Oxford: Clarendon Press.

_____. 1979. *The Existence of God*. Oxford: Clarendon Press.

_____. 1977. *The Coherence of Theism*. Oxford: Clarendon Press.

Tennant, F. R. 1930. *Philosophical Theology, vol. II*. Cambridge: Cambridge University Press.

Timpe, Kevin, ed. 2009. *Arguing About Religion*. New York and London: Routledge.

Walsh, M. 1971–1973. "Notes on Philosophy of Religion." Unpublished.

Waterhouse, Eric S. 1938. *Philosophical Approach to Religion*. London: The Epworth Press.

Zagzebski, Linda. 1993. *Rational Faith: Catholic Responses to Reformed Epistemology*. Notre Dame: University of Notre Dame.

CHAPTER SIX

SOCIOLOGICAL APPROACH

INTRODUCTION

A profitable study of sociological approach in religion requires a basic understanding of the two components. This is possible only with working definitions of the two phenomena so as to determine
the dynamics of interaction between them. Thus, the questions must be asked, What is sociology? What is
religion? What are the interlocking or interacting elements which give rise to the influence of one over the
other?

First, what is sociology? As in the cases of definitions of other subjects, the definition of sociology has
been subjected to controversies due to the application of different definitions by various people. In fact, some
have tended to postulate that sociology is synonymous with socialism or social work. However, our interest here is not to sort out the controversies. To satisfy our purpose here, we may define sociology as, "the
academic discipline concerned with the systematic study of human social relationships in the most general
sense" (Aderibigbe, 2001). What does this mean? We may use an analogy to drive the point home. If we
take, for example, that an academic discipline is organized to study the social life of, say, ants, what should be
important to those undertaking the study would not be individual ants, but the relationship among the ants,
which are abstract in the sense that though they are observable, they are not physical. What would ultimately
be discovered is that there is a group when the ants come together, and within this group there would be
structures of social, political, and economic dimensions.

The same thing applies when sociology is considered from the human angle. It is concerned with the
relationship that exists among human beings, in which some are regarded as subordinate and others super-
ordinate, which in turn is a result of inner feelings known as attitudes, which also derive their origin from
economic, religious, social, and educational conditions.

So what a sociologist is primarily concerned with is not Mr. A. or Mr. B, but the relationship between
the two and the effects of this on them and the society in which they live, as well as the influence of society
on them. These are the interactions that take place among them. These, with their consequences, are what
constitute the subject matter of sociology.

Second, what is religion? A meticulous compilation of the definitions of religion, that is, what religion is or its subject matter would run into as each person or group of persons define it in such a way that would reflect subjective dispositions from the standpoint of interests. Again, for our purpose here, and without prejudice to our view in Chapter One, we would take the definition of religion as offered by Emile Durkheim. Though it is not without its weakness, it does, however, suit our purpose here. Durkheim (1912) says:

"Religion is that which deals with the sacred, with things set apart and forbidden."

In fact it is with the takeoff from this definition that the fundamental attitude to religion was most conservative, in the sense that religion was regarded as the relationship between man as an individual and the sacred entity to which he is aligned. It was then not particularly out of place to hold that this relationship does not necessarily have to involve others in the society as such, so as to warrant the study of relationships, not only between men and the sacred entity and the relationships and its consequences on the adherents of religion, but as well as those outside the particular religion. If religion were limited to the relationship between men and God, then there would likely be no need for sociological approach in religion, as God is evidently outside the scope of society. However, it is in the realization that religion is a dynamic which combines the relationships not just among the adherents of religions as an extension of these with the object of religions, and their consequences not only on the adherents but on others who cohabit with them, as well as the effects of these on their overall relationships, that the sociological approach to religion takes its proper place.

If it is accepted that religion is one of the major facets of human life, which is institutionalized in every known society, one is then tempted to conclude that no society can exist without at least a semblance of religion. (Some dispute this, pointing to modern secular states.) Whichever way it is considered, the presence and dominance of religion are assured, from the fact that there are manifestations of religion in every society and in every era. When we also consider the fact that religions have practices, beliefs, and doctrines, and that these could be institutionalized—in which case they constitute what we know as "organized religion" (Judaism, Christianity, Islam, Buddhism, etc.)—the interactions of such organizations necessarily attract the particular interest of society from the sociological point of view.

First, as interaction and consequences of this among the adherents of each organized religion; second, among the organized religions; third, of those within the religions and society at large; and fourth, of the society with the religions. Also, academic considerations and the desire for a better understanding of religions and their practitioners (which would, in effect, lead to the peaceful coexistence of various adherents of different religions) may constitute the why and benefits of the sociological approach in religion. These considerations have led to the propagations of how these relationships evolve and operate in the form of theories.

SOCIOLOGICAL THEORIES OF RELIGION

Before the consideration of the practical involvement of religion in societal functions and institutions, it is worthwhile to give attention to general sociological theories of religion. This is because the sociological approach to religion has a very theoretical tradition, whereby sociology's renowned theorists have made a lot of effort. They have interpreted religion's value for human society as well as its negative consequences, and have traced religious influences in major trends of world history. A consideration of a few of such theories and their protagonists become relevant here.

Durkheim: Religion as Worship of Society

In the period preceding World War I, Emile Durkheim wrote one of his most significant contributions to functionalist sociology, *The Elementary Forms of Religious Life* (1912). In the book, he asks two questions: What is religion? and What are the functions of religion for human society? It struck Durkheim that religion was very much a "social thing." He felt that to understand it at all, one must focus upon its origin and its contribution to maintaining collective life. Although he began his analysis by interpreting the religious experiences of Australian aborigines, he felt that he had arrived at an understanding of general phenomena that applied to other societies, including his own.

Durkheim sees human experience as divided into two radically different spheres: the sacred and the profane. The profane is the ordinary experience in everyday life, while the sacred evokes awe and reverence. Durkheim decides that religion's purpose is to maintain the radical segregation of the sacred sphere from the profane through the practice of rituals. Today, many people assume that the most important feature of religion is the private internal experience of the individual, and that the ritual observances within group meetings are only trivial external manifestations that have little bearing on one's deep experience. Durkheim, however, considered the practice of the ritual cult to be of central importance.

According to him, people everywhere worship sacred objects, but what they consider real differs greatly from one place to another. Thus, in Durkheim's view, people everywhere worshipped the same object, although they symbolized it in very different terms. He then concludes that this object of reverence and awe is the society. To Durkheim, "God" is the society, which becomes a personalized living entity. Ultimately, religion sacralizes the traditions upon which society ultimately rests. Within this dynamic, society is greater than the individual. It gives a person strength and support, and is the source of the ideas and values that render the person's life meaningful. It makes her or him a social being. In sum, it is the conclusion of Durkheim that the worship of God is seen as the disguised worship of society, the great being upon which the individual depends. Religion's purpose is therefore to preserve society. It points out the values of society for mankind and makes it an object of reverence. In its worship, society reaffirms itself on symbolic acting-out of its attitudes, which strengthens society itself.

Although primarily interested in the group rather than in the individual, Durkheim did recognize the supportive role of religion for the believer. He believes that religion gives the believer a feeling of comfort and dependence. Thus, by communicating with his "god," the believer becomes stronger, with more fortitude to either endure the trials of existence or to conquer them.

Marx: Religion as Ideology

Marx's views on religion are most commonly discussed in connection with a controversy between his followers and those of Weber, concerning how much of independent casual status to attribute to religion. Marx is the champion of those who submit that the only basic forces in society are economic and technological. This is the school of thought that considers religion to be an effect of other factors. On the other hand, the school of thought to which Weber belongs sees it more as a cause of other factors.

Marx held that groups of people tend to adopt belief systems (or ideologies) that can be used to justify the pursuit of their own economic advantages. However, because some social groups have leisure and an opportunity to communicate with one another, they may develop very clear and plausible doctrines that support their dominance quite eloquently. On the other hand, other groups, made up of workers and especially peasants, have neither the free time nor the occasion to discuss their situation, and they may not be fully conscious of the fact that they are exploited. Indeed, the ruling group may be able to get the workers to believe that their rule is proper and that rebellion against them is sin.

To Marx, religion is just a doctrine, an "opiate" lulling the masses into compliance, and it forestalls their revolution. It has to have some casual significance if it is used by the ruling classes to subordinate the workers. However, Marx did not expect religion to be a source of social change, and Marxist sociologists have generally ignored the study of religion, regarding it as an unimportant factor of social life.

Weber: Religion as the Source of Social Change

It is against the background of this Marxist assumption that Weber's book, *The Protestant Ethic and the Spirit of Capitalism* (1904), arguably stands out in such bold relief. Weber, like Marx, was curious about what caused industrial capitalism to develop. In the book, he shows a full appreciation of the organizational, technological, and economical prerequisites of capitalism. He does not mean to suggest that capitalism sprang fully armed from John Calvin; nevertheless, he is determined to show that the spirit of capitalism was a result of Protestantism, a result that early Protestant fathers foresaw and deplored.

The Protestant Ethic

Weber observed that in his day a disproportionate number of European business leaders were Protestants. Recalling that the Industrial Revolution began shortly after the Protestant Reformation, Weber considered the possibility that the Reformation was somehow a precondition for this revolution. His reasoning was sociopsychological. The character traits that the Protestant value system fostered were precisely those traits that a man would need if he were to thrive as an entrepreneur. And yet it was by no means the intention of the Protestant fathers to encourage the acquisition of material goods; they were concerned only with the salvation of souls. Protestantism did not cause acquisitiveness—that trait is as old as human nature—but it did create a system of legitimate rational acquisitiveness. Several aspects of Protestantism contributed to this effect: (1) the legitimizing of interest on loans; (2) the concept of secular work as "calling," by which God is served; and (3) the anxiety that each person is preordained to go either to heaven or hell.

The Catholic Church had prohibited Christians from lending money at interest. The rationale was that this process allowed the individual to gain profit from the misfortune and needs of others. This meant that a Catholic was not allowed to amass capital and lend it to businessmen for the establishment of industry or for other worthy purposes. Where such a rule was observed, capitalism was impossible. Jews were allowed to accept interest, and during the middle ages, towns very much needed the services of Jews for ongoing business transactions. Sometime after Calvin's day, Protestantism began to tolerate the taking of interest, and this freed devout Christians to engage in rational investment.

Protestantism furthermore taught that one's work in the world could be a "calling" from God. Consequently it was taught that one ought to devote his life to worldly tasks with the same spiritual zeal that hermits or priests had for religious matters. It was therefore not necessary for one to turn away from worldly things in order to serve God. The work of the world was God's work, and it required asceticism no less rigorous than that of a monk. A person was required to forego pleasures of the flesh and work instead industriously and prudently to administer the profits of his labor, which are God's.

Finally, Protestantism (especially Calvinism) generated a terrible sense of loneliness and anxiety by emphasizing that God, being wholly transcendent, could not be comprehended by man's mind, and had decreed whether each man was to be saved or damned. Man could not earn salvation and should never permit himself to rest assured that he had been chosen. Indeed, in the minds of early Calvinists, there could be no clue as to whether one belonged to the elect or the damned. Man must live out his life in society, waiting to learn of his eternal fate.

By the time Protestantism had reached full swing, however, this chilling doctrine had been revised in a direction that was crucial for the development of capitalism.

Although one could not earn salvation, one could measure how well he was carrying out God's work on earth by how well he prospered. Thus, the wealthy businessman who succeeded in his "calling" would seem to be acceptable to God. Money was thus a means of reducing a person's anxious concern as to his state of grace. Conversely, a person's poverty was evidence that he was not applying himself with the proper moral fervor and was probably not worthy of salvation.

Because the hardworking Protestant was not supposed to spend his money on luxurious living, and because he ought not to interfere with his impoverished neighbors by helping them in their own "calling," he acquired riches that he could neither spend nor give away. Happily, Calvinism allowed him to invest his money. This was conducive to capitalist entrepreneurship. Very early in the Reformation, some leaders foresaw the effects that Weber would spell out later in retrospect. Thus, John Wesley (1755) wrote:

> I fear, wherever riches have increased, the essence of religion has decreased in the same proportion. Therefore I do not see how it is possible, in the nature of things, for any revival of true religion to continue for long. For religion must necessarily produce both industry and frugality, and those who cannot produce both industry and frugality, and those who cannot produce riches. For as riches increase, so will pride, anger and love of the world in all its branches. How then is it possible that Methodism, that is, a religion of the heart, though it flourishes now as a green bay tree, should continue in this stage? For the Methodists in every place grow diligent and frugal; consequently they increase in goods.

Wesley's fears were well grounded. The ethic of world asceticism declined among the Protestants over time, and modern Methodists are not recognizably different in character from members of other religious communities. Before this transformation occurred, however, Weber argued that the Protestant ethic did much to produce industrial capitalism.

This, then, is the basic outline of the "Weber thesis," one of the most "debatable" theories in the history of sociology. Although it has stimulated countless other studies, there is hardly anything left standing of the thesis itself.

The theory has been severely criticized based on some quite obvious lapses. For example, it has been established that capitalism was not unknown in the Catholic world. Several pre-Reformation Catholic religious orders rivaled the Puritans in their hospitality toward capitalism in general and even usury in particular. Perhaps the most serious weakness in Weber's thesis is that it is still possible, even today, to maintain the Marxist position that capitalism caused Protestantism, rather than the other way around. Further objections to Weber's thesis consist, for instance, in responses from scholars such as Fanfani (1935), who insisted in his book, *Catholicism, Protestantism and Capitalism*, that Calvin imposed ethical restraints upon business activity just as great as those imposed by the Catholic Church, and that Calvin's ethics, not his theology, were in fact largely derived from Catholicism. Also, it was quite obvious, as against the presumption of Weber, that Calvinists did not always become rich. This is well demonstrated by Johnson's (1976) observation that no religious beliefs are sufficient in themselves to make people rich, unless circumstances are favorable. Finally, in agreement with Fanfani, there is incontestable evidence that capitalism was flourishing long before Calvin.

Conclusion

An overview of the theories examined above clearly indicate that many sociologists view the gods or God as a product of the collective imagination of a society. God, then, is a mere "projection" and not a real being. God is often created by the society for social purposes, e.g., to gain greater control over individuals. Sociologists view belief in God as providing a social point for the shared values of a society, particularly the values taken to be holy. On the other hand, there are other sociologists who view religion(s) as a catalyst dictating social ideology.

In the first category, French sociologist Emile Durkheim emphasizes that religious beliefs contribute greatly to the cohesion and harmonious functioning of a society. Also, Marx viewed society as being permeated by conflict and strife, and therefore religious belief was related to class conflict. For him, religion is the "opium of the people," and most often the ruling class uses it to justify the status quo and to pacify the oppressed classes. At the same time, Marx recognized religion as an implicit protest against the status quo, a longing for a better world which directly indicts the actual world.

From Durkheim and Marx, it is possible to conclude that the particular forms of a sociological theory of religion often do reflect the characteristics of particular forms of sociological theory. However, this line of thought has been disputed. For example, against Durkheim's theory of God as a symbol of the power and authority of society, H. A. Farmer (1998) offers an objection. He insists that such a theory actually does not account for the universal scope of the teachings of the higher religions. Moreover, it does not explain the reasons for the power to criticize society in a prophetic manner.

Against Marx's approach, C. S. Evans notes that, though religion(s) and its vestibules may constitute grounds for social oppression, there equally exists portent evidence that religious beliefs have also motivated many to stand up against oppression. He gives the example of the abolitionists in nineteenth-century America.

Thus, a sociological approach in religion can provide a very positive understanding of both religion and the society in the way both influence each other—the way social contexts shape religion and the way religion influences society.

SOCIETAL INSTITUTIONS AND RELIGION

We do know that human society in various ways influences the individual acceptance of religion, and consequent commitment to its societal factors. These factors, such as environment, institutions, age, sex, etc., have a lot to do in the religious life of an individual. On the other hand, religion and its practices (arguably) also have a lot to contribute to the proper development, progress and orderliness of the society. It would be worthwhile to examine some of these mutual functions. We begin by examining some societal institutions that may influence religious acceptance and behaviors in individuals.

Family: Parents

The family is the first social institution that the individual encounters. The attitudes of parents and other family members can go a long way to determine the religious attitude of the individual, positively or negatively.

There can be little doubt that the attitudes of the parents are of great importance in the formation of religious tendencies. When people, particularly students, are asked to identify what had been the greatest influence informing their religious attitude and beliefs, they usually point to their parents, home, or mother. This has been proved in detailed researches globally. This is particularly so when there is a close relationship between parents and children, even more so in firstborns, who, to a large extent, have closer relationships with their parents. This influence seems to be particularly high where the children are still living at home. In this regard, the mother is adjudged in majority of studies to be more influential than the father.

In all, it is more likely that the children will be loyal to the religious beliefs of the parents, particularly where they hold the same faith; where they are divergent, the children are more likely to follow the mother.

Educational Institutions

Attendance of educational institutions can go a long way to influence religious attitudes of students. This is more so in religiously oriented schools, particularly where the teaching of religion and moral injunctions are stressed. If we take the establishment of educational institutions in Nigeria (an African country) as a case study, one discovers that the majority of these are products of missionary activities with the objective of conversion. In fact, there have been cases where prospective students of such schools were expected to be converted first before being enrolled. However, the religious influences of schools, according to studies, have been known to be more pronounced in relation to formal church membership and church attendance, rather than lasting religious commitments.

Also, it should be pointed out that the level of schooling may be a major determining factor. This is because schooling that falls within the adolescent age generally tend toward a lower level of church attendance and an equally lower level of religious beliefs and attitudes. The reason for this is not farfetched. This is a period when students are less orthodox, less fundamental, and less likely to believe in God and think of Him as a person. On the other hand, as Michael and Benjamin point out, very few students become atheists or agnostics. This is because they are likely to modify their beliefs, thinking that they need some form of religious orientation so as to attain a fully mature philosophy of life.

Again using Nigeria as an example, the saga of religiousness has been very much on the increase in university campuses, with the seeming craze for membership in all kinds of Christian fellowships and Muslim youth societies in the campuses. The reasons for this trend have been traced to mostly sociological and psychological dispositions. In most cases, people have come to the conclusion that the students so involved employ the religious commitments as a panacea for personal life frustrations. More objective studies need to be undertaken to understand the actual objectives of students belonging to these groups. There is no doubt, however, that the presence of such groups in campuses has tremendous influence on the religious attitudes of students there. This phenomenon is obviously absent on college campuses in the United States, where religious expressions are largely out of the public domain.

The Influence of Social Groups and Contacts

Aside from the home and educational institutions, the formation of religious attitudes in terms of beliefs and religious functions and attendance can be developed through belonging to particular groups and other forms of social contacts. Like other life attitudes, religious attitudes are very much susceptible to the social influences of groups, participation in evangelistic meetings, and listening to lectures, seminars, and symposia.

Groups

While it is true that people may belong to a group for nonreligious reasons (for example, a person may like some members of the group), invariably, through the influence of the group leaders and others, the religious inclinations of the individual may change. This may result from a number of reasons:

i.   the inclination of the individual to identify himself with popular beliefs of the group for fear of being rejected if he deviates;
ii. in the belief that the others in the group are experts; and
iii. the cognitive disposition of the individual is likely to change as a result of exposure to the group's ways of thinking and talking.

However, a person may set out to belong to a group just because the group is a religious one, for example, the Scripture Union, Christian fellowships, Muslim youth organizations, etc. So also it is possible for a person to join such a religious group for nonreligious reasons, but only to conform to the religious attitudes and beliefs of the group as a result of exposure to strong pressures from members of the group.

On the whole, evidence abounds from various sources to buttress the submission that influences from friends in the groups to which one belongs are more often than not likely to produce shared religious attitudes and beliefs.

Evangelical and Other Meetings

Quite a number of individuals have found the sources of their religious commitments through attendance of evangelical meetings. These are, of course, very easy to come by and many religious bodies have thrown a lot into this form for conversion to one kind of religion or another. Evangelical meetings so abound all over the place that one can hardly fail to notice them. The emotional scenes associated with such meetings and the claims of miraculous feats have been and are sure attractions to people. Activities at such meetings are easily predictable. Emotions stirred by the singing of moving hymns, the powerful preaching of evangelists, speaking in tongues (through displays of violent jerking and twitching), collapsing senselessly on the ground, and finally, the glorification of God for miracles performed by the coming forward of those cured of various diseases.

One is normally struck by the large number of people who attend such meetings, many of whom are from different religious denominations, many attending for the first time and getting converted. Evangelical groups that sprang up have been so well organized that they have become quite impressive and viable institutions. Prominent ones that readily come to mind are those of John Wesley in England, which metamorphosed into the Methodist Church, Billy Graham, an American Christian evangelist, and in Nigeria we have the likes of the late Benson Idahosa in Benin, Obadare of Akure, Eunuch Adeboye of the Redeemed Christian Church of God in Lagos, and a lot of others springing up on an almost daily basis.

All things said, one is tempted to conclude that these evangelical meetings serve more as problem-solving campaigns on the side of attendance, and (one wishes one were wrong) a lucrative economic venture on the side of the organizers, rather than a catalyst of lasting religious attitudes and commitments. Only time can determine which is which. In relation to the above, the mass media have also been sources of germination and sustenance of religious attitudes and practices. Not only do evangelistic groups use the media, the regular churches also use them to broadcast services to homes. So also do the print media devote some of their pages to religious matters which are meant to influence the reading public, not to mention religious organizations with their own newspapers and other forms of mass media.

ROLE(S) OF RELIGION IN THE SOCIETY

So far, we have discussed how societal institutions and other factors can influence religion through the cultivation of religious attitudes and practices in individuals in the society. As we mentioned earlier, religion and its practices also influence society in its various facets. This is particularly true of organized religions. Religion, primarily, should be seen as a spiritual pilgrimage that is mainly characterized by:

i.   the search for and recognition of some superhuman power;
ii. man's humble acceptance of his limitations and dependence on superhuman power; and
iii. the adoption of ways and means, via doctrines, attitudes, behaviors often reflected in empirical moral living to find solutions to basic problems in man's existence (Aderibigbe, 2001).

The attempt by humans to attain the above has been largely responsible for their coming together under the umbrella of organized religious traditions, which have, from the very beginning, had both individual and social consequences and repercussions on the society. Many would want to limit the role of religion, per se, in society to that of its sanctification. However true this may be, there is equally the realization of religion's important role(s) in the society and/or individuals constituting that society. This is concretely reflected in religion's involvement in various forms of social institutions. This is why religion's role(s) is better examined through the strategies of institutionalized or organized religions in the society. The actualizations of these strategies are demonstrable through three basic dimensional questions:

- what should be the orientation of organized religions in terms of working spirits and qualities? In other words, what qualities are expected of religion?
- what role(s) has religion played in the society in the past? (Here, Nigeria is taken as a case study.); and
- what future role(s) is expected of religion if it is to continue its relevance to society?

Expected Qualities

A religion that intends to live up to expectations in the society should possess creative, progressive, and dynamic dispositions. Not only should it be adaptable, but it must also be progressively dynamic, with a knowledgeable, compassionate, and generous leadership. This leadership should be one that carries with it the people to avoid the often common predicament of turning the religion into a clergy-cult religion.

There must also be a conscious effort to make use of indigenous materials, not only in its doctrine, but also in its leadership structure; and in response to the local situation. However, care should be taken that this does not jeopardize the unique elements of the religion that make it one with the same religion internationally.

Creativeness

The creativeness of a religion involves its being original, pioneering, and also exploring, so that it can be advantageously related to the people involved in its practice. As a means of realizing these ideals, it must be ever ready to accept new ideas in such a way that necessary changes can take place when appropriate.

Progressiveness

The progressive nature that a religion must possess should make it strive to be on the move at all times, refusing to put new wine into old bottles, as it were. The pitfall of turning conservative in the bid to maintain the status quo should be avoided. Not only should it identify itself with the society in its changing nature, it must also address itself to the pursuant of societal ideals, such as liberty, justice, human dignity, human rights, and democracy within its area of operation.

Cultural Applications

A strive toward getting itself rooted in the culture of the people among whom it finds itself is essential for any religion waning to make headway in such a society. This is what will help carry the people along with it. For example, it is believed in many quarters that Islam spread more rapidly in Africa because of its affinity with the cultural disposition of the people. On the other hand, Christianity found it more difficult to penetrate equally well because of its disdain and isolation from the culture of the people. In fact, until recently this attitude was very prevalent among the orthodox churches, and has led to the establishment of what came to be known as Independent African Churches, whose liberal attitudes toward, and to a large extent, adoption of the cultural setting of the people have attracted large numbers of Africans to join such churches, to the disadvantage of the orthodox churches. Interestingly, the orthodox churches are beginning to take a clue from these churches and are now Africanizing their looks. It all boils down to the very important point that not only should a religion appreciate the culture of the people, it must, as much as possible, avail itself of its services wherever appropriate. Anything less turns religion into a distant and alien institution that can hardly induce the spirit of total belonging by its adherents.

VISIBLE ROLES OF RELIGION IN THE SOCIETY

Over the centuries, religion per se and in the form of organized institutions has played significant roles in the lives of not only the adherents, but in society at large. These roles have not been limited to only religious services to the people; they have cut across other aspects of everyday living of the people and society, ranging from political, moral, social, educational, and even to economic ones. Some salient roles are briefly examined here:

Religion and Politics

Religion and politics are two phenomena that really affect individuals and the society globally. Earlier, it was mentioned that religion as a phenomenon is very important in man's life. It is also a common saying that every human is a political animal, that is to say, there is no individual without an element of politics in him or her. If, as pointed out, the two phenomena have such a strong hold on individuals and the society, what then has been the relationship that exists between the two in the contexts of individual living and societal political dynamics? Historically, what has been the relationship between religion and politics?

In the ancient Greek world, as exemplified by classical political thinkers such as Plato and Aristotle, religion was seen as being crucial to political life, with the submission that religious homogeneity was necessary if there were to be political stability. This being so, it seems that these classical political thinkers would subscribe to a closer relationship between the two. However, it is not clear if they would support an identical religious and political life.

In contemporary scholarly debates, proponents of both positive and negative relationships between religion and politics have emerged. Thus, the relationship that should exist between religion and politics has been approached from fundamentally two occasionally exclusive positions. These have been located in submissions for a place for religion in politics and the countersubmissions of discrediting any role for religion in politics. The proponents of a place for religion in politics insist on the benefits thereof, while the opponents are only too happy to point out the insignificance and dangers of politics embedded in religion.

Before discussing those two opposing "stations," it might be worthwhile to briefly examine the very basic conceptual groundings of religion and politics as human engagements and the diverse perspectives of their dynamics and agencies in human affairs as individuals and corporate institutions.

Religion is usually regarded as an enigma. Thus, it can be explained in different ways. It can also be manipulated to suit subjective persuasions. As a result, some have come to see it as an instrument of fashioning positive, strong, and reliable characters. For example, Ejizu (1986:143), in submitting to this positive view of religion, says: "man's value systems and attitudinal orientations are basically the functions of one's religious beliefs." Also echoing the same view, Makosi (1988:3) remarks: "religion presupposes epiphany—a divine manifestation or revelation to man and man's response to the call in appreciation of the reality and consequences of the revelation."

However, there are those who have taken opposing positions regarding religion as a Hydra-headed monster, inflicting fear upon people, and it therefore should be discouraged as an influence on individuals and the society. For example, both Lucretius and Voltaire have voiced opinions that give credence to this negative view of religion. Lucretius (from Makosi, 1988:3) says:

> *Tantum religio suadere malorum* (such were the lengths of wickedness to which religion could persuade human nature to go).

And Voltaire (from Durant 1921:224), being more direct in his attack on religion, says:

> Crush that monster religion and set western man's spirit free from pursuing his glorious enterprise of raising his culture by Olympic heights.

The opposing views on religion above vividly demonstrate the fact of the influence of religion on society. It is another ball game altogether, whether it is considered a positive or negative agency. Its reality confronts the individual and the society as a value system that has significant bearing on cultural and attitudinal orientation in human civic or political domains, either as a harbinger of progress or a monster out for destruction (Madu, 1995).

Politics is usually regarded as an integral feature of man's social existence and interaction (Madu, 1995). The term actually derives from the Greek polis, which means city-state. This meaning denotes politics as the art of governance. This art of governance represents the dynamic process of mobilizing human and other resources for the managing, directing, and enforcing the affairs of public policies and decisions toward regulating social order (Durant, 1921). Consequently, politics, holistically speaking, applies to different forms of organizations and direction of human interests at various levels of society. These may be family, village, national, international, church, etc. From this general class, different kinds of political systems have emerged: aristocracy, socialism, democracy, anarchism, oligarchy, etc. Whatever the format or the *dramatis personae*, the ultimate is the structuring of a process for achieving some articulated goals (Durant, 1921). These goals are directly or indirectly linked to the realization of a commonwealth in a state. However, it is instructive to point out that no political ideology is created in a vacuum. There must be the attendant historical and cultural fabrics. Inadvertently, whatever political dispensation adopted, it must be built on a political philosophy that shapes the lives of the people operating the political dispensation.

Perhaps it is this fundamental demand of politics, which also strikes a common chord in religion as a religious philosophy, and acts as shaping agents in men's lives, that accounts for the claimed positive or negative interactions of religion and politics. This fluctuating relationship of religion and politics becomes quite understandable from the perspective of the fact that both religion and politics proceed from human conducts essentially derived from man's nature. This nature, one or the other, strives for the holistic welfare of individuals within a given community to live in harmony, freedom, and solidarity befitting human dignity, and indeed enhance the attainment of social justice and peace (Madu, 1995).

Based on these conceptual relationships between religion and politics discussed above, we may now proceed to present the case for and against the influence of religion in politics as advanced by respective opposing schools of thought.

Arguments for Religion in Politics

There are those who have argued for the involvement of religion in politics (at least from the Christian perspective) based on the very nature of man as derived from God. This ultimately makes man dependent on God, the foundation of his (man's) activities—which are actually dynamics of the mandate given by God to man to control and subdue the earth. In consequence, whatever powers exercised by man are subject to the providential sovereignty of God. Within this context, politics becomes an essential aspect of the divine design for man's individual and public good (Aderibigbe, 1995). Based on this argument, politics per se is abstract. Its concreteness emerges when it is cohered in an individual or a community of individuals, whose very nature is religious. How then do we separate the religious man from the political man? This argument concludes that both religion and politics have common human actors—they are created by man for the good of man and society. Consequently, in a way, the relationship between religion and politics becomes that of cosmic necessity.

Indeed, this line of argument has been pursued by some American political scientists in the past. For example, Ernest Griffith, John Plamenatz, and J. Rolland Pennock (1956) have argued that some elements of the American creed originated from some conception of divine presence. Indeed, they attempted to list the beliefs, which according to them are essential to the survival of democracy and that each of these basically depended on religious (Judeo-Christian) heritage. These beliefs consist in:

1. Love for and belief in freedom; best based upon belief in the sacredness of the individual as a child of God;
2. Active and constructive participation in community life; best based upon the obligation of the Christian, the Jew, and other believers to accept responsibilities, cooperating with and working for their brethren;
3. Integrity in discussion; best based upon the inner light of truth being primary in a world God meant to be righteous;
4. The freely assumed obligation of economic groups to serve society; best based upon the Christian insight into the nature of society as set forth, for example, by the parable of the body and its members;
5. Leadership and office holding regarded as public trust; best based upon or inspired by the example and teachings of religious prophets such as Jesus, who accepted such a service "to the death";
6. Attitudes assuring that passion will be channeled into constructive Ends; best based upon religious faiths that unite an obligation to love and serve with recognition of the primacy of individual personality;

7. Friendliness and cooperation among nations; best based upon the vision of world brotherhood derived from a faith that we all are children of a common heavenly Father.

Apart from the link of cosmic necessity of religion with politics based on the nature of man derived from God, some other proponents of the case for religion in politics have built their argument on principles which should empirically sustain partnership between religion and politics. For example, policies on human rights are claimed to be basically derived from religious principles. These principles are in conformity with the divine injunction of the "Golden Rule," which demands that one do unto others as he would wish to be treated. The implication of this is that one loves the other person as himself and by doing so, others would love him in return. From this standpoint, the supporter of religion in politics argues that religion in fact provides the standard for judgments which are essential in giving meaning to highly treasured human values, such as fairness , justice, goodness, and dignity—all hallmarks of good and beneficial politics. Indeed, this line of argumentation may be extended by submitting, as Richard J. Neuhaus did, "that religion supplies a counterweight to the greatest threat faced by democracy—a slide into totalitarianism" (Neuhaus, 1984).

Perhaps the arguments of this school of thought, making a case for religion in politics can be summed up in the figurative designation of religion as a leg of the tripod upon which rests the spirit of human governance, the others being morality and politics (Ajayi, 1992). This, to them, totally debunks the notion that religion and politics could be separated on the basis that the first is spiritual and the second, material. The two should be interwoven for the good of humanity they inclusively serve.

Arguments against Religion in Politics

While the advocates of religion in politics have drawn on the dependence of man's nature on the divine as the source of cosmic connection between religion and politics as well as the political benefits derivable from religious principles, the advocates of separating religion from politics have argued their case, largely by insisting on the dysfunctional dynamics of religion. Kenneth Wald and Allison Calhoun-Brown (2007) have highlighted three of such dynamics and their consequences, as advanced by critics of the involvement of religion in politics. These are: non-compromise, dogmatism, and fundamentalism. Though the dynamics could be discussed separately, they are inclusive in their dysfunctional influences on politics.

The first of such dynamics is the non-compromise stances of religious zealots in defending their positions against other people's religious views, or even general social issues. Once these positions are based on particular religious beliefs or principles, it becomes very difficult—if not impossible—to arrive at compromising solutions, so as to accommodate the views and positions of others who do not hold the same beliefs or principles. This is usually irrespective of the fact that they live in the same system of governance along with these other people. Such uncompromising attitudes, in the view of critics, could definitely jeopardize governance and the polity of the state.

The non-compromise dispositions could both be the cause or the product of dogmatism. Whichever is the case, religious values based on rigid and unbending positions usually encourage, and quite often perpetuate, contempt for an alternative point of view. In most cases, traits of dogmatism portend grave danger of not just accidental, but intended commitment to the rightness, truthfulness, and confidence of one's position against those of others. This may result in extreme subjective application of standards of truth and justice, and the determination to bring all of society under one's own banner without respecting the motives and views of opponents. As Liebman (1988) points out, this becomes more foreboding when the religious believers are convinced they are under the direct command of God. When this is the situation, an opponent may be regarded as not just being misguided or confused, but actually evil and malevolent. Indeed, Martin Buber (1937) puts it more succinctly by saying "religious faith may drive a person to treat an opponent as an 'it' rather than 'thou.'"

A third leg of the dysfunctional dynamic of religion is fundamentalism, which in practical terms is the end product of non-compromise and dogmatism. Opponents of religious involvement in politics have always insisted that fundamentalism poses grave problems for political democracy. Thus, according to Nagata (2001):

> Fundamentalism is an agency driven by the quest for certainty, exclusiveness and unambiguous boundaries ... propelled by the determination to chart a morally black and white path out of the gray zones of intimidating cultural and religious complexities.

A direct result of this kind of exercise is the building of a wall of demarcation between "true" believer and those outside the "circle," whom the believers treat as "the other" and consider not just a dangerous enemy, but a threatening one.

Arising from these perceived inclusive dysfunctional dynamics of religion in politics, opponents of religion in politics have identified two principal consequences. These are intolerance and the resultant violence that may ensue in furthering religious ends. There is no doubt that situations of intolerance and ultimately religious conflicts ending up in violence with everyday loss of life and destruction of properties have become part of human history in different parts of the world. Such ugly scenes have been and are still being played out, particularly in nations with a contending plurality of religions, and where followers of these different religious traditions compete for supremacy and dominance using religion to advance the course of political power, and ultimately embracing and sustaining antidemocratic politics.

In sum, the arguments of the advocates of religion in politics and those with contrary positions have shown that we can hardly have a consensus in determining the kind of relationship that should exist between religion and politics. Desiring one or the other in a balancing of views by taking a middle position may have to stem from a dispassionate consideration of the involvement of religion in concrete terms in the body politic of different democracies of the world. This should involve dwelling on salient points such as governance, the public sphere, test of quality leadership, indicators of the preference of leaders, and the overall benefits of religion in societal politics.

In the traditional societal setting, the Yoruba traditional society in Southwest Nigeria could serve as a model that captures the African dominating format. From all records available, there was a complete and absolute relationship between religion and politics. It seemed no distinction was made between the two. This is vividly demonstrated in the role of the *obas*, who were the natural rulers of the people. They were not regarded only as political leaders, but they also led their people in religious matters. In fact, among the Yoruba the political powers of the *obas* were guaranteed in their religious contexts. They were regarded as holding power in trust for Olodumare, the Supreme Being, and generally greeted as "Igbakeji Orisa," i.e., second in command to the divinity. Even today, when Western civilization and foreign religions have made the Yoruba people followers of different religions, the *oba* of a given town is still regarded as belonging to as many religions as his subjects participate in. Thus we find the *oba*, no matter his religious affiliations before his becoming king, performing his leadership role in the traditional religious life of his people. All these point to the fact that we cannot talk of a dichotomy between religion and politics in Yoruba land, a position very much the same in parts of Africa where the institution of traditional authority still exists.

When the history of Christianity is considered, we would see that, while there was what could be referred to as internal politics (if we consider, for example, the electoral process of casting lots to elect a replacement for Judas in the group of the Apostles, and the election of the Seven Deacons), the Christians maintained a distance from the practical politics of governing at its early stages, which was probably responsible for the persecution the Church went through.

However, from the time of Emperor Constantine of Rome, Christianity began to enjoy state protection and gradually became a virtual state religion, so much so that in the middle centuries Catholic popes were not only religious leaders, they also had enormous political powers. At this time, it was difficult to distinguish between their religious and political powers, as they essentially ruled the world, with the enthronement and dethronement of the then emperors and monarchs securely in their hands.

The sixteenth-century Reformation brought about a different situation, especially in England during the time of Henry VIII, who, because of his dissatisfaction over his marriage, broke with the Church in Rome and established the Church of England. Henry controlled this church, thus uniting religious and political authorities under the English monarchy. However, by the 1500s, the English crown, having passed through many hands, religious pluralism and separation of state from a single coercive church came to be established in England.

As of today, there is hardly any nation, except, of course, the Vatican, where the pope is head of state, that Christianity as a religion could be said to be united with political power so as to have what could be regarded as a "theocratic state." This is not to deny the fact of Christianity as a religion affecting, to a large extent, the policies of the governments of nations, which are predominantly Christian.

In the case of Islam, the situation is quite different. From the very beginning, Islam as a religion has been regarded as a way of life. So everything in human life is included; politics, of course, is not excluded. Muhammad, Islam's founder, combined political power with religious leadership. This stand has been maintained ever since. Consequently, the Islamic religion could be considered as the only religion that conveniently combines politics with religion, as exhibited by various Islamic nations in the world. Examples abound, particularly in the Arab world, such as Iran, Libya, Saudi Arabia, et al.

In contemporary times, the controversy over the connection between religion and politics has become prominent particularly with reference to governance and leadership expectations. Though the predominant situation now is the separation between the religious and political governing of nations, except as mentioned earlier. The majority of nations now are secularly administered, with freedom granted to citizens to belong to any religion of their choice, with followers of various religions taking part in the governance of such nations. However the connection between religion and politics in the body politic of these nations has continued to be a subject of interest and controversy, particularly with regard to governance. In most cases in such "secular" states, even when there are constitutional provisions for the separation of religion and politics, these have only been de jure in essence, while the role of religion in the body politic of the states has remained de facto.

This dynamic was significantly played out in the political-cum-religious embellishments surrounding the 2008 presidential race in the United States of America. The 2008 presidential election in the United States was spectacular in a number of ways. At the inception of the campaigns, both at the intraparty levels and then the interparty campaigns, it was clear that the nation was at the threshold of a historical phenomenon. The country would end up having one of the three historical landmark personalities becoming president: the first woman president, the first African American president, or the oldest president ever elected in the United States. However, over and above this personality election, the factor of religion became very prominent at every stage of the campaign.

We should, however, point out that it is not as if religion has not been part of electing American presidents in the past. For example, in 1928, Al Smith became the first Roman Catholic to run for president, but he lost. The major reason for this was attributed to the belief that a fair number of Americans at that time would not accept a Roman Catholic as their leader. To head off a similar fate, John Kennedy had to address his Catholicism, pledging to strictly govern on the principle of separation of religion and state, and not to be subjected to the dictates of the pope, the head of the Roman Catholic Church. Thus, in a way, the issue of religion in presidential elections in the United States has evolved from a contradiction thrown up by two historical events in American history and political development. The first was the ratification of the secular Constitution in 1789, and the next was the second great awakening and the rapid rise of evangelism. As Dr. Harvey (2008) points out, the first foresaw a tight regulation of religion in politics, and a distinct separation. The second made such a separation impossible.

What this situation established was a de jure separation of church (religion) and state and a complementary de jure vision of the separation of the religious from the political. However, when the history of religion and politics in the United States is closely examined, there emerges a particular de facto intermingling of the two (Paul Harvey, 2008).

While it is true that the founding fathers intended and indeed operated a de jure separation of religion and state and therefore willed the exception of religious prerequisite—or as it is put, "tests" in determining the election of political leaders, historical de facto mingling of religion with politics has made "religious testing" prominent consideration in electing leaders. Thus, religious "testing" seemed to have gained a central position in America to such an extent that it may not be possible for a candidate with the same moral or religious views as George Washington to make it to the White House in contemporary United States.

The prevalence of the de facto mingling of religion and politics over the de jure separation of religion and politics, and thus the application of "religious testing" for electing leaders, became significantly obvious in the 2008 U.S. presidential election. This was both at the primary stage of the campaigns in the two political parties—Republican and Democratic—and then at the stage of the battle between McCain, a Republican and Obama, a Democrat. The "religious testing" of the presidential candidates for the 2008 elections found its way into the limelight right from the intraparty primaries. For example, on July 10, 2008, a report from the Press Forum and the Project for Excellence in Journalism stated that media coverage of religion in the presidential primary campaigns from January 2007 through April 2008 rivaled coverage of race and gender combined.

For the Democratic Party primary, the controversy on religion and politics beset candidate Obama the most. The first controversy, which was short-lived, had to do with which religion Obama practices, Christianity or Islam? There was a report in relation to his being a Muslim while living in Indonesia. As the research center found out, even though "the inaccurate belief that Obama is a Muslim appears to have virtually no effect on Republican voters, but Democrats, who share the misperception are significantly less likely to support him" (Pew Forum on Religion & Public Life, 2008). Obama has to puncture this misperception by "showcasing" his church membership in the Rev. Wright's church in Chicago. Paradoxically, his membership of the church and relationship with the Rev. Wright soon became an albatross around Obama's neck because of the "radical" and claimed anti-American stances of the pastor. Even though Obama attempted to ride the wave of the criticism, he finally had to not only distance himself from the radical beliefs of the Rev. Wright, but had to resign his membership of the church outright. In spite of this proactive move, the problem remained a major issue for him, both in the primaries and the presidential contest against McCain.

On the Republican side, religion also played an active role, particularly at the primaries. For example, Mitt Romney had to show why he should be accepted as a Mormon, in order to lead the United States. In the fashion of John F. Kennedy's explanation to the country of his Catholic faith, Romney had to speak publicly about his religious faith, and pledged to be independent from the Mormon church authority in his duties as president of the United States, if he were elected.

However, in the December 5, 2007, speech at the George H. W. Bush Presidential Library, Romney insisted on the connection between religion and politics. Quoting John Adams, he said: "Our Constitution was made for a moral and religious people." Romney also subscribed to the notion that: "The Constitution established the United States as a Christian nation." To buttress this positive link between religion and political democracy, Romney insisted that "Freedom requires religion just as religion requires freedom. ... Freedom and religion endure together or perish alone ..." (Teachable Moment, 2008).

Still, in the Republican primaries, religious affiliations were identified for the reasons Romney fell behind Mike Huckabee, a former Baptist minister (Pew Forum on Religion & Public Life, 2008). In the same vein, Huckabee was able to remain in the Republican primaries for so long because of the support of evangelical Christians. Indeed, Huckabee's insistence on the significant role of faith in his political life (which drew evangelical Christians to him) was well articulated in his campaign ad: "Faith doesn't just influence me, it really defines me. I don't have to wake up every day, wondering 'what do I need to believe?'" And as he speaks, the screen, in capital letters, flashes "CHRISTIAN LEADER."

The central stage enjoyed by religion in the U.S. 2008 presidential election was not limited to just the religious connections of the presidential candidates. Other agencies of the American public waded in to give credence to this prominence. For example, the mass media had a field day in assessing the role of religion in the election. Both Obama and McCain granted interviews, and actually had debates on their religious affiliations. Apart from the event hosted by the Rev. Rick Warren on August 16, 2008, Obama and McCain made statements on their plans to build on President George W. Bush's faith-based initiative. In addition, both presidential candidates highlighted their backgrounds, which indicated their affirmation of religious good in individual and public services. For example, McCain dwelled on his prisoner-of-war experience in Vietnam, and how the mercy showed to him by his captors affirmed his religious faith. Obama, on the other hand, drew on his experience as a community organizer in Chicago through a black church to embrace faith.

These experiences for the two candidates were "faith stories" that explained their belief that religion could and should actually impact public life (Pew Forum on Religion & Public Life, 2008).

We must, however, not shy away from the strong submission in some quarters, that no matter how large a role religion played in the 2008 presidential campaigns, the ultimate factors were made-up variables having to do with charisma, the need for change, and the emerging economic problems during the last months of the presidential campaigns. The above position notwithstanding, we cannot but give significant consideration to the public and private spiritual stuff such as the revivalism that grew as the last days of the campaigns approached, when religious congregations and individuals prayed for the success of the candidates of their choice through vigils and other religious activities. At least, as Harold Dean suggests:

> One group emerged convinced that its prayers were answered ... Those who believed that they would never see an African-American president in their lifetime, attributed Barack Obama's victory to divine intervention.

What more could have indicated the limitation of the de jure separation of religion and politics and give credence to the de facto mingling of religion and politics in the 2008 U.S. presidential election? Finally, for different reasons and from different standpoints, we share the view of Richard B. Miller that: "The 2008 presidential contest between Barack Obama and John McCain will likely be remembered for engaging religion at two levels: one thematic, the other cultural and demographic."

Unity, Peace, and Stability

Religion is also important in making these available in the society; its method of producing them is two-dimensional:

(a) it may be through prayer services and other rituals; or
(b) it may also be in the form of concrete participation in the life of society.

In the first method, on numerous occasions and among different communities all over the world, religionists have been asked to offer prayers in moments of stress and difficulties; services are offered for the unity of the nations, e.g., prayers before national days, for the survival and well-being of the nations and the citizens.

In concrete terms, the living style of various followers of religion has started to demonstrate an attitude of understanding in which they are ready to live mutually together as brothers and sisters, taking part not only in common social activities, but sometimes in common religious activities at the invitation of one another, e.g., harvests, festivals, at Christmas. The intention is to provide a conducive environment for followers of various religions to live together in peace and harmony, thus creating stability and a peaceful society. Also, all religions, at least theoretically, stand for justice and fairness and are mostly disposed to aiding the oppressed, thus standing as the last hope of the common man when all else fails. The Old Testament is full of stories of prophets like Amos and Nathan, who both stood up for the poor. Jesus Christ, in the New Testament, is portrayed as the best friend of the poor. The prophet Muhammad of the Muslims fought for the social mobility of the poor.

Educational Roles

The role of religion in the education of society, both informally and formally, has been considerable. The literary development of the world always has to do with religionists. Not only this, with the casting away of religion's suspicion for literary works, scientific inventions, and morality, education has come to mean much to all religious organizations. The current trend now is to find points of unity, or more specifically, compromise between faith and reason. In the search for making religion acceptable to man, many Christians have involved themselves in literary pursuits. Thus, various Christian philosophers like Thomas Aquinas have made their marks in world literary development in the bid to prove the existence of God, employing rational process.

Far from the time of the controvercy with Charles Darwin on his knowledge, the Christian world has come to allow its followers to engage in free investigations into things not only on earth but in outer space as well; and the general belief is that, rather than the knowledge turning people away from God, it actually brings more vividly to the forefront the wonders and greatness of God and His creative power and authority over the whole universe.

The Bible has also led the aspiration for more knowledge. On one hand, especially among laymen, the desire to read the Bible has led many to struggle for knowledge; on the other hand, the desire to read, interpret, and understand via critical methods the contents of the Bible has also been a stimulus for the search for knowledge. Christianity has also had to use education to enhance the spread of faith. The work of evangelization had to be accompanied by formal education: first to train interpreters, and then successors to the missionaries. Islam, too, has not been left out. It is claimed that after Muhammad's death, Muslim rulers and scholars began a wave of expansion of scholastic activities, on which it is claimed our present-day civilization rests. And, as with Christianity, Muslim philosophers also made their mark on the literary world, so also in the world of science and astronomy.

On the formal aspect of education, using Nigeria in Africa as a vivid example, religious organizations (until the 1970s when state governments began to take over schools) had been in the forefront of establishing schools at various levels. In fact, Christianity (all denominations of it) has been quite impressive on this point, when the fact that all the formal education and the initial establishment of schools in this part of the world were the products of Christian missionaries. There is hardly any part of Nigeria where the story is different. It is always the case that Christianity brought formal education to the people. While its objective or aim in doing so is quite another question, the fact remains that Nigerians owe the existence of formal education today to the missionaries. Islam, too, has contributed, though in small measure, to the formal education of Nigerians. It is also the case that many colleges and universities in the United States were established by different religious organizations. Indeed, today such organizations have private colleges and universities located in different parts of the United States.

Religion and Economy

As we have observed in the basic thesis of Max Weber, the interaction between religion and the forms and goals of economic life gave rise to modern capitalism in the Western world. Modern capitalism developed in the seventh century and differed from traditional capitalism as a result of the form in which the capitalists practiced it. They became:

- More rational in their methods.
- More impatient with traditional restraints on technological innovation and the scope of the markets.
- Motivated by the ethical spirit, which was believed to give the capitalist enterprise the dignity of being in service to God, as well as the fulfillment of His wishes for man. It was an ethical spirit that was conspicuously shown by Protestants, especially Calvinists. It must be remembered that Catholics were either other-worldly as required by Catholic doctrine, or rarely worldly in a peculiar way, and thereby subject to feelings of guilt for their deviation from the teachings of the Church. In contradistinction to the Catholics, Calvinists were inner-world ascetics.
- The circumstances of the period were favorable for the emergence of modern capitalism. There were many inventions, discoveries, and political events that actually had their origins in the previous four hundred years or more.
- The hold of Catholicism over secular life had become weakened considerably by the rise of nationalism; this, in turn, strengthened Protestantism.

The effect of all these on religion was tremendous, but perhaps the lasting legacy bestowed on succeeding generations was what has now come to be called secularization. Religion itself became secularized. Norman Vincent Peale has epitomized this process in his *Ten Rules for Getting Self-Confidence*, the first of which is highly revealing.

Overall, the adoption of new religious views, etc., often leads to modification of the previous life, especially with regard to marriage (polygamy, monogamy in the African setup).

The essential qualities of religion in relation to the roles expected of it and the various roles it has played in the society act as takeoff points for more relevant roles that it should plan in society. The changing complexity of the society and its orientation toward a pragmatic stance will, no doubt, present heavier challenges and demands on religion, particularly the organized ones. It is the meeting of such societal challenges and demands that will, in the long run, guarantee the survival of religion, in whatever form one may think of it.

FUTURE EXPECTATIONS

It may be true that today religion is meeting the emotional, psychological, and day-to-day practical needs of people, and in some ways striving to satisfy the mundane expectations of vast numbers of religious followers who seek answers to their various "life" problems. However, as solutions to these "life" problems begin to emerge in man's empirical and epistemological developments, religion should rise to meet more fundamental demands of society to justify its existence.

This will consist primarily in identification with certain ideals of the society and fighting a progressively sustained battle for the realization of these ideals. Religion in its various forms promotes human ideals, such as human dignity, freedom, and fundamental human rights. It must be ready at all times to stand resolutely for these. The liberty and freedom of man should be vigorously pursued. There must be openness of truth. Religion should not be shy of change. It must also not only allow innovations, but, in fact, encourage them.

Religion, in whatever form, must be committed to the problems of the society. It must work relentlessly for the welfare of society, transcending mere lip-service to various shades of religious rivalries and fanaticism.

Not only should religion pursue a theoretical campaign of seeing that peace and justice prevail, more than this, its gospel of justice and peace must find an empirical expression. It is only through this that religion will come to be seen as the agent of social harmony, progress, and prosperity, and at the same time justify and thence guarantee its survival in a modern society. On a general basis, the functional and dysfunctional roles of religion consist of the following, among other things:

(1) Religion is capable of offering amelioration for man in the society when confronted with disappointment and reconciliation with society when alienated from its goals and norms. This role of religion can be dysfunctional, too. In consoling those who are frustrated and reconciling those who are alienated, religion may inhibit, protest, and impede beneficial social change. By postponing reforms, religion can contribute to the buildup of explosive resentments that may eventually lead to revolution.

(2) Religion offers man contact with ultimate reality through worship ceremonies and provides authoritative teaching of beliefs and values. This priestly function contributes to emotional stability, to security, and to order. Thus, it gives a worshipper a firmer identity amid the uncertainties that he must confront during the course of his life. The corresponding dysfunction is that this process may sacralize (make sacred) erroneous ideas and provincial attitudes. This may retard a society's knowledge of its environment and man's efforts to control nature. The trial of Galileo for the "crime" of suggesting that the earth revolved around the sun is an example of this kind of dysfunction.

(3) Religion "sacralizes" the norms and values of established society, maintaining the dominance of group goals over individual wishes by reinforcing the society's pattern of rewards. This is religion's social control function. Moreover, because people do not always manage to live up to society's standards without deviation, some method must be found of handling the guilt of the deviant. Religion presents ways—often rituals—through which guilt can be expelled and the individual reintegrated into the social group. However, the social control function of religion can also have dysfunctional aspects. It can retard adaptation to changing conditions. For example, for a long time, the Church refused to permit members to lend money at interest, despite the great functional need for this activity in a situation of developing capitalism. The sacral freezing of norms is a source of many social conflicts, as shown by the contemporary debate over birth control in the Catholic Church.

(4) Religion may provide standards of value in terms of which institutionalized norms may be critically examined and found seriously wanting. We have this function in its clearest form in the Hebrew prophets, who were "troublemakers" in their own society, berating the shortcomings of established procedures. Hence, we call this the prophetic function. The conflicts between the priestly and prophetic functions of religion play an important role in biblical history. The prophetic functions occasionally generate social protests against established forms and conditions, but it had dysfunctional consequences also. Prophetic demands for reform were suspected to constitute an obstacle in the working out of more practical solutions to social problems. By issuing its demands in the name of God, religion may render compromise between them and the general society impossible.

(5) Religion performs important identity functions. Kingsley Davis writes that:

Religion gives the individual a sense of identity with the distant past and the limitless future. It expands his ego by making his spirit significant for the universe and the universe significant for him.

However, religious identification may cause divisions in societies. Moreover, by making sacred the identity it provides, it may worsen and, in fact, promote bitter conflicts, as witnessed in many parts of the world today. Religious substitutes such as communism and nationalism are also symbolic systems that give people an identity and tend to intensify intergroup conflicts.

SOCIOLOGICAL DIMENSIONS OF TRADITIONAL RELIGION

Discussion on traditional religion in relation to its sociological value to the African society should be a fitting conclusion to this chapter. However, the discussion here depends largely on experiences derived from the Yoruba society of Western Nigeria.

Traditional religion, as it exists among Africans, does not enjoy an elaborate organization. There is diversity of the religion in terms of objects of veneration (apart from the belief in one Supreme Being), between men and supernatural beings, the ways and methods of worship, the demands of objects of worship, and the followers. Also, traditional religion is not conversion oriented. However, the above having been said, it does not mean ATR has no sociological dynamics. It does, and to a very large extent might be considered to be more sociologically based than the so-called organized religions, in the sense that traditional religion is all-society involving. Individuals have important roles to play, and are related in a special way to other followers and the object of worship or veneration in the sense that his actions, good or bad, have effects on the whole society. So also the actions of others and the society impact co-survival, occupation, progress, a peaceful life, etc. For example, the wrong actions of a single adherent may bring disaster to all, including the performer. The following are agents of sociological dynamics in African (Yoruba) traditional Religion.

Oracles

The significance of oracles, not only among African religionists but among all peoples in the world, arises from the fact that man is never content with the knowledge he has or his position or fortune. There is therefore the desire to seek out knowledge, in addition to the burning desire to know what the future has in store for him. For example, among the Yoruba as traditional religionists, Orunmila is regarded as the embodiment of wisdom and knowledge, from whom knowledge about things not disclosed to ordinary men could be known, and could also precisely foretell future happenings. Today, the wisdom of Orunmila and his codes of knowledge as concentrated in *Ifa* oracles are used also to know the past wishes and will of God and ancestors.

Sociological Use of Oracles

There are many ways in which traditional religionists use oracles. In fact, the consultation of oracles starts for a child at birth, when his parents approach a diviner or a priest to know not only the type of child they have on their hands so as to know how to care for it, but also to find out what sort of person he would grow up to become. When it is time for the child to choose his career, the oracle is consulted again to know which work would be best for him. At marriage, a return trip is again made to the oracle to make sure that he or she gets a suitable partner. Even at death, if the circumstances surrounding his death are cloudy, the oracles are asked to clarify matters.

Societal Level

Oracles may be consulted to find out the cause of tribulations in the society and the solutions. When an *oba* is to be appointed, it is oracles that make the final selection. Oracles are also consulted before going to war, both to inquire if to undertake the campaign and the disclosure of the secrets of the opponents so that victory may be ascertained. Even today, with all the influences of foreign religions, people still indulge in attempts to find out about the future. There is the constant return to the roots to complement modern life and religion, particularly when the going gets tough.

Shrines

Shrines are places dedicated to one god or another. It could be both individual and societal. When such shrines are dedicated to family ancestors, they are found in houses or graves of these ancestors. If the shrines are societal, belonging to divinities, they are generally found in places that are traditionally connected with the presence of these divinities. However, it must be noted that even here there may be numerous shrines for a particular divinity, even in a locality.

Consequently, we notice that important activities of a society may, more often than not, take place in these shrines in order to give legal and religious contexts that would make decisions reached binding. Thus, *obas* may have to be crowned in shrines; favors are sought from the divinities at their shrines. As shrines are regarded as holy, their presence in a society has protective effects, enhancing plenty, peace, and stability in that society. So also any act of disrespect to the shrines, e.g., an intruder, may have adverse effects both on the intruder and society in general as a result of his actions. People also use shrines for blessing, material things and children; a shrine could also be a sanctuary for people in trouble.

Taboos

This is a word derived from the Polynesian term, *tabu*, meaning forbidden. Among the Yoruba it is called *eewo*, that is, something one is not expected to indulge in. The forbidden may be a thing or a person. Once something is designated as taboo, it must not be done or touched. Anyone who does something or touches it becomes a taboo himself until he is purified.

There are different kinds of taboos. It may be a religious taboo, in which case it is connected with one's object of worship; e.g., some food and drink are taboo to some divinities, so their followers must not touch them (for example, an *Orisanla* among the Yoruba drinks no palm wine). Taboos may have to do with personality. Kings and priests are often surrounded with taboos. Once a man becomes king, he becomes sacred. For example, he must not strike or be struck. He must not walk barefooted, etc. So also priests have some taboos to observe. (There are some having a hunter not hunting on certain days.)

Sociological Use

The sociological functions of taboos include the following:

i.   They are regarded as a body of "do's" and don'ts," which serve as guidelines to the morality of the people.
ii. They also fulfill a socialization role for the mastering of these taboos by the children and the society in general.
iii. They actually provide members of the community with the rules and regulations by which they can be accepted or rejected by society. A child's adequate knowledge of them and compliance gradually integrates him with his society, not only on the moral aspects but also knowledge-wise.

The impact of taboos on society is also of great importance. The breaking of a taboo may result in hazardous consequences for the society. As an example, it is said that if an *oba* walks barefooted, the ancestors would bring misfortune on the whole tribe. So there is the realization that the consequences of breaking a taboo does not end with the punishment of the person responsible alone; the whole tribe may become unholy by his action, and a general misfortune results. The consciousness of this by the people and the attempt not to be a bringer of woe not only to oneself but to the society in which one lives could act as a deterrent factor. With this, the morality of the society is enhanced. Peace, harmony, prosperity, discipline, and blessings would be the lot of the society, since the gods are happy with the society. The reverse is better imagined than actualized.

REVIEW QUESTIONS

1. From the pool of definitions of religion available to you, in your view which one best describes the sociological approach in religion?
2. Durkheim's sociological theory of religion designates society as the object of religious worship. How would you respond to this view based on the religiosity of individuals?
3. Karl Marx sees religion from the prism of oppression and subjugation of the masses. Is this a justified and viable social theory of religion?
4. Protestant ethics propagated by Calvinists designate religion as a social catalyst in promoting—if not actually originating—capitalism. Is this a fair assessment of Protestant ethics?
5. What would be your response to those who look for an intimate relationship between religion and politics?
6. What qualities and roles should religion acquire to be socially relevant in an increasingly materialistic and scientific global environment?
7. Using the Yoruba model, explain how religious elements such as shrines, oracles, and taboos could be employed as sociological tools.

BIBLIOGRAPHY AND FURTHER READING

Aderibigbe, Gbolade & Deji Aiyegboyin, eds. 2001. *Religion: Study and Practice*. Ibadan: Olu-Akin Press.

_____. 1995. *Religion and Politics*. Ibadan: Olu Akin Press.

_____. 1993. *Religion and Nation Building*. Ibadan: Olu Akin Press.

Allinsmith, W. and B. Allinsmith. 1948. "Religious Affiliation and Politico-Economic Attitudes: A Study of Eight Major U.S. Groups." *Public Opinion Quarterly* 12.

Allison, J. 1968. "Religious Conversion, Regression and Progression in an Adolescent's Experience," *Journal of Scientific Study of Religion*.

Buber, Martin. 1937. *I and Thou*. Edinburgh: Clark.

Bellah, R. N. 1968. "Religion: The Sociology of Religion," *International Encyclopedia of Social Sciences*.

Berger, P. L. and T. Luckmann. 1963. *Sociology of Religion and Sociology of Knowledge*. NY: Oxford University Press.

Bertocci, P. A. 1971. *Psychological Interpretation of Religious Experience*. London: Blackward Publishing.

Broom, L. and N. Green. 1966. "Religious Differences in Reported Attitudes and Behaviors," *Sociological Analysis*.

Calhoun-Brown, A. and K. Wald. 2007. *Religion and Politics in the United States*. New York: Rowman & Littlefield Publishers Inc.

Clark, E. T. 1929. *The Psychology of Religious Awakening*. New York: Macmillan.

Cochran, Clark E. 1990. *Religion in Public and Private Life*. New York: Rutledge Press.

Christiano, Kevin J. et al. 2008. *Sociology of Religion: Contemporary Developments*. UK: Rowman & Littlefield Publishers Inc.

Davenport, E. 1915. *The Elementary Forms of the Religious Life*. London: Allen & Unwin.

Dawson, Christopher. 1930. *Religion and the Modern State*. London: Oxford University Press.

Durant, W. 1921. *The Story of Philosophy*. New York: Simon & Schuster.

Ejizu, C. I. 1986. "Continuity and Discontinuity of Igbo Traditional Religion," in E. I. Metuh, ed. *The Gods in Retreat*. Enugu: Dimension Publishers.

Elkond, D. 1971. "The Origin of Religion in the Child," *Review of Religious Research*.

Farmer, H. H. 1943. *Toward Belief in God*. New York: Macmillan.

Fenn, R. K. 1992. "Toward a New Sociology of Religion." *Journal of Scientific Study of Religion*.

Freud, S. 1913. *Totem and Taboo*. London: Hogarth Press.

Glock, C. Y. 1984. "The Sociology of Religion," in R. K. Merton et al., eds. *Sociology Today*. New York: Basic Books.

Goldman, R. J. 1964. *Religious Thinking from Childhood to Adolescence*. London: Routledge & Kegan Paul.

Griffith, E. et al. 1956. "Cultural Prerequisites to a Successful Functioning Democracy." *American Political Science Review*, vol. 50.

Hart, Brad. 2008. "History of Religion and Politics in Presidential Elections: An Historical Perspective." *BlogSpot*.

Hoult, T. F. 1958. *The Sociology of Religion*. New York: Holt.

James, W. 1902. *The Varieties of Religious Experience*. New York: Longman.

Jones, E., ed. 1951. *Essays in Psychoanalysis*. London: Hogarth Press.

Juergensmeyer, Mark. 2003. *Terror in the Mind of God: The Global Rise of Religious Violence*, 3rd ed. Berkeley: University of California Press.

Liebman, Charles. 1988. *Deceptive Images*. New Brunswick, NJ: Transaction.

Luckmann, T. 1967. *The Invisible Religion*. New York: Macmillan.

Madu, J. E. 1995. "The Interplay of Religion and Politics in Nigeria: A Mutual Symbiosis," in Aderibigbe and Ayegboyin, eds. *Religion and Politics*. Ibadan: Olu-Akin Press.

Marx, K. 1964. *Early Writings*. New York: McGraw-Hill.

Makosi, A. O. 1988. "Religion and Politics in Independent Nigeria: A Historical Analysis," *Nigerian Journal of Theology*, vol. 1.

Nagala, Judith. 2001. "Beyond Theory: Toward an Anthropology of Fundamentalism," *American Anthropologists*, vol.103.

Neuhaus, R. J. 1984. *The Naked Public Square*. Grand Rapids: Eerdmans.

Nottingham, E. K. 1954. *Religion and Society*. New York: Doubleday.

Nwanaju, Isidore. 2005. *Christian-Muslim Relations in Nigeria*. Ikeja: Free Enterprise Publishers.

Olupona, J. K. ed. 1992. *Religion and Peace in Multi-Faith Nigeria*. Ile-Ife: University of Ife Press.

Phillip, H. L. 1956. *Freud and Religious Belief*. London: Rockcliff.

Reagan, Ronald. 1990. *An American Life*. New York: Simon & Schuster.

Stark, Rodney. 2005. *The Victory of Reason: How Christianity Led to Freedom, Capitalism, and Western Success*. New York: Random House.

Swatos, William H. 1993. *A Future for Religion? Paradigms for Social Analysis*. Newbury Park, CA: Sage.

Weber, M. 1904. *The Protestant Ethic and the Spirit of Capitalism*. London: Allen & Unwin.

_____. 1922. *The Sociology of Religion*. Boston: Beacon Press.

Weibe, D. 1982. *Religion and Truth: Toward an Alternative Paradigm for the Study of Religion*. New York: Mouton Publications.

CHAPTER SEVEN

ETHICAL APPROACH

INTRODUCTION

The possibility of a significant connection between religion and ethics has been an issue of constant interest and controversy, particularly between religious believers and some humanist philosophers. While the former insist on an identical nature of the two, particularly when ethics is considered from its practical term—morality—the latter, especially in contemporary times, are disposed to regarding religion and ethics (morality) as logically and empirically distinct, with no significant connection, not to mention being identical. However, there is no denying the fact that the two human phenomena have always been seen as striving to bring out in man the aspects that prompt him to do right or good things, rather than the wrong or bad ones. This notwithstanding, one cannot but be convinced of considerable levels of differentiation after a sober and critical reflection on the definitions, procedures, and goals of religion and ethics.

RELIGION: DEFINITION AND GOAL

Defining religion is not only a complicated task, but also an interestingly rich experience. This is because, according to W. Hall, for example, "the term religion means many things to many people." Also, says D. Wiebe, "there are numerous definitions of religion." Thus, Yinger indicates that "given a good library and an hour or two, a list of a hundred or more could easily be compelled." Invariably, to ask, What is religion? is not only to ask an ambiguous question, but to irresistibly indulge in ambiguity. In the final analysis, the kind of answer one gets from this question may have to depend largely on one's area of interest or emphasis. If, for example, one wishes to emphasize belief, the definition of religion in *Webster's Third New International Dictionary* would be most appropriate. It states:

> Religion is a belief in an invisible superhuman power, together with the feeling and practices that flow from such a belief.

On the other hand, if it is value that is to be stressed, the *American Collegiate Dictionary* is of use. It defines religion as: "… the quest for the values of the ideal life and for the quests of achieving them and includes a worldview that relates this quest to the surrounding universe."

A definition from the perspective of interest abounds in the meanings given by an array of professionals such as anthropologists, sociologists, psychologists, and philosophers too numerous to mention here. However, for the purpose of this discussion, we may simply define religion as:

> … the means by which man discovers the face of God, formulates a dependent relationship with Him in communication of practices, as the infinite creator of the universe (Aderibigbe, 2001).

We have adopted this definition principally in anticipation of why religion maintains certain positions. While defining religion may involve a lot of ambiguities, the situation is definitely less so when the question of the goal(s) of religion is raised. There is, to a large extent, an overall consensus as to what religion strives for and which has made it the strongest dominating factor in human history.

Over and above any other goals or objectives, religion has as its main goal the attainment of an afterlife for its followers—that is, the salvation of their souls. Any other goals are supporting ones to enhance this singular aim in ensuring that humans lead a good life by doing the will of the Supreme Being. This ultimate goal of religion is tied absolutely to the belief in the life hereafter and the conception that this could only be attained through the practice of religion.

ETHICS: DEFINITION AND GOAL

Ethics has been defined in a number of ways to adequately reflect not only its subject matter, but also its functions and procedures. Unlike religion, the definitions given to ethics are, to a large extent, complementary. This is vividly shown in some of the definitions of ethics provided here. For example, it has been defined as:

> … an aspect of philosophy which examines human actions and conducts inasmuch as they are judged good or bad, right or wrong. Thus it is also a subject that concerns itself with matters of duty, obligation and moral responsibility of individuals (Aderibigbe, 2001).

It has also been defined by Aderibigbe as:

> A branch of philosophy which is concerned with what is considered to be morally good or bad and the ability of human beings to choose between these two alternatives.

In another definition, Asaju (2001) sees ethics as:

> … the rules of human conduct in human society. In other words, it deals with the dos and don'ts of societal morality.

In the same vein, W. T. Jones (et al.) (1973), says:

> In one sense, the term is a pattern or norm or code of conduct actually adopted by a group of people (although, of course, not necessarily always obeyed) … an activity of appraising and perhaps revising the codes. … It should also be seen as a philosophical inquiry in the attempt to do more critically and more systematically what everyone does on these occasions.

In line with these definitions of ethics—which are in no way exclusive—the ultimate goal of ethics may be said to be represented by two major perspectives. First, there are those who conceive the goal of ethics as producing in man the qualities that would ultimately make him do what is good and what he ought to do. Secondly, to others (particularly Aristotle and those in his school of thought), what is demanded of ethics is to perfect the process of making man to be himself and know himself. These are attained by means of reasoning and the utilization of various talents. When this state has been reached, man, according to Socrates, becomes whole. It is then that he, as Aristotle opined, could find supreme happiness.

When these two perspectives are synthesized, one may surely consider the overall goal of ethics as that of producing a reasonable man who, in making use of his talents and rationality, is able to know himself, and consequently choose rightly for himself through a discriminating capability that has gone through the mill of sound and healthy reasoning.

RELATIONSHIP BETWEEN RELIGION AND ETHICS

If the goals that both religion and ethics pursue are to be used as the basis of determining the kind of general relations that should exist between them, then one can proffer that these would consist of areas of agreement and disagreement.

Areas of Agreement

Comparing religion and ethics from a viewpoint of striving toward the same goal will certainly reveal a major fact—that ethical or moral doctrines have had a very central place in religion. In fact, religion, either as definitive or institutionalized, can hardly be considered without ethical groundings. Consequently, we speak of religious ethics as against secular ethics. Also, all known religions of the world contain ethical grounds that guide both membership and the conduct of followers who belong to particular religions. Thus we have Christian ethics, Islamic ethics, traditional ethics, etc. Apart from this, but most probably as a culmination of it, all the great religions of the world are built on absolute demand of obedience from followers. Thus, there is the prescription of laws by which members must live. This is done in the bid to stipulate the type of behavior expected of members. In these regards, religion may be said to be one with ethics, whose main preoccupation may be seen primarily as that of cultivation of the attitude of the obedience to given rules and regulations, and the attitude of always choosing the right from the wrong. Some moral philosophers, such as Immanuel Kant, have stressed this area of agreement between religion and ethics to posit the concept that religion and ethics are identical. Kant (*Groundwork for the Metaphysics of Morals*, Section 11) in particular strongly propagated this notion and consequently concluded that "religion consists in regarding our moral duties as divine commandments."

Conceptual Differences

While there is a general agreement between religion and ethics of the sort enumerated above, when peculiarities are critically considered, a seemingly unrecognizable "divide" develops between religion and ethics. This may be concrete, as expressed in the following series of comparisons.

First, the prescriptions given to the way of life by the religionists are quite different from those given by moral philosophers regarding man's life being completely controlled by the supernatural. The moral philosopher sees no rationale in such a relationship.

Second, for the moral philosopher, ethics can be undertaken with the notion that the Supreme Being is dispensable. This is considered to be so inasmuch as the relationship between the Supreme Being and morality is an independent one, in which the Supreme Being is said to approve of certain actions because they are morally right, not that they are morally right because the Supreme Being approves of them. Thus, in ethics, the moral rightness or wrongness of an action is independent of the Supreme Being. Religion would certainly not agree with this position. It would, in fact, uphold the very opposite—that what is right or wrong is so because the Supreme Being ordains it.

Third, religionists are not slow in indicting ethics, particularly secular ethics, of ignoring the most essential thing in man's existence—the Supreme Being, who is the creator and controller of all things. This accounts for the reason why in religion the golden rule seems to be "I ought to do this, but it is only by God's grace that I can do it." For ethics, on the other hand, man himself is the final determining factor. Thus, it posits: "I ought to do this thing, therefore I must and I can."

Fourth, there is the concept that ethics, strictly speaking, succumbs to the narrow utilization of man's capabilities of the intellect and the conscience, while religion, on the other hand, is said to involve the whole of man's personality—the intellect, the conscience, the imagination, and the emotion. That is why to a large extent mystical elements that are evidenced in the lives of holy men are totally absent in ethics.

Fifth, and perhaps most significantly, the demand by ethics for human goodness is usually seen as strictly for the betterment of the individual in relation to making humanity and the world he inhabits a more humane and better place to live in. On the contrary, humanity and the world are secondary in religion's exhortation of man to be good. The primary objective is for the reunion with the Supreme Being, his creator. Thus, to some extent, while ethics may be said to be limited to moral or mundane aspirations of man, religion transcends this world for the next, and, in fact, justifies man's hopes in immortality. It is important to point out here that the conception of a significant level of differences between religion and ethics has led quite a few contemporary humanist philosophers to insist on empirical and logical distinctions between religion and morality (ethics).

APPROACHES, CHARACTERISTICS AND SOME THEORIES IN ETHICS

Having discussed the two-faced relationship between religion and ethics, with the conclusion that vividly shows that the two concepts are quite independent of each other, we may now proceed by highlighting the nature of ethics. This essentially consists in the classification of ethics as a subject of study, the two major ways of approaching ethics: its characteristics and limits, as well as some selected theories that have been propagated in ethics, however these are presented in their introductory forms. For in-depth and detailed study, the reader should find ample materials in the list of books provided at the end of the chapter.

Classification of Ethics

Ethics, as earlier defined, is an aspect of philosophy which examines human actions and conduct, inasmuch as they are adjudged good or bad; right or wrong. It is also a subject that concerns itself with matters of duty and obligation and the moral responsibility of individuals. In defining ethics, the question of free will becomes relevant in order to know the limitations of the subject. This is because, when a person behaves out of his own free will, then he can be judged in accordance with this behavior. Since not all actions of man come under ethics, actions that are carried out under any form of pressure, consciously or unconsciously, do not come under ethical considerations. For example, the action of a soldier who kills in a war cannot be ethically assessed, so also are actions carried out under severe provocation, hypnotism, and an unconscious or unsound state of mind. The contention here is that the person carrying out actions under these conditions is not exercising his free will, and therefore could not be held responsible for them.

The question of whether ethics could be regarded as a science has often been raised. In determining this problem, science would be divided into two main approaches: the narrow and the wider perspectives. Under the narrow perspective, science could be defined as the phenomenon that deals with observation, the postulation of hypotheses, and the production of tested facts using the positives, empirical or descriptive methods. Examples of subjects under this disposition are biology, physics, and chemistry. When science is approached in a wider perspective, it could be defined as the systematic study of any phenomenon according to some fundamental principles. The knowledge acquired from this process is known as scientific knowledge.

In light of this dichotomy, it is generally accepted that ethics cannot be regarded as scientific if the narrow definition of science is used as a parameter. It is agreed, however, that the subject can rightly take its place under the wider definition of science as a social science.

Approaches in Ethics

The study of ethics has generally been approached from two main dimensions. As a result, the subject has been divided into two classes: Normative ethics and metaethics.

Normative Ethics

This is concerned with principles. These principles determine which kinds of things are accepted as good or bad, right or wrong. It deals with questions such as, What ought I do? or What should I do?

Metaethics

This deals mainly with the meaning of the words, terms, and expressions used in ethics. For example, when we use the words "right," "wrong," "bad," or "good," what do we mean? When we say stealing is bad, what meaning do we intend to communicate?

It must be noted that the distinction between metaethics and normative ethics is not clear-cut. This is because the meanings of ethical terms and judgments go a long way to clarify and sometimes influence the principles upon which ethics is based. So also it will be very difficult to make any meaningful ethical statements without being familiar with some principles upon which the statements are based. In other words, the two approaches in ethics complement each other, and there is no way ethical standards can be accepted with the exclusion of any of the two approaches.

Characteristics of Ethical Statements

As earlier discussed, the subject matter of ethics is the situation presented in man's everyday life. But not every human situation comes under the scope of ethics. For a situation to be judged ethical, it must fulfill one or more of the following conditions.

Social

Any situation that falls under ethical judgment must be social. That is, the actions, attitudes, and behaviors exhibited must involve a relationship between one person and another, or between one group of people and another. Actions, behaviors, and attitudes that terminate on an individual or personal level deserve no ethical judgment.

Rational

Before an action or situation can be adjudged ethical, it must be rational. That is, such an action or behavior must deal with the conscious aspect of a person, and the person must have the benefit of applying his sense of discrimination through the act of reasoning. This condition certainly rules out any action, behavior, or attitude carried out either unconsciously or under any form of pressure or severe intimidation. For example, the action of a man who has a gun pointed at his head and commits murder cannot be ethically judged.

Universality

To come under ethical consideration, an action must have universal appeal. That is, such an action should be in conformity with principles that are generally accepted in the society in which one lives. The dictates of one's surroundings are very important in the ethical evaluation of a person's action, behaviors, and attitudes.

Limitations of Ethical Statements

Having seen the nature of ethical statements, it is only proper to identify the limitations of such statements, since we realize that ethical statements do not cover the totality of human endeavor.

- The first limitation of ethical statements is that they are not casuistry. This is because they are not interested in demanding change. This is where there is a lot of difference between ethics and religion. While the principal objective of religion is to bring about a change in any man who practices it, ethics only deals with the actions of man as they are presented, and does not strive for any change in human conduct.

- Also, ethical statements do not deal with private actions. For example, one's actions in preferring one type of food to another or sleeping instead of going to a party do not come under the scope of ethics. This is because the study plays no part in the acts of individuals that have no social bearing on the society.

- Equally, ethics does not concern itself with unconscious acts. Behaviors that are beyond the control of individuals and for which they cannot be held responsible are clearly outside the scope of ethics. For example, if someone who is insane carries out an act, he cannot be held responsible for it, because he is by the nature of his state of mind not in control of his deeds.

Ethical Theories

Various theories have been propagated, both in normative ethics and metaethics, in the attempt to provide guidelines for the interpretation and formulation of principles and meanings on which ethical standards may be based. Some of these theories are briefly discussed here.

Normative Theories
(1) Utilitarianism

The general position of the exponents of utilitarianism is that the only standard by which what is right or wrong is judged is the principle of utility. This principle claims that what is morally sought as an end is the greatest balance of good over evil. Over the years, this general position has been approached from two main perspectives, namely, Act-Utilitarianism and Rule-Utilitarianism.

Act-Utilitarianism

Believers in this principle hold that the right act to perform in any given situation is that which, when alternatives are presented, will produce the greatest balance of good over evil.

Rule-Utilitarianism

While the principles of utilitarianism are still the same, believers in rule–utilitarianism (unlike act-utilitarianism, which evaluates particular situations) apply rules. Thus, an act is judged right if it is in keeping with a rule that promotes the greatest good over evil.

Critical Considerations

As attractive and superficially convincing as the theory looks, a closer and critical consideration of it presents some problems that cannot be overlooked and which makes ready acceptance of the theory difficult. Some of these are:

- The attempt to calculate the evil and the good actions will not only be difficult, but outright impracticable in man's daily moral decision making.
- The criterion demanded for judging an action right or wrong may be more than the amount of good over evil they produce. For example, an act with the highest score may involve the breaking of other moral codes, like not fulfilling a promise, telling a lie, or violating some rules.
- If the utilitarian principle is accepted, acts which are ordinarily considered to be bad may be made out to be good. For example, a poor man may be justified to steal from a rich man to feed his family.
- There is also the difficulty of distributing the good and evil among the population. One wonders as to the basis on which this would be done.
- A major problem with utilitarianism is that it does not provide for the long-term effects of moral actions, since it is not possible to assess their rightness or wrongness of an act without experiencing its efforts. We may have to wait for some time, when the effects would become manifest, before passing judgment as to the rightness or wrongness of the action. Since utilitarianism does not provide for this possibility, it is not unlikely that in the long run, some acts with short-term good effects may have negative consequences.
- Another prominent problem of utilitarianism is its rejection that motives behind an act should be used in evaluating it. Its position that the end justifies the means may produce a situation in which, for example, if a person intends to cheat and ends up with an act of good consequence, then the man's action should be considered right.

(2) The Deontological Theories

There are various deontological theories of ethics. Our discussion here, however, will be limited to two of such theories: The will of God theory and Kant's theory.

(i) The Will of God Theory

It is the intention of this theory to submit that the only standard by which an action could be adjudged right or wrong depends on its being commanded or forbidden by God. This position, no doubt, is an extension of the theistic belief in the existence of a Supreme Being, whose commands are used in defining ethical terms, good, right, bad, or wrong.

As would be expected, the atheists and agnostics have painted out some of the inconsistencies involved in the theist's position. This has consequently raised some salient questions. Among these are: Is something right because God commands it to be so? Or does He command it because it is right? If we hold the first view (a thing is right because God commands it), it means that if God commands evil, killing, cheating, and stealing, these acts would be seen as right. On the other hand, if God commands a thing because it is right, then the criterion for evaluation is independent of God's command. This position has also given rise to the question of why we must obey God's command. To the exponents of theological ethics, our obedience of

God's commands is imperative because not only is God good and loving, He also has our interest in mind at all times. Failure to obey his commands leads to punishment, while adherence to his commands fetches rewards.

Seen in light of the above, the will of God theory is mostly reduced to a type of prudential ethics, in which case morality comes to be regarded as the pursuit of self-interest and could be compared to ethical egoism, which has been roundly rejected. We do not see how the will of God theory can escape the same fortune.

(ii) Kant's Theories

Instrumental and Intrinsic Good

It is Kant's view that when all the things man values and desires are considered, some of them would be discovered to be means to a higher end, while others are ends in themselves, since they are desired for no other reason but for their own sake.

Desires and values that are means to some other ends are considered instrumental and are seen as possessing extrinsic good, while those that are ends in themselves possess intrinsic good. A consideration of the set of value and desires below will reflect the two basic classes of good (extrinsic and intrinsic). It may be worthwhile to note that sometimes situations and practical options may not allow for strict adherence of one value to a particular class. For example, a desire or value that is considered as possessing intrinsic good may become extrinsic in nature due to circumstances and applications.

Some of man's values and desires are pleasure, health, life, knowledge, peace, money, power, and self-realization. We hesitate to divide the values and desires into intrinsic and extrinsic classes because of the limitations discussed above. With this at the back of his mind, Kant opines that the highest good (intrinsic) is a moral quality, examples of which are kindness, loyalty, fidelity, goodwill, dedication, love, etc. However, it is his firm belief that whatever is considered good in the world or beyond it has to be qualified. The only exception, he believes, is goodwill, which he says is the only good without qualification. This is because goodwill is not good because of what it accomplishes or because of the adequacy in achieving some desired end. It is simply good.

Kant goes further to consider acts that are done from inclination and those done "from duty" (out of respect for the moral law) to determine if they, or some of them, come(s) with moral considerations. Man as a free agent is known to act either from inclination (acting according to his tastes or what pleases him), or from duty or obligation (doing what is expected of him, whether it pleases him or not). It is the stand of Kant that only acts that are performed from duty are moral, since they are done out of respect for the moral law.

There is no doubt that this position of Kant's looks strange as it attempts to exclude acts of man that are born out of his free disposition without the compulsion of the law. It is our belief that the moral judgment of an act may have to be independent of whether it is done as fulfillment of a laid-down regulation, or from the free choice of the actor. The determining factor of moral judgment certainly goes beyond mere consideration of free choice or choice in accordance with known laws. The fundamental issue in judging an action as moral or not should depend on facts such as rationality, universality, and sociality, as discussed earlier, and in conjunction, the end result of such an action. There is no way in which man's acts from inclination (free choice) could be separated from moral evaluation.

Moral Law and the Categorical Imperative

It is the function of moral law to prescribe what ought to be done and what ought not to be done to bring about whatever is the highest good. That is why Kant holds that a will that acts out of respect for moral laws is the highest good. With the above position taken for granted, he goes on to postulate that since moral law prescribes what we ought to do, it could be referred to as the unconditional or categorical imperative, with a universal application. Kant believes there is also what he calls a hypothetical imperative, which tells man to act in a particular way because a certain result will be produced. Here, the expected result conditions the need for the action. This is in opposition to the categorical imperative, which commands man unconditionally and seeks obedience as a matter of duty. In this case, the only reason that is given for acting morally is that it is one's duty or obligation to do so. Kant then goes further to distinguish between actions that are in agreement with duty (acting according to duty) and actions that are performed from duty. While the former, according to Kant, are not necessarily moral acts, the latter are compulsorily so. He also prescribes the principles under which the categorical imperative can operate. These are mainly two:

i.   That one must act only on the maxim which one desires to become a universal law. In other words, if an action is right for me, it must be right for everybody else under the same conditions.
ii. One must act in such a way that people could be treated as ends in themselves and not as means, for to treat people as means is to turn them into instruments of achieving one's selfish needs (ends).

Metaethical Theories

As we pointed out in our discussion on approaches to the study of ethics, metaethics has to do with giving meaning to, explaining, and clarifying ethical words and statements. This is why theories in metaethics are largely concerned with the definition and nature of moral judgments, causing the field of inquiry to be referred to as philosophical analysis. There are many of these theories, but the principal ones are:

i.   Ethical intuitionism;
ii. Emotivism;
iii. Prescriptivism; and
iv. Ethical naturalism.

(a) Ethical Intuitionism

Exponents of this theory are of the view that all moral truths are known by intuition. This is because, according to them, such truths are self-evident. This is essentially a non-naturalist position, claiming that there is no empirical observation by which the truth of a moral position is knowable.

(b) Emotivism

This is a claim that all moral words and statements are simply the expressions of the feelings, emotions, and attitudes of the speaker. Thus, to say something is good is to express a favorable attitude of the speaker. So, to say something is good is to express a favorable attitude toward it, while to say something is bad is to express one's unfavorable attitude toward it.

(c) Prescriptivism

This is a more recent doctrine, which claims that what all moral judgments seek to do is influence, prescribe, and guide human conduct. For this reason, moral judgments should not be seen as mere expressions of emotion or statements of fact. They are determinant in nature, since they tell people what to do or what not to do.

(d) Ethical Naturalism

Ethical naturalists claim that ethical statements are translatable into nonethical ones without any change of meaning. They claim that ethical words, moral values, and obligations should be understood in "natural" terms.

When all the above theories are closely considered, it will be discovered, that they are all centered on some philosophical controversies. The most popular of these controversies is the one between naturalism and anti-naturalism. More often than not, this dispute is discussed in the realm of distinction between evaluating and describing, the "is/ought" problem. We shall give some consideration to this controversy here. The anti-naturalists are against the presupposition of the naturalists that moral words are definable and nonmoral (natural) ones. It is their opinion that there is an unbridgeable logical gap between the moral and nonmoral (natural). Therefore, any attempt to move from one position to the other will necessarily lead to committing what G. E. Moore refers to as a "naturalistic fallacy." It is claimed that for the naturalist to hold his position, he must be committed to one of the following positions:

+ That the activity of describing is distinct from that of evaluating, but the latter is reducible to the former; or
+ He must totally deny the distinction between the activities of describing and evaluating.

The contrary position of the anti-naturalist seems to advocate two views in holding that describing is different from evaluating:

+ That distinct classes of expressions are used for descriptions and evaluations;
+ That there are insurmountable differences between the activities of describing and evaluating.

The controversy between naturalists and anti-naturalists in respect of the relationship possible between describing and evaluating has also been approached through the "is/ought" question. Moore calls the move from descriptive to the evaluative a "naturalistic fallacy" because, according to him, the relation between stating facts and passing judgment on them is a contingent and not a necessary one. Moore is not even impressed by the attempt of Hobbes's system of ethics, which defines the moral in terms of the peace, security, and preservation of society, and since man desires all these they ought to pursue them because, according to Moore, any system of ethics that attempts to build its conception of the moral good or bad on the "observable" facts of society is logically invalid, for there is no way we can derive the moral "ought" from a set of propositions about human nature or society.

Moral philosophers such as J. Kemp, J. R. Seale, and P. Foot have disagreed with Moore, denoting that there is a necessary connection between the "is" and the "ought" (description and evaluation). For example,

Kemp holds that there is no logical error committed in claiming that once a man desires something, he must immediately proceed to attain it. Seale, in his "promising game," puts up five statements in deductive logical order which, according to him, show that from a major premise that is a factual statement, an evaluative conclusion could be attained without any faulty logical move.

1. Jones extends the words, "I hereby promise to pay you, Smith, five dollars."
2. Jones promised to pay Smith, five dollars.
3. Jones placed himself under obligation to pay Smith five dollars.
4. Jones is under obligation to pay Smith five dollars.
5. Therefore, Jones ought to pay Smith five dollars.

On a scale of 1–5, Seale has been able to demonstrate that from the mere assertion, "I promise to pay you," an ought-to statement could be attained.

Foot is of the firm opinion that there is a logical relationship between the descriptive (is) and the evaluative (ought). To show this, she analyzes the concept of "rude." She says "rudeness" is a morally evaluative notion. This notion is tied to that of "offense," so if a person is said to be rude, there is the acceptance that conditions for offense have been met. However, to commit an offense is simply behaving unconventionally. Using the above position, Foot tries to demonstrate the logical connection possible, using the following example:

i. Jim offended his father by pushing him out of the armchair.
ii. Therefore, Jim is rude.

If one accepts (i) as true, argues Foot, he cannot logically deny (ii). This would, of course, show that there is a necessary relation between the two statements, the first being descriptive and the second evaluative.

Ethical Relativism

In general terms, the claim of ethical relativism is that there is no one moral standard that is generally applicable to all men in all places and at all times. Therefore, morality is said to be relative to age, place, and circumstance. There is no absolute morality. Three areas of relativism have been identified for morality:

i. Cultural relativism, which holds that the correctness of ethical standards depends on the culture of the person concerned.
ii. Class relativism, which states that it is the class of the person concerned that determines the ethical standard to apply.
iii. Historical relativism, which claims that it is the time in which a person lives that can determine the correct standard of applicable ethics. Relativists are quick to point out the things that may not come under the scope of ethical relativism. Among these are:

- Disagreement of two particular actions in their judgment of a particular action, since both or all of them may still be applying the same standard. For example, there is likely to be a disagreement in the method a swimmer and a nonswimmer would want to adopt to save a drowning person.
- There could also be disagreement in the belief or knowledge of the facts of a situation.

Justification for Relativism

The claims of ethical relativism find support in the following considerations:

- One is likely to discover, even within the same culture and the same period, that judgments of people differ depending on the situations in which they find themselves. Therefore, one can only speak of relatively correct standards.
- The moral ideas of men are based on emotions; what men regard with resentment and disapprove of they call immoral, and that which they admire and approve they call moral. What displeases one may please another. So, ethical relativism is true.
- The advancement in knowledge by man, particularly in the anthropological fields, has shown that the moral codes of men have never been consistently the same: While some tribes regard aggression and cheating as moral virtues, in others these are regarded as immoral. Thus, there are no objective standards to apply. So, ethical relativism is true.
- If there is to be an absolute command, then there must be a universal commander from where a universal command could have derived its authority. Since it is difficult to find the universal commander issuing such an authority, it would then be better to take ethical relativism as morality if the codes are accepted to be relative to time, place, people, and circumstance.

REVIEW QUESTIONS

1. With the background definitions of religion and ethics offered in this book, what would you consider the main goals of the two phenomena?
2. Identify and discuss the existing similarities and differences between religion and Ethics.
3. To what extent would you align with the materialist philosopher that there should be both logical and empirical distinction between religion and ethics?
4. Purely from the religious believer's perspective, how can religious ethics be justified?
5. What would you consider the main strengths and weaknesses of ethical utilitarianism?
6. Ethical relativism is usually justified on the diversity of dynamics observable in human conduct. How far is this defensible?

BIBLIOGRAPHY AND FURTHER READING

Abraham, W. J. 1985. *An Introduction to the Philosophy of Religion*. Englewood Cliffs, NJ: Prentice-Hall Inc.

Aderibigbe, G. 1988. *The Study of Religion*. Ilesa: Jola Publications Ltd.

Augustine. 1993. *On the Free Choice of the Will*. Indianapolis: Hackett Publishing Co.

Brandt, R. B. 1976. *Ethical Theory and Militarism in Contemporary British Philosophy*. London: Oxford University Press.

Bird, Frederick. 1981. "Paradigms and Parameters for the Comparative Study of Religious and Ideological Ethics," *Journal of Religious Ethics*. 9.2.

Bohman, James. 1991. *New Philosophy of Social Science*. Cambridge: MIT Press.

Brandom, Robert. 1994. *Making it Explicit: Reasoning, Representing, and Discursive Commitment*. Cambridge, MA: Harvard University Press.

Fischer, J. M., ed. 1989. *God, Foreknowledge and Freedom*. Stanford, CA: Stanford University Press.

James, R. & A.T. Frank. 1972. *Philosophical Issues: A Contemporary Introduction*. New York: Harper & Row Publishers.

Green, Ronald. 1978. *Religious Reason: The Rational and Moral Basis of Religious Belief*. New York: Oxford University Press.

Hauerwas, Stanley and Alasdair MacIntyre, eds. 1983. *Revisions: Changing Perspectives in Moral Philosophy*. Notre Dame, IN: University of Notre Dame Press.

Kim, Jaegwon. 2006. *Philosophy of Mind*. 2nd ed. Cambridge: Westview Press.

Little, David and Sumner B. Twiss. 1973. "Basic Terms in the Study of Religious Ethics." In *Religion and Morality: A Collection of Essays*, eds. Gene Outka and John P. Reeder, Garden City, NY: Double Anchor Books.

Little, David. 1978. *Comparative Religious Ethics: A New Method*. New York: Harper & Row.

Lovin, Robin W. and Frank E. Reynolds, eds. 1991. "Teaching Comparative Ethics." In *Tracing Common Themes: Comparative Courses in the Study of Religion*, ed. John Braisted and Steven P. Hopkins. Atlanta: Scholars Press.

Hare, Richard. 1952. *The Language of Morals*. London: Oxford University Press.

Hastings, James, ed. 1987. *Encyclopedia of Religious Ethics*. London: Oxford University Press.

Hursthouse, Rosalind. 1999. *On Virtue Ethics*. Oxford: Oxford University Press.

MacIntyre, Alasdair. 1988. *Whose Justice? Which Rationality?* Notre Dame, IN: University of Notre Dame Press.

_____. 1981. *After Virtue: A Study in Moral Theory*. London: Duckworth.

_____.1966. *A Short History of Ethics*. New York: Macmillan & Co.

Mackie, J. L. 1977. *Ethics: Inventing Right and Wrong*. Middlesex: Hammondsworth.

Mitchell, B. L. 1967. *Morality and Religion in a Secular Society*. New York: Oxford University Press.

Moore, G. E. 1954. *Principal Ethics*. Cambridge: University Press.

Nowell Smith, P. M. 1903. *Ethics*. London: Macmillan.

Omoregbe, Joseph. 1993. *Ethics: A Systematic and Historical Study*. Lagos: Joja Educational Research and Publication.

Rudd, Anthony. 1993. *Kierkegaard and the Limits of the Ethical*. Oxford: Clarendon.

Segal, Robert, ed. 2006. *Blackwell Companion to the Study of Religion*. Oxford: Blackwell Publishing.

Singer, P. 1979. *Practical Ethics*. London: Cambridge University Press.

Sizemore, Russell. 1990. "Comparative Religious Ethics as a Field: Faith, Culture and Reason in Ethics." In *Ethics, Wealth, and Salvation*, eds. Russell Sizemore and Donald Swearer. Columbia: University of South Carolina Press.

Steinberg, Allen. 1995. "The Foundations and Development of Moral Values." *Journal of Assisted Reproduction and Genetics*, vol. 8.

Stevenson, C. I. 1944. *Ethics and Language*. New Haven, CT: Oxford University Press.

Stout, Jeffrey. 1983. "Holism and Comparative Ethics: A Response to Little." *Journal of Religious Ethics*. 11.2.

Taylor, Charles. 1989. *Sources of the Self*. Cambridge: Cambridge University Press.

Unison, J. O. 1953. "The Interpretation of the Moral Philosophy of J. S. Mill," *Philosophical Quarterly*, 3.

Vogel, Lawrence. 1994. *The Fragile "We": Ethical Interpretations of Heidegger's Being and Time*. Evanston, IL: Northwestern University Press.

Wellman, C. 1975. *Morals & Ethics*. New York: Foresman & Co.

William, Bernard. 1985. *Ethics and Limits of Philosophy*. Cambridge, MA: Harvard University Press.

Williams, B. M. 1976. *Morality*. Cambridge: University Press.

Woodruff, Paul. 2001. *Reverence: Renewing a Forgotten Virtue*. Oxford: Oxford University Press.

Yearly, Lee. 1990. *Mencius and Aquinas: Theories of Virtue and Conceptions of Courage*. Albany: State University of New York Press.

CHAPTER EIGHT

COMPARATIVE APPROACH

INTRODUCTION

A comparative approach to religion serves a number of purposes. The principal ones essentially involve the expansion of one's understanding of the philosophy and theologies of various religious traditions. Also, such a tool should be considered important and needed for religionists in their attempt to understand the reasons behind the differences in beliefs, values, and methodologies of these religions. Comparing religions should not be limited to just making a list of pros and cons. It should indeed be involved in the objective study and discourse of different religions, but also the meanings of the history that each religion presents and why followers hold their unique beliefs should be considered. Such dispositions generate and entrench beneficial competitiveness without disintegration into negative rivalry controversies. This chapter examines the meaning and the process, as well as the dynamics, of the advantages and disadvantages involved in the comparative approach to religion.

DEFINITIONS–MEANINGS AND PROCESS

The terms "comparative" and "religion" have been defined from different standpoints. For instance, defining religion, as discussed in the very first chapter of this book, has been shown to be quite complicated. However, for the purpose of the discussion in this chapter, the model definition offered at the end of that chapter is adopted. It states:

> Religion, in its essence, is the means by which man discovers the "face" of God, and formulates a dependent relationship with Him in communication of practices as the infinite creator of the universe (Aderibigbe, 2001).

The concept of "comparison" is seen as vital in the process of individuals making decisions in virtually every facet of human endeavor. This exercise is usually tied to the dynamics and strategies influencing one's or other people's opinions through a process of comparing and contrasting objects and situations. Indeed, it has been shown that comparison has become a tool to be deployed, even as a consumer searching for an item that will suit his needs in a store. In such situations, there is no denying the influence of the levels of popularity and universal acceptability of the item as dictated by the current trend of acceptability and interaction by peers and others within proximity.

As in other human attitudes and behavior, comparing religion(s) both as an individual engagement and/or as a scholarly profession, has become an obviously fashionable phenomenon globally, so to speak.

At the individual level, a comparative approach in religion reflects diverse cultural and family backgrounds in constructing religious beliefs, very often without ever questioning the individual's grounds, process, and method of these beliefs.

An example of such dynamics is the belief (or nonbelief) in an afterlife, which arguably constitutes an essential part of all religions. The belief in "life after death" is the ultimate desire of many religious believers. However, taken at the individual religion level, the context and method of attaining the "hereafter" become significantly diverse. For instance, for the Christians, the central doctrines of attaining salvation (life after death) revolve around living a holy life, the practice of prayer, biblical study, and complete faith in God. On the other hand, for the followers of Confucianism, the path to eternal purpose involves honesty, politeness, and a correct understanding of your role in society.

At the scholarly and hopefully objective level, the characteristics employed in the exercise are expected to essentially depict tools that are simple and based on logical reasoning. With such strategies, it should be possible to focus on the real subject matters having to do with finding the unique similarities and differences. While such factors may not often be immediately obvious, a painstaking and specific thought process of analyzing available data objectively should do the trick. As Deming (2005) points out, religions compared on just the surface can only give the general thought process. However, when truly and deeply compared, the uniqueness of the religions can be accounted for—thereby, allowing a meaningful exploration of the similarities and differences among the religions.

SAMPLED COMPARISONS OF THE ESSENTIAL BELIEFS AMONG FOUR RELIGIONS (JUDAISM, CHRISTIANITY, ISLAM, AND AFRICAN TRADITIONAL RELIGION)

1. The Belief in One Supreme Being

The belief in one Supreme Being can be found in the four religions listed above. However, there are certainly differences in approaching and teaching this belief. Judaism, up to the exile, believed in one Supreme God—Jehovah—and acknowledged also that other nations might worship their respective deities. But after the period of exile, the Jews were consistently monotheistic. Islam's belief in one Supreme Being is all involving, hence its monotheistic stand is thorough to the point that it continuously stresses the oneness of the

Supreme Being as having no equal and with no relatives nor children. It specifically disagrees with the Trinity conception in Christianity and God's fatherhood of Christ. On the other hand, Christianity does not see any contradiction in its doctrine of the Trinity and belief in one Supreme Being. To Christianity, the three persons in the Trinity—the Father, the Son, and the Holy Spirit—are one and inseparable, and are shades of one and the same person.

In the case of African Traditional Religion, there is the concept of diffused monotheism, whereby there is the belief in one Supreme Being who is worshipped through the lesser god, regarded as His subordinates. It is only in Christianity, and not in Judaism and Islam, that we find the conception of the Supreme Being as a deity who, in the concern for the redemption of mankind, sent His representative—not less in moral character—into human history. It may be concluded that of all the religions discussed, only Judaism, Islam, Christianity, and African Traditional Religion actually believe in teaching about and worshipping the Supreme Being, thereby reflecting genuine monotheism.

2. Supernatural Origin of the Founder

With the exception of Judaism and African Traditional Religion, which originated with the people, all other religions considered lay claim to founders. As far as the religions are concerned these founders were not ordinary men. Rather, they were products of mysterious circumstances and events that to them fundamentally justify supernatural origins. Particularly, their births are known to be surrounded with unusual occurrences, and in most cases have become legendary. For instance, in Christianity the event of Christ's conception and birth in the New Testament Gospels demonstrates the authenticity of the claim that he is the Son of God and the second Person of the Trinity. Not only was Christ recognized by others as this figure, but He also portrayed himself as having come from God, who is a father to Him and with whom He lived in constant intimacy.

In Islam, even though Muhammad has often been created with humble and ordinary origins, this was restricted to the early period of the religion. In later development, he has come to be regarded as a superhuman. In fact, both the Sunnis and Shiites have accepted the traditions that claim preexistence for Muhammad before the creation of the world.

3. Universal Application

This had to do with the intentions and aspirations of the religions to become world religions. This would, of course, mean how evangelical- or missionary-oriented each of the religions is in the attempt to make its belief and doctrines accepted and to gain followers all over the world in preference to other known religions. Judaism has clearly expressed in its sacred scriptures the hope of the universal application of the religion. Even though Judaism's early belief was to regard this religion as meant for the *Jews* alone, the efforts of prophets like Jeremiah and Isaiah changed such beliefs. They advocated that Yahweh's (the God of Israel) intention was to use the Israelites to reach other people of the world. Thus, they saw missionary and conversion activities as imperative for Judaism. Islam and Christianity have always been characterized by plans of becoming universal religions. Today, Islam can be considered the greatest rival of Christianity in attaining this plan. From the very beginning, the religion has always been committed to the propagation of the Islamic faith. This has been through military conquests, traders, and conscious missionary activities. The result is that today there is no continent in the world that the Islamic faith has not penetrated.

Also there is the claim that the injunction of making Christianity a world religion was given by Jesus the founder himself when he instructed his disciples, "Go therefore and make disciples of all nations" (Matt. 28:19). That injunction has been exploited to the fullest by the monumental spread and influence of Christianity from the very first missionary activities of Paul. Today, Christianity in its numerous denominations is found in every part of the globe.

African religion is not a universal religion because it is not missionary-oriented. Consequently, unlike other religions, it does not pursue an aggressive conversion program.

4. Moral Behaviors

All these religions support a morally upright life. According to the religion, this also teaches that it should be reflected in the way and manner each member of the society deals with the other so as to bring harmony and peace in the society. As a way of realizing this religious injunction of love and consideration for others in the society, each religion has presented what could be regarded as idioms or philosophical sayings to guide their followers.

These are reflected in the traditions and/or the scriptures of the religions. For example, Judaism stresses the injunction by directing: "Take heed to thyself my child in all thy works and be discreet in all thy behavior. And what then thyself hated do to no man" (Tobat 4:1415).

As the founder of Christianity, Jesus was very concerned with the moral behavior of his followers. He directed: "… and then love your enemies and pray for them that persecute you. …" (Matt. 5:44). This, according to him, should be done in order to be a good representative of God. On the whole, the Christian attitude to this injunction is best reflected in the words of Jesus: "All things therefore whatsoever you would that men should do unto you even so do you also unto them" (Matt. 7:11).

Islam also places a premium on moral uprightness. This is why the believer's approach to life should be different from that of the non-believer. One must continually do the right things and avoid the wrong acts.

African religion, like Christianity, considers morality a nonnegotiable element of religion and religious-based. It is believed that moral attitude is a necessary condition for religion. Moral attitudes are necessarily embedded in the nature of religion. Thus, the African is in accord with St. Augustine's concept of natural law (*Lex Christianorum 4 Tatura*) and Romans 2:15 that "the demands of the law are written in their hearts. Their conscience bears witness together with that law and their thoughts will accuse or defend them."

5. The Problem of Evil

All of the above religions have one thing or another to say about the problem of evil in the world. This ranges from that of total denial of its presence to that of acceptance of its crushing reality. The consideration of the problem has been approached by attempts to find answers to some basic questions on the problem, such as:

i.   Who is responsible for evil in the world?
ii. How extensive is evil?
iii. What things can we refer to as evil?

iv. What types of evil do we have?

v. How can man avoid evil to gain salvation?

As expected, answers to these questions vary from one religion to another. For example, Islam states that it is difficult to ascribe responsibility, since the insubordinate attitude of man does not, strictly speaking, make him responsible. And God, who is omnipotent and does everything, is so divinely "insulated" that no responsibility may be charged against him. In this case, Islam sees evil as really not existent, and if existent at all, not that much. Any evil that may be in existence must be the result of a lack of submission; this constitutes the only evil that could be imagined. To avoid it, man submits to the will of Allah and in addition undertakes an aggressive propaganda for the spread of Islam, with this salvation assured.

Christianity holds that while God might be said to be responsible for the possibility of evil in the world by giving man free will, the actual transmission of evil is through man and his various organizations. In addition, responsibility is placed on individuals for choosing evil rather than good. Thus, for Christianity, evil is not only real but also very terrible and widespread. Evil for Christianity is the selfish use of the free will given to man by God and any injury inflicted on moral personality.

To the African, sin is the commission of a wrong, not only against another human, but more importantly and ultimately against the Supreme Being. Sin goes along with attendant punishment and forgiveness. The punishment involves suffering and pains which may be physical or psychological. The suffering caused by sin even when committed by just one person may affect not only that person but other members of the family, town, and surrounding communities. Forgiveness of sin can only come when the necessary repentance and atonement have been made.

The Jews also believe that man should continually aspire for the holiness of Yahweh. Not following this injunction results in moral laxities, which will not go unpunished by Yahweh. For instance, when the children of Israel began to take part in Canaanite festivals and religious practices and did not keep the teachings of Moses to maintain the undiluted religion of Yahweh, they received the ultimate punishment of going into exile. Therefore, in Judaism, the problem of evil arises when man consciously departs from the laws and ways acceptable to Yahweh.

6. Life After Death

All the religions see a life beyond this physical world for man. However, as may be expected, there are differences in conceptions as to the type of life this would be or if such a life would have any lasting benefits to the desires of man. Most, if not all, religions present the physical world as temporary in nature. In fact, some of them consider it to be only an illusion. Thus, the next world or the place to which man proceeds after death is seen as being permanent and real. It must also be added that the religions have conceptions of a dual nature for man. That is, man is composed of two elements, the body and the soul. It is the soul element in man that has the capability of surviving death. Here again, there are varying opinions on how the soul of man survives death and what happens to it after the survival and separation from the body.

Islam acknowledges life after death. It presents the picture of what it would look like. A place where there would be judgment, reward, and punishment awarded, depending on the type of life the person concerned has led while in the physical world.

Christianity also teaches there is an afterlife. Here, the afterlife finds unique expression in the resurrection that awaits the dead on the final day. There is also the belief in the judgment day and the just allocation of rewards and punishments, as the case may be.

Africans believe that there is a heavenly abode to which man goes after his death. In fact, the conviction is prevalent that the world is just for a while and that heaven is the last home. Thus, the Yoruba of Nigeria have a popular saying that *aye loja, orun nile* ("the world is a market and heaven is home"). Running through most religions is the concept that in order to live a prosperous life in the hereafter, man must have lived a worthy life here in the physical world. This is because of the belief that each person has to account for what he has done here on earth.

Assets and Limitations of the Comparative Approach in Religion

In a situation where we have many religions competing for the "hearts" of men, we cannot but have a comparison of religions, either for positive or negative intentions. Comparison of religions could be of great benefit to man if approached with the right attitude. However, on many occasions, attempts to compare religions have been undertaken for the sinister motives of slighting, condemning, and seeking for the total eradication of another religion. When this happens, it seems the comparison comes from a competitive sense and the desire to claim superiority for one's own religion over and above others. In this kind of comparison, the negative aspects of the other religions are unduly highlighted or at best, the good and positive aspects are misinterpreted and presented out of context and sometimes with deliberate "lies."

However, comparison of religions can be undertaken and employed not only for having adequate knowledge of religions other than our own, but also as a means of encouraging and maintaining interfaith dialogues. This is so that there could be complete understanding among men of different faiths living together. Undoubtedly, such a situation could bring about a tolerant and accommodating society devoid of religious "wars" that tend to breed a fearful and unstable society. There is no doubt that a positive comparison of religions could be done. But to achieve this, the minds and attitudes of those who indulge in the exercise must overflow with spirits that reflect sympathy for the religions they are comparing, the recognition of the inherent values of these religions' critical discriminating ability to separate the genuine from the fake and respect for the spiritual worthiness of the religion. Above all, those concerned should have deep and accurate knowledge of facts about the religions being compared. It would indeed be disastrous to compare from a position of partial or total ignorance as many have done in the past. To do this, such things as their histories, followers, and impact on society should be taken into account. This is because each category gives a more in-depth comparison into religion as a whole. In terms of history, comparing this allows a further insight into how it was formed, accepted into a culture, and how it has been shaped over time.

As with history, a lot of differences can be found when comparing the followers of various religions. Each religion is unique in itself, having its own set morals, rules, and impact. Therefore, believers are often constricted to react to situations based on their beliefs.

Comparing the impact religion has on society, however, takes the most analysis. This is because society has the power to dictate religion; therefore, this will have an overwhelming impact. Depending on the area, some religions may be more socially welcoming and available, thus giving a greater range of comparison and thought. However, other religions are not and comparing them assists in defining how their complexities differ. The important thing to remember is that religion obtains a constant state of change, whether it is from the symbolic meaning of sacred items (Deming, 2005:87–92), or coming from the evolution of society as a whole.

Religion is something very special that cannot be ignored. Whether someone believes in a particular religion or not, this phenomenon is inescapable. It is so important that people have dedicated their lives to study its beneficial effects on themselves and others. Furthermore, it can be very advantageous to compare different religions. Different religions share common aspects and characteristics. These similarities include the beliefs and practices of the religion, scriptures, and the use of symbols (Harding and Rodrigues, 2009:136). Advantages of comparing religions include the accumulation of knowledge and understanding.

Comparing religions can be beneficial because it can expand one's knowledge and understanding, which ultimately leads to better appreciation of other people's religious values and qualities. It is advantageous in the sense that through an exercise, one can come to a better understanding and appreciation of one's own religion.

However, some very fundamental disadvantages occur in comparing religions. Some of the most common and obvious are related to conflicts that are usually generated through the exercise. Over the centuries, comparison of religions has led to fundamental and irresolvable differences among different religious groups, ultimately causing and perpetuating not just verbal and written sparring, but actual warfare.

It is quite understandable that people tend to subscribe to subjective vision when it comes to the religion they practice. The dynamics usually favored are those that conform with their way of thinking and acting within the context of the beliefs and practices of their religion, while consciously shutting out any other form of perspectives. As such it is usually very difficult to respect other people's religious values while strongly holding on to those within one's religion. This is why it is very conceivable to hold that, as long as humanity exists and people within it subscribe to different religious traditions, there will always be conflict in religious attitudes, experiences, and practices.

It is also important to point out that conflict expressed through the disposition above usually brings about another form of comparative disadvantage. This ultimately involves an elitist configuration in religious relationships. Thus some people that belong to a certain religion regard their religion to be exclusively superior to the will of others. With this elitist mentality, discrimination against other religions becomes prominent and fashionable. To avoid the situations enumerated above, it is imperative that the task of comparing religion(s), both at the individual and professional levels, should subscribe to a set of objective rules and regulations to create and sustain a level playing field in order to be equitable and fair.

The advantages and disadvantages discussed above are indicative of the controversial but necessary nature of the comparative approach to religion. Religion is—and always will be—in existence. Thus, there will always be, as there always have been, comparisons among different religions in different societies. This is in tandem with the inescapable human nature to engage in comparisons of events, concepts, and practices to identify similarities and differences. It then becomes almost impossible to exclude religion from this dynamic.

The universal and obvious impulse is to compare, based on knowledge and or observation of one's own religion to other people's religions at the individual level. At the academic level, the engagement is characterized by the attempt to identify the values, doctrines, theologies, scriptures, etc., found in different religions and subject them to comparative evaluation. However, at both levels, the preoccupation should not be exclusively targeted at pointing out what one religion is doing wrong versus what another is doing correctly. Comparison should be used as a tool to gain a better understanding and appreciation of the religions involved.

REVIEW QUESTIONS

1. With background definitions of religion and the concept of comparison, attempt a critical review of the process of the comparative approach in religion.
2. How is the individual comparison of religion and the professional or scholarly comparative study of religion distinguished?
3. Identify and compare some basic beliefs of the religions discussed in this book.
4. Identify and explain the fundamental advantages and disadvantages of the comparative study of religion(s).

BIBLIOGRAPHY AND FURTHER READING

Aderibigbe, Gbolade and Deji Aiyegboyin, eds. 2001. *Religion: Study and Practice*. Ibadan: Olu-Akin Press.

Clark, Peter et al., eds. 1998. *The World Religions*. London: Routledge.

Coogan, Michael D., ed. 1998. *The Illustrated Guide to World Religions*. Oxford: Oxford University Press.

Cousineau, Madeleine, ed. 1989. *Religion in a Changing World: Comparative Study in Sociology*. Connecticut, London: Praeger Westport.

Deming, Will. 2005. *Rethinking Religion*. New York: Oxford University Press

Glazier, Stephen D., ed. 1997. *Anthropology of Religion: A Handbook*. London: Praeger Westport.

Gort, Jeral D. et al., eds. 2006. *Religions View Religions: Explorations in Pursuit of Understanding*. Amsterdam, NY: Rodopi.

Green, Ronald M. 1988. *Religion and Moral Reason: A New Method for Comparative Study*. New York: Oxford University Press.

Harding, John S. and Hillary Rodrigues. 2009. *Introduction to the Study of Religion*. New York: Routledge.

Jordan, Louis Henry. 1905. *Comparative Religion*. Edinburgh: T &T Clark.

Molloy, Michael. 2005. *Experiencing the World Religions*. 3rd ed. London: McGraw-Hill.

Patton, Kimberly and Benjamin Ray, eds. 2000. *A Magic Still Dwells: Comparative Religion in the Postmodern Age*. Berkeley: University of California Press.

Peterfield, Amanda. 1998. *The Power of Religion: A Comparative Introduction*. New York, Oxford: Oxford University Press.

Valea, Ernest. 2011. *A Comparative Analysis of the Major World Religions from a Christian Perspective*. Electronic Publishing.

_____. 2006. *The Buddha and the Christ*. London: University Press.

_____. 1990. *The Problem of Evil in World Religions*. New York: Arcade Publishing.

PART III

RELIGIOUS TRADITIONS

CHAPTER NINE

AFRICAN TRADITIONAL RELIGION, NATURE, AND BELIEF SYSTEMS

INTRODUCTION

Religion is found in all established human societies in the world. It is one of the most important institutional structures that make up the total social system. There is hardly a known race in the world, regardless of how primitive it might be, without a form of religion to which the people try to communicate the divine. This religion becomes inseparable with the total life experience of the people. It thereby permeates into every sphere of the people's lives, encompassing their culture, the social, the political, and the ethical, as well as the individual and societal expectations in their ups and downs. As is the case of nearly every other people in the world, religion is one of the keystones of African culture and is completely entwined in the people's lifestyle. A basic understanding of African religion will provide an awareness of African customs and belief systems.

Perhaps no religion has been so confused in the minds of Western audiences as the African Traditional Religion. The images of this religion have been presented as hopelessly savage and full of ugly superstition. This is solely because the earliest investigators and writers about the religion were mostly European and American anthropologists, some missionaries, and colonial administrators who had no knowledge of the true African spiritual situation. Their works portrayed a distorted image of a religion drawn from half-truths and fertile imaginations. However, an increasing number of African theologians are conducting valuable studies in the African Religion. They have been able to unveil the position that the tenets, spiritual values, and satisfaction which are found in the other world religions—namely, Christianity, Islam, and Buddhism, to mention a few—could also be found in African Traditional Religion. Furthermore, it is imperative to say that these researches have left a positive impact, in the sense that they have helped highlight the general truths, concepts, and trends about the religion, thereby dispelling most of the popular misconceptions about the religion.

The emphasis of this chapter will be on the basic concepts of African Traditional Religion. These are its nature, characteristic features, and its conceptual framework.

THE NATURE OF AFRICAN TRADITIONAL RELIGION

The African Religion is the religion of the Africans and strictly for the Africans. It is not a religion preached to them, but rather a part of their heritage that evolved with them over the years. They were born and not converted into it. It has no founder, but rather a product of the thinking and experiences of their forefathers who formed religious ideas and beliefs. Therefore, its existence cannot be attributed to any individual as in other world religions, such as Christianity, Islam, Confucianism, Buddhism, Hinduism, and so on.

Through the ages, the Africans have worshipped without being preoccupied with finding names for their religions. It was the investigators of religion who first supplied labels such as paganism, idolatry, and fetishism, to mention a few. In order to correct the misconception of such derogatory terms, it became important to designate the religion with a name that describes its true and real nature.

The name African Traditional Religion has been used by scholars to describe the religion. The name was not coined in order to brandish the religion as primitive, local, or unprogressive—rather, it is employed to reflect its location in geographical space and to underscore its evolution from the African personal experience (Aderibigbe, 1995). Furthermore, it is used to distinguish the religion from any other type of religion, since there are other religions in Africa that did not grow out of the African soil but were brought from outside. This shows that the religion is particular to the people, and it would be meaningless and useless to try and transplant this religion to an entirely different society outside of Africa (Mbiti, 1975).

To the African, religion is a hidden treasure secretly given by the Supreme Being solely to the African as a vehicle of communicating and for expressing himself before the sacred entity. In order for a non-African to see and appreciate the wealth of spiritual resources embedded within the religion, he needs to actively participate in order to unveil the nature of the religion, which cannot be understood by mere casual observation. This is why the true nature of the African Religion has been wrongly described and expressed by many, particularly foreign writers and scholars who were outsiders and had no deep knowledge of the experience of the true African spiritual dynamics. These unfortunate misconceptions have been variously demonstrated in derogatory terms for the religion, the denial of African concepts of God (Aderibigbe, 1995), and as ugly superstition that is demon-oriented. It therefore lacks the spiritual fulfillment necessary for the salvation of the soul. Consequently, their works are full of fabrications, exaggerations, half-truths, and biases against the religion and its adherents.

Nevertheless, their works have left a significant impression on most Westerners. Most people remember the African Religion with the image of a missionary in a cannibal's pot about to be cooked and eaten or an evil witch doctor trying to cast a voodoo spell upon a victim. However, with the increase of scholars in the field of African theology such as E. B. Idowu (1962) and Mbiti (1975), there have been some successful attempts to correct some erroneous ideas about African Religion and its belief systems, thought patterns, rituals, and culture generally. The true nature of African Religion cannot be based on erroneous claims of the Europeans concerning the Religion, but rather on what the Africans think and feel about their religion. The true nature of African religion is hinged on the embodiment of the religion in a belief system and functionalism that are actualized in the everyday life of the indigenous African.

A basic understanding of the religion will provide an awareness of African customs, belief systems, concept of God, relationship with the divinities, spirits, ancestors, and the view of death and life beyond death.

CHARACTERISTIC FEATURES

The fact that African Traditional Religion has no sacred scriptures like other world religions does not necessarily mean that it is devoid of organized religious beliefs and practices. The religion is characterized by a belief system which consists of the totality of the African beliefs, thought patterns, and ritual practices. The religious beliefs of African Religion are in two inclusive categories: the major beliefs and the minor beliefs. The major beliefs are in a fivefold classification. The major beliefs in their hierarchical order have significant relevance on the totality of African religious belief systems.

The above diagram represents an overview of the belief system in a hierarchical order.

Belief in the Supreme Being

In the religious belief system, the belief in the Supreme Being is fundamental to all other beliefs and is firmly entrenched in African belief and thought. This is contrary to the Western view that the primitive African is not capable of having any conception of a single Supreme Deity. As Idowu points out:

> Those who take one look at other people's religion and assert glibly that such people have no clear concept of God or no concept of God at all should first look within themselves and face honestly the question, "How clear is the concept of God to me ..." (Idowu, 1973).

The Africans believe in the Supreme Being and recognize Him as the ultimate object of worship. He is not an abstract power or entity, neither is He an idle Negro king in a sleep of idleness occupying Himself only with His own happiness (Baudin, 1885). Rather He is actively involved in the day-to-day affairs of the people. The people strongly attest to the fact that He is the creator and author of all things in heaven and on earth. The names and attributes of God clearly connote the people's belief in Him. He is regarded as omnipotent, holy, the creator and source of all other beings that originate from Him and are in turn responsible to Him. The exalted place of the Supreme Being as above other creatures gives rise to His worship in various African societies, either fully as is the case of the Ashanti of Ghana and the Kikuyu tribe of Kenya, or with partial worship as the Ewe and Abomey peoples of Togo do. Among the Yoruba and Igbo of Nigeria, the lack of an organized cult such as temples, shrines, altars, or priests for Him does not in any way diminish His presence and significance. He is believed to be present everywhere. At the same time, this is why He is not limited to a local shrine or

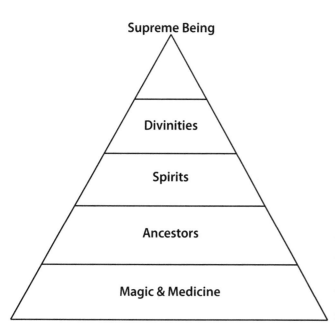

represented in images or symbols. God is real to the Africans—His name is constantly on their lips. Each people have a local name which uniquely belongs to Him. The names by which the Deity is called in Africa are descriptive of His character and emphatic of the fact that He is a reality and that He is not an abstract concept (Idowu, 1973). As Westermann (1937) observes:

> The figure of God assumes features of a truly personal and purely divine Supreme Being … it cannot be overlooked that he is a reality to the African who will admit that what he knows about God is the purest expression of his religious experience.

The Yoruba people refer to Him as Olodumare—Almighty God; Olorun—owner or Lord of Heaven; Aterere Kari aye—Omnipresent God. The Igbo refer to Him as Chukwu—the Great Source Being or Spirit; Chineke—the Source Being who created all things. The Akan of Ghana refer to Him as Onyame—the Supreme Being, the Deity. The Memde of Sierra Leone refer to Him as Ngewo—the Eternal One who rules from above. These various names and their meanings give us a vivid understanding of the African concept of the Supreme Being. To Africans, God is real, the Giver of Life and the All-Sufficient One.

Belief in Divinities

The belief in divinities form an integral part of the African belief system. The divinities were created for specific functions and do not exist of their volition. The relationship of the divinities to the Supreme Being is born of African sociological patterns. Most African countries have a king or chief as the head of the society, and he is always approached by other chiefs who are lesser in rank to the king. This is due to the belief that the king is sacred and must not be approached directly. The role of the divinities like the lesser chiefs as intermediaries between the Supreme Being and man is that of serving as a conventional channel of communication, through which man believes he should normally approach the Supreme Being. This distinctive role of the divinities led to the erroneous conclusion of the Europeans that the Supreme Being is never approached directly by Africans.

To the African, divinities are real, each with its own definite function in the theocratic government of the universe. The divinities are halfway as a means to an end and can never be ends in themselves. The real and final authority comes from the Supreme Being. This is why after each prayer and supplication before the divinities the Yoruba end the devotions with -ase, meaning "may it be sanctioned by the Supreme Being." The divinities have different names in different African societies. The Yoruba call them Orisa. To the Igbos, they are known as Alusindiminuo. The Akan address them as Abosom. There are numerous divinities in Africa, and their number varies from one community to another or from one locality to another. Their number ranges between 201 and 1,700 in various Yoruba localities. The names of divinities depict their nature or natural phenomenon through which they are manifested. For example, the divinity first associated with the wrath of God among the Yoruba was Jakuta, meaning "he who fights with stones." The same god among the Igbos is known as Amadioha. Among the Nupe the same divinity is called Sokogba—Soxo's ax.

The divinities in African concept can be classified into three categories. First are the primordial divinities. These are believed to have been in existence with the Supreme Being before and during the creation of the world. They are believed to have partaken in the creative works of God. Their origins are not known and are beyond man's probing. One of such divinities is Obatala, a Yoruba divinity believed to have been entrusted with the creation work of the physical part of men. Consequently, he is popularly referred to as Alamorere (the fine molder). He is also called Orisa-nla and designated as an arch-divinity; he is believed to be the deputy of Olodumare, deriving his attributes from those of the Supreme Being.

The second are the deified ancestors—those who were heroes during their lifetime by living extraordinary and mysterious lives are deified after their death. They are no longer mere ancestors, but absorb the characteristics of an earlier divinity. A vivid example is Sango, the deified Alaafin of Oyo, who assumed the attributes of Jakuta, the erstwhile thunder divinity in Yoruba land.

There are also divinities that found expression in natural phenomena. Such divinities are spirits associated with natural forces such as rivers, lakes, trees, mountains, forests, etc. Their habitations are considered sacred, and there are usually priests who are custodians of such places and through whom the spirit may be consulted. An example of this is the Olokun (water divinity), which is common among the Yoruba and Edo people.

Finally, divinities are believed to be ambidextrous. With this nature, they are capable of being good and bad simultaneously. Positively, they help in solving people's various problems by helping in procreation, fertility, increasing man's prosperity, and so on. On the other hand, when denied veneration, they could inflict misfortunes on a community.

Belief in Spirit

Africans believe in and recognize the existence of spirits referred to as apparitional beings who inhabit material objects as temporary residence. According to African belief, spirits are ubiquitous and can inhabit any area of the earth because they are immaterial and incorporeal beings. Though divinities and ancestors are sometimes classified as spirits, they are, however, different from the kinds of spirits being discussed here, in the sense that they are more positively associated with the people. They are, in fact, described as "domesticated" spirits. While men venerate, respect, and communicate positively with the divinities, he associates with the spirit out of fear and awe. Spirits are normally synonymous with inimical activities detrimental to man's prosperity, so the people try to placate them so that their progress may not be hindered. Spirits inhabit such places as rivers, hills, water, bushes, and trees. Such places are naturally sacred. For instance, among the Yoruba, the Akoko (known by the Igbo as Ogilisi) is reputed to be an abode for spirits.

Spirits have been classified into groups. Among the Yoruba, there are spirits known as Abiku or Ogbange. The Igbo refer to them as born-to-die children. These are considered sadistic spirits that specialize in entering into the womb of women in order to die at a specific period, thereby causing their victims pain and anguish. Such spirits could plague a particular woman several times if treatment is not applied. This is why in Yoruba land pregnant women are not allowed to walk about at noontime, because it is believed that this is the time the spirits roam about and they are capable of ejecting the original fetus of the pregnant woman and implant themselves as substitutes for the ejected fetus.

The second category of spirits is believed to be spirits of the dead whose souls have not been reposed. These are spirits the dead whose bodies have not been buried with due and correct rites. It is believed that their spirits will not be admitted to the abode of the departed. Thus, until they are properly buried, they will continue to wander about. Such spirits could also belong to those who engaged in wicked works while alive and also died wicked. Such spirits could haunt the community, wreaking havoc if not continually appeased.

The spirit of witchcraft belongs to the third category of spirits. It is a human spirit, and it is believed it can be sent out of the body on errands of havoc to other persons or the community in body, mind, or estate. Such spirits may cause diseases, miscarriages in women, insanity, or deformity in human beings.

Finally, Africans recognize spirits in anthropomorphic terms since they are believed to possess the same human characteristics such as tastes, emotions, and passions.

Belief in Ancestors

This belief is based on the concept that the world is dual: it is comprised of the physical world and the spiritual world. The spiritual world is recognized as an extension of the physical, thereby controlling it. Africans have a strong belief in the continued existence of their dead. The communal and family bonds are held to continue even in the next world. They are usually referred to as ancestors or the living dead. They are closely related to this world, but are no longer ordinary mortals. The Africans believe they can come to abide with their folks on earth invisibly to aid or hinder them to promote prosperity or cause adversity. This is why belief in them is not only taken seriously, but is also one of the most important features of the African Religion. The ancestors are factors of cohesion in the African society. This is because of the respect and honor given to them as predecessors who have experienced the life the living are now treading.

However not all the dead are ancestors. There are conditions laid down that must be fulfilled before assuming the exalted status of an ancestor. The first condition is that the dead person must have lived a good and full life. Second, he must have died a good death and not an abominable death caused by accident, suicide, or a violent or unusual death such as from chronic diseases. Finally he must have died in old age and be survived by children and grandchildren. When these conditions are fulfilled, he automatically becomes an ancestor and receives veneration so intense as to be erroneously regarded as worship. Idowu has this to say of the African belief in ancestors:

> To some extent, they are believed to be intermediaries between the Deity or the divinities and their own children; this is a continuation of their earthly function of ensuring domestic peace and the well-being of their community, to distribute favors, to exercise discipline or enforce penalties, to be guardians of community ethics and prevent anything that might cause disruption (Idowu, 1973).

Based on this belief, the Africans bury their dead in the family compound in the hope that they will continue to influence their lives. In the African societies, there are various ways of venerating the ancestors. It may be by pouring a libation of food and drinks and/or by prayers. It may be carried out by individuals or on a communal basis. Furthermore, there are also religious festivals which are usually carried out in the ancestral cult. In Yoruba land, the Oro and Egungun festivals are the symbolical representations of the ancestral cult.

Almost all the tribes in Africa have one form of ancestral cult with festivals associated with it for the veneration of the ancestors. An example is the Ashanti of Ghana, where we have the sacred Golden Stool, which is the ancestral symbol of the Ashanti. Other tribes in Africa with ancestral cults are the Mende of Sierra Leone, the Lugbara of Central Africa, and the Ovambo of Southern Africa.

Belief in Magic and Medicine

Magic and medicine form a significant part of the traditional beliefs of Africans. By definition, magic is an attempt on the part of man to tap and control the supernatural resources of the universe for his own benefit (Idowu, 1973). Through the use of supernatural powers, he tried to achieve his own desires through self-effort. Man's use of this power could either be positive or negative, depending on his conception of the power. Medicine, however, is the science or art of the prevention, treatment, and cure of disease. The art of medicine is important because man recognizes that health can be lost and medicine helps the body return to its normal state.

Basically, the difference between magic and medicine is that in the use of magic, man tries to enforce his will by using supernatural powers at his disposal; while through the use of medicine, man tries to utilize the powers at his disposal to prevent or cure any form of misfortune which might befall his body or estate. This is clearly seen in the words of R. S. Rattray, concerning the Akan belief about medicine:

If God gave you sickness, he also gave you medicine (Rattray, 1923).

This is why medicine men, known as traditional doctors, abound in Africa. They regard their powers as a gift from God through the divinities. They claim they are given the art of medicine by divinities through dreams or through spirit possession. Among the Yoruba, the tutelary divinity of medicine is Osanyin. The divinity is believed to be the custodian of the art of medicine. Though magic is negatively viewed, when it is associated with medicine, the two become so interlinked that it becomes difficult to know where one ends and the other begins. This is because both employ supernatural powers and can be employed for both evil and good, depending upon the individual involved.

Another common trait about magic and medicine highlighted by Awolalu and Dopamu in writing about the religion of West Africa is that some tribes in Africa have a common name for magic and medicine. For example, the Yoruba call oogun, *egbogi*, and *isegun*. The Igbo call them *ogwu*, while the Akans of Ghana call them *suman*.

Finally, it is essential to point out that both magic and medicine constitute a part of the mysteriousness of the African Religion. This is because they derive their supernaturalness, efficacy, taboos, and custodians from the religion. This is why incantations and rituals are common features of magic and medicine in the African Religion.

Other Beliefs in African Religion

There are some other beliefs within the African Religion that are basically derived from the five major beliefs discussed above. They complement the major beliefs, and together they form the totality of the African Religious Belief. They are referred to as minor beliefs.

Belief in the Hereafter

Like all other world religions, the concept of a life after death is firmly entrenched in the people's belief: African Religion also holds the view that life exists beyond this physical world, which is considered the temporary abode of men while heaven is the spiritual and real home of man. Africans believe that man is made up of both body and soul. The soul does not die like the physical body, but rather it returns to the Supreme Being, who is believed to reside in heaven. The Supreme Being is the final destination of man to whom he belongs and must return. This belief is clearly illustrated in the Yoruba adage *Aye loja orun nile*—that is, the world is a marketplace and heaven is home. No one sleeps in the marketplace. After each day's transactions he or she returns home to rest.

However, not everyone is qualified to enter into heaven. Only those who have engaged in good works while on earth would be granted eternal rest with the Supreme Being, the Supreme Judge of all men. Among the Yoruba there is a saying which encourages man to do good while on earth in order to earn eternal life: *Serere to ri ojo ati sun*—do good so you can earn eternal life. It is believed that those who live an ungodly life on earth will be banished and separated from the Supreme Being.

Belief in Morality

Morality in African Religion is religiously based, since every sphere of the African life is closely associated with being religious. This is why Adewale (1988) asserts that the ethics (morality) of Africans from one to another is religious. Africans have a deep sense of right and wrong, and this moral sense has produced customs, rules, laws, traditions, and taboos which can be observed in each society (Mbiti, 1975).

Morality deals with human conduct, and this conduct has two dimensions, the personal and the social. It guides people in doing what is right and good for both their sake and that of their society. It evolved in order to keep society in harmony, which is achieved through the system of reward and punishment. African morality is centered around some basic beliefs. It is believed that morals are God given and were instituted simultaneously with creation. Therefore, its authority flows from God and must not be challenged. For his part, man is compelled to respond appropriately to these moral demands; failure to comply could incur the wrath of God. This is why certain calamities which may befall a community or person are often interpreted as a punishment from God.

Furthermore, Africans believe that some supernatural beings like the ancestors and the divinities keep watch over people to make sure they observe moral laws. They could punish or reward moral behavior. This further strengthens the authority of the morals. Human beings also play an active role in controlling the morality of the people. The individuals keep a close watch on those with bad moral attitude and often uproot them before they turn the society into an immoral one. This is based on the belief that the welfare and solidarity of the people are closely related to the moral action of individuals. Good deeds are normally encouraged, for these bring harmony, peace, and prosperity. On the other hand, misdeeds could bring calamities of all kinds.

Finally, the importance of morality to Africans cannot be overemphasized. It is evident in their myths, legends, and proverbs, which stress the need to keep the moral demands of human conduct.

Belief in Worship

The act of worship is an integral part of any religion and African Religion is not excluded. It is believed that through worship, one turns to his object of worship in adoration and supplication. Worship in African Religion is directed to the Supreme Being and veneration to the divinities. It is believed that if there is effective worship of both, there will be peace and harmony between the supernatural beings and man.

There are various forms of worship in African Religion. There is the formal and also the informal, the direct and the indirect. In parts of Africa with a direct form of worship, it is characterized by altars, priests, and sacrifices. This is especially so with the worship of the Supreme Being. In the case of indirect worship, there are no temples or priests specially designed for the Supreme Being.

The veneration of divinities could be done regularly on a communal level or individually. This is because they are frequently called upon for one favor or another. On the individual level, the informal type of veneration is carried out privately at the personal shrine normally located in the compound. At the communal level, the formal kind of veneration is carried out at the public shrine, where everyone within the community participates, including family heads, clan heads, priests, priestesses, and traditional rulers.

The main components of worship and veneration are prayers, songs, libations, invocations, and offerings. On the whole, worship or veneration in African Religion is employed to show adoration of and communication with the supernatural beings. It is believed that when these beings are adequately worshipped or venerated, they will bestow upon man the necessary blessings required for successful living on earth.

SOURCES OF INFORMATION ON AFRICAN TRADITIONAL RELIGION

Africans have a rich cultural heritage, which has been handed down from one generation to another. The richness of their heritage reflects in all spheres of their lives, especially in the area of the Traditional Religion. Though the religion does not have a sacred scripture like other world religions, it has means by which its religious beliefs and practices can be known and appreciated. These devices are categorized into oral and non-oral. The oral devices are proverbs, myths, pithy sayings, legends, liturgy, everyday speech, songs, and Theocratic names. The non-oral devices consist of artistic expression.

Oral Traditions

This is regarded as the scriptures of African Traditional Religion. The lack of knowledge in the art of reading and writing caused the African society to employ a means of preserving and transmitting their religious beliefs and practices through oral traditions. They are testimonies of the past, which are transmitted from person to person over the ages. Some of them are records of actual historical events memorized by the people. Others are created by the people's imagination. Consequently, some are regarded to be more reliable than others. For example, proverbs, pithy sayings, and names are believed to be more reliable than legends, myths, daily speeches, and folktales, which are often distorted and cannot be regarded as authentic for grasping the people's beliefs and practices. Here are some forms of oral traditions and their functions:

Myths

In the African traditional society, storytelling at night is the most common recreation in many homes enjoyed by the children and young people. Myths attempt to explain certain things, especially the origin of man and the world. They are vehicles for conveying certain beliefs about man's experience in his encounter with the created order and with regard to man's experiences in the supersensible world. Through myths, man tries to find explanations for certain things. For example, how death came into world; why only women conceive; why they must labor before giving birth to children; why different languages in Africa came into being. Answers to such questions are conveyed in stories which help to preserve them in the memory, making it easier for retention. Myths give us an insight into some of the religious concepts of the Africans who evolve them. Myths are variable sources of information in African Religion because they serve as practical ways of preserving the nonliterate beliefs for possible transmitting without losing their theological themes, since most of these myths are popular stories that draw from beliefs and ideas familiar to the people. Some myths, especially those used during rituals, may enjoy a high degree of authenticity. Such myths could provide the basis for the scriptures of African Religion.

Proverbs

Proverbs are a major source of African wisdom and a valuable part of her heritage. They are a rich deposit of the wisdom of many generations and are held in high esteem. There are hundreds of such proverbs in different African societies which carried with them theological instructions, moral teachings, and metaphysical significance (Jacob, 1977). These proverbs reveal a lot about African religious beliefs, since they are mostly formulated from human experiences and reflections that fit into particular situations of life throughout the ages. It is no gainsaying that among Africans, proverbs are cultivated as an art form and cherished as an index of good oratory. For example, among the Yoruba, proverbs are regarded as "horses for retrieving missing words" that are used for conveying deeper meaning. From some of these proverbs one can learn the various attributes of God as creator, omnipresent, holy, merciful and upright, etc. Thus, we find many proverbs referring to God as an object of religious beliefs, such as the Akan proverb "If you want to tell God anything, tell it to the wind"; "God drives away flies for the cow with no tail" (Yoruba); "God has both the yam and the knife, only those whom he cuts a piece can eat" (Igbo). The importance of proverbs to Africans cannot be overemphasized, and this is clearly expressed in the Igbo adage, "A child who knows how to use proverbs has justified the dowry paid on his mother's head."

Names of People

Names are given immediately upon birth and considered to be very much a part of the personality of the person. In most African countries, the name of the Supreme Being is often made part of the child's name (Mbiti, 1969). This shows that they recognize the Supreme Being. Such names are used as practical demonstration of people's religious feelings, an expression of worship, and the events prevailing at the time of birth. This practically demonstrates how much the people associate the Supreme Being with the continuation of life and the birth of children. There are many names which signify a particular attribute of the Supreme Being.

This would mostly depend on the circumstances surrounding the child's birth. Among the Yoruba, we have such names as Oluwatobi (God is great), Oluwaseun (God is victorious). The Burundi name their children Bizimana, meaning "God knows everything." A careful study of various names by researchers of African Traditional Religion could give a deeper insight into the people's religious beliefs, especially their belief in the Supreme Being.

Prayers

Prayers are an essential part of religion. They constitute the act of communicating with the Supreme Being, which is the essence of religion. Like other world religions, prayers are an integral part of African Traditional Religion. Africans pray to the Supreme Being for guidance, blessings in matters of daily life, good health, protection from danger, etc. These prayers are directed to Him, the deities, and the ancestors requesting for one favor or another. The prayers may be made privately by an individual or communally at public meetings and for public needs. When Africans pray, their prayers are always short and straight to the point. They do not "beat about the bush." There are different modes by which the people pray to the supernatural beings. There is the direct form of prayer, where people communicate with the Supreme Being without the help of intermediaries. However, the indirect form of prayer is when people pray on behalf of others. These include priests (both men and women), rainmakers, chiefs, kings, and sometimes medicine men (Mbiti, 1975). Africans pray because they believe the Supreme Being listens to them and accepts and answers their prayers. He is believed to be everywhere simultaneously. Here are a few examples of prayers in African Traditional Religion as illustrations.

For example, in the morning, the Yoruba have prayers like, "God, let us be successful today." Before worshipping, the Yoruba also pray, "Father, accept our offering and supplication to you."

When there is drought, Africans pray, "God, give us rain"; "Help us, O God"; "God, pity us." In times of sickness, African prayers implore the Supreme Being: "God, heal our sickness, let the sick be well again"; "Take this sickness away from our house, our town, our tribe." When a journey or other forms of a project are to be embarked on, Africans pray for God's protection and successful completion of the project. Prayers such as, "May God go with you"; "May God help you," etc., are offered. There are also general prayers of blessings, such as "God preserve you and keep you." Prayers are also offered for long life, such as "May God spare you to see your children's children."

It must be stressed that in all situations, the Africans pray to show their belief in and dependence on the Supreme Being. The prayers also provide information on the African concepts about the Supreme Being. These concepts form the center of the African Traditional Religion.

Non-Oral Sources

Apart from the oral sources, through which valuable information on African traditional religion is secured, there are some non-oral devices which provide valuable information on the beliefs and practices of Africans where their religion is concerned. These non-oral sources are identifiable in three forms: (i) artifacts; (ii) wooden masks; and (iii) the sacred institutions (Abioye, 2001). These three non-oral traditions are essentially artistic expressions that in concrete terms "showcase" the African traditional religion in all its ramifications. Here is a brief discussion of each of them.

Artifacts

All African societies are very rich in artifacts. These artifacts have become concrete reflections of African belief and devotion to the Supreme Being, the divinities, and the ancestors. The artifacts associated with the African Religion are in two categories. There are objects that are products of archeological findings. Artifacts in the second category are made up of the works of contemporary artists. Archeological excavations have, in some cases, led to more information and better understanding of certain African beliefs and practices. An example of this is the discovery of the temples and altars of Onyame, the Ashanti Supreme Deity, by R. S. Rattray. This singular discovery has gone a long way to show the inadequacy of the foreigners' usual claim that Africans had no organized worship of the Supreme Being because they did not have the idea of God. Indeed, the discovery has led to the search and successful discovery of many other different forms of organized worship among various African tribes. In addition, contemporary artifacts comprising of dance staffs, apparatuses for divination, musical instruments, votive figures, and many other forms of ritual objects provide information on African religious beliefs and practices. Many of these objects are found in shrines, while others are part of the general stocks of artistic works of many African artists attempting to recapture the rich African cultures in different forms.

Wooden Masks

These are concrete forms of covering the face in the attempt to hide the identity of the persons putting on the masks. The practice of putting on masks covers the whole of Africa and is regarded as a part of basic rituals, particularly having to do with the ancestral worship and the cult's expressions of the African people. In the first form, people who are regarded as incarnations of the spirits of the ancestors put on masks to conceal the earthly personality behind the mask and give cogency to the belief that the person wearing the mask is an ancestral spirit. In the second form, members of secret societies in Africa put on masks. Examples of mask usage are found among the Ogboni in Yoruba land and the Poro among the Mende of Sierra Leone.

In addition to the masks, there have been stools found in shrines. They are regarded as having religious implications in their artistic expression. The stools become objects of religious expression by the fact that they are not only found in shrines, but also in some other places. For example, among the Akan of Ghana, the stools have become altars upon which the head of the Akan lineage offers food and drink to their ancestors on appropriate occasions, thereby praying for the protection of the lineage. He also prays for good health and long life with an abundance of harvests.

Sacred Institutions

Beliefs of Africans in the Supreme Being and all other aspects of their religion are reflected in the several traditional institutions all over Africa. Traditionally, these institutions are regarded as sacred. An example of such institution is the traditional ruling institution. Among Africans, the traditional rulers are not mere political heads. They indeed represent the Supreme Being. Thus, the authority they have is in trust for the Supreme Being. This is why traditional rulers are not seen as ordinary persons. They are sacred. For example, the Yoruba call an *oba Igbakeji Orisa* (deputy of the Supreme Being). Among the Ashanti, the golden ornaments the king wears symbolize the belief that the Supreme Being is personified by the sun. Thus, when the Ashanti king wears the golden ornaments, he signifies the eternal fire of the sun (Abioye, 2001). In addition, among the Yoruba and the Akan, the cult of thunder has become a kind of sacred institution. In both African societies, the ax has assumed the symbol of the Supreme Being's judgment. The Supreme Being is regarded as the ultimate judge, and he can express his wrath against evildoers. The ax is the tool for this wrath. For the Yoruba, the divinity executing Olodumare's wrath is Sango. Consequently, axes are found in his shrines. Indeed, the original thunder divinity among the Yoruba was Jakuta, which literally means "one who throws stones." The stones are also found in the shrines of Sango, the new divinity of thunder. The Akan of Ghana refer to the ax as *nyame akuma* (God's ax), and the ax is found in the shrines of Onyame as a symbol of his wrath.

REVIEW QUESTIONS

1. To what extent should African Traditional Religion be regarded as the "window" of African heritage?
2. In your opinion, what features of African Traditional Religion constitute the unique nature of the religion?
3. Examine and explain the context and significance of the words "African" and "Traditional" in constituting the name of the religion.
4. Why has it been so easy for "outsiders" to give misleading nomenclatures to African Traditional Religion?
5. Describe how the "fanatical" veneration of divinities by devotees of African Traditional Religion reflects African sociological values in the traditional society.
6. African traditional religion professes monotheism. Compare this form of monotheism to the that found in Christianity and Islam.
7. What challenges and future do you envisage for ATR in the global competition for religious space and relevance?

BIBLIOGRAPHY AND FURTHER READING

Abioye, S. O. 2001. "African Traditional Religion: An Introduction," in G. Aderibigbe and D. Aiyegboyin, eds. *Religion: Study & Practice*. Ibadan: Olu-Akin Press.

Abraham, W. E. 1982. *The Mind of Africa*. London: Weidenfeld & Nicolson.

Aderibigbe, G. 1995. "African Religious Beliefs," in A. O. K. Noah, ed. *Fundamentals of General Studies*. Ibadan: Rex Charles Publications.

Adewale, S. A. 1988. *The Religion of the Yoruba: A Phenomenological Analysis*. Ibadan: Daystar Press.

Awolalu, J. Omosade. 1979. *Yoruba Beliefs and Sacrificial Rites*. England: Longman.

Awolalu, J. O. and P. A. Dopamu. 1979. *West African Traditional Religion*. Ibadan: Onibonoje Press.

Bascom, William. 1969. *Ifa Divination: Communication Between Gods and Men in West Africa*. Bloomington: University of Indiana.

Courtlander, H. 1973. *Tales of Yoruba Gods and Heroes*. New York: Crown Publishers.

Ekpunobi, E. and S. Ezeaku, eds. 1990. *Socio-Philosophical Perspective of African Traditional Religion*. Enugu: New Age Publishers.

Ellis, A. B. 1894. *The Yoruba-Speaking People of the Slave Coast of West Africa*. London: Chapman & Hall.

Idowu, E. B. 1973. *African Traditional Religion: A Definition*. London: SMC Press.

_____. 1962. *Olodumare: God in Yoruba Belief*. London: SMC Press.

Jacobs, A. B. 1977. *A Textbook on African Traditional Religion*. Ibadan: Aromolaran Press.

Kayode, J. O. 1979. *Understanding African Traditional Religion*. Ile-Ife: University of Ife Press.

Kierman, Jim. 1995b. "African Traditional Religion in South Africa." In Martin Prozesky and John de Gruchy, eds. *Living Faiths in South Africa*. Cape Town: David Philip.

_____. 1993c. "The Impact of White Settlement on African Traditional Religions." In Martin Prozesky and John de Gruchy, eds. *Living Faiths in South Africa*. Cape Town: David Philip.

King, M. O. 1970. *Religions of Africa*. New York: Harper & Row Publishers.

Lucas, J. O. 1948. *Religions in West Africa and Ancient Egypt*. Lagos: CMS Books.

Mazrui, Ali A. 1986. *The Africans: A Triple Heritage*. London: BBC Publications.

MacVeigh, Malcolm J. 1974. *God in Africa: Conception of God in African Traditional Religion and Christianity*. Cape Coast: Claude Stark.

Mbiti, J. S. 1991. Introduction to African Religion, 2nd ed. Oxford: Heinemann.

_____. 1982. *African Religion and Philosophy*. London: Heinemann Educational Press.

_____. 1970. *African Concept of God*. London: SMC Press.

Merriam, A. P. 1974. *An African World*. Indiana University Press.

CHAPTER TEN

JUDEO-CHRISTIAN TRADITION

INTRODUCTION AND BACKGROUND

The term Judeo-Christian tradition derives from the set of values, beliefs, and issues central to the practices of Judaism and Christianity that are regarded to have evolved from inclusive, yet independent, religious traditions. These values are essentially centered on the belief in monotheism, and grounded on the twin principles of election and messianism found in the Old Testament, which constitutes the Jewish scriptures, and a section of the two parts of Christian scripture.

The principle of election by God, based on the concept of divine predestination, has also become a central doctrine of Christianity. It has a vivid background in the Jewish election as a people and nation by Yahweh, through a covenant that was consummated and sealed on Mount Sinai. However, this conservation of the covenant was to activate the outcome of a continuing promise made to Abraham and preserved through a series of elective patterns of choices comprising of Isaac and Jacob and politically established in the house of David.

It is instructive to point out that the covenant made with the "Exodus people" was located in teachings which stipulated conditions that Israel must meet in order to preserve the special relationship with God. That condition became the delimiting principles to direct the socioreligious life and even the political life of Israel thereafter (Davidson, 1970).

Within the construct of the covenant and the condition as the guiding principles to the political life of Israel, Israelite politics assumed a theoretic dynamic in which Yahweh was the sovereign and the judges and subsequent kings were just His representatives (Bauer, ed., 1962).

With the election of the house of David, its dynasty, and by extension, Israel as a kingdom (so it seemed) had become everlasting.

However, this was not to be. The failure on the part of the Israelites to fulfill the conditions of the covenant with Yahweh eventually led to the end of both the Davidic dynasty and the kingdom of Israel. Judah was overrun in 587/586 bc by the Babylonians, and both king and leading citizens were taken into exile.

This situation, contrary to the promise made to Abraham, was perplexing to the Jews. What had become of Yahweh's promise, which was to be everlasting! It took the intervention of the prophets, such as Jeremiah and Ezekiel, to point out to the Jews that the situation in which they found themselves was a deserved punishment for their betrayal of Yahweh's sovereignty and that Yahweh's promise remained valid, but could only be reclaimed through repentance (Bright, 1981).

After the exile and return of the faithful remnant, Deutero-Isaiah, Haggai, and Zachariah as prophets strengthened the validity of Yahweh's promise through a reformation that was to be effected by the messiah to be sent by Yahweh. This would once again restore the permanency and glory of the Israelite kingdom as well as the Davidic dynasty (Wilken, 1987).

The expectation of this messiah and the establishment of an everlasting kingdom have not only sustained Judaism till today, but have actually constituted the major links and departure between Judaism and Christianity.

While Judaism has been in expectation of a political messiah with a mandate of an earthly and physical Jewish kingdom with the ultimate vanquishing of all enemies, Christianity has prescribed a different stance. To Christianity, the expected messiah was a spiritual one. The messiah has indeed come, as he is Jesus Christ, the son of David. As foretold by the prophets, he has indeed established the spiritual kingdom of God. The Christian Church is just a physical manifestation of God's kingdom on earth. In addition, through his death on the cross, Jesus has enacted a new and everlasting covenant between God and those who belong to His new kingdom, which has completely overshadowed the Sinaitic covenant. Thus, symbolically Christians have become the new elect and the new Israel. Judaism is separated from Christianity today because it has rejected Christ as the expected messiah and currently still awaits His arrival with a political mandate of deliverance.

CHRISTIANITY–ORIGINS

Based on the background enumerated above, it is generally accepted that Christianity grew out of Judaism. This is evidenced and established by many studies and in the literature. Foremost among these is the three-volume study of the Bible by Wilfrid J. Harrington. The work is titled *The Record of Revelation: The Bible; The Record of Promise: The Old Testament;* and *The Record of the Fulfillment: The New Testament* (Hardon, 1968). Within this context, right from its inception, Christianity has regarded itself as the direct successor of the Old Testament transitions. This claim has been vividly demonstrated in first, the origin of its name, and second, the historical and theological configurations of its founder—Jesus Christ.

The word Christ (from which the word Christianity is derived) comes from the Greek word *Christos*. This is equivalent to the Hebrew word *mashiah*, which translates to "messiah" in English. The etymological meaning of the word in the three languages is "the anointed one." It denotes someone who is given a specific mandate of undertaking a national responsibility. Secondly, the term "Christian" was first used in Antioch to describe the followers of Christ by the observation of their behaviors.

Jesus, the founder of Christianity, historically lived in Galilee in Palestine in the early first century bc. Facts about his birth and mission come almost exclusively from the Christian Bible (the New Testament). His birth is claimed to be miraculous, having been conceived of the Holy Spirit and born by the Virgin Mary. He is, however, regarded as a descendant of David through linkage with Joseph, his foster father, to whom his mother, Mary, was betrothed. The mission of Christ, which became the foundation of Christianity, lasted about three years. During this period, Jesus traveled all over Judah. He chose twelve men to become his apostles. In their company, he preached about the kingdom of God.

This kingdom was distinguished from an earthly one. Though it was foretold by the prophets, it turned out to be a heavenly kingdom against the expectation of the Jewish people. The central message of Christ was that in this heavenly kingdom, salvation is spiritual rather than physical or political. The worship would be spiritual in nature. In addition, the members would live by the truth and have brotherly love toward one another. By his words and actions, Jesus presented himself as the expected messiah foretold by the prophets. His principal mission was to save the world and establish the heavenly kingdom. He was credited with many miracles (mighty works) to give credence to his messianic power. Ironically, it was the messianic claims of Jesus (the Son of God) that got him into trouble with the official Jewish establishment, which eventually had him delivered to the Roman authorities and executed.

Apart from his disciples and other followers, Jesus had no organized group as such. In addition, he did not write anything down, but his preaching and activities became preserved in the New Testament, consisting of the Gospels, the Acts of the Apostles, and the Epistles. It is instructive that the violent death of Jesus on the cross, although initially disappointing to his disciples, his resurrection, appearance, and ascension reassured them of his power and the truth of his promises. Finally, the events of the Pentecost—through which the apostles experienced the coming of the Holy Spirit as promised by Christ—not only emboldened them but also (and more significantly) "officially" constituted the first winning over of souls to the movement later called Christianity.

THE CHRISTIAN DOCTRINES, BELIEFS, AND PRACTICES

Though the mainstream doctrines of Christianity are found in the Apostles' Creed, the various interpretations they have witnessed have constituted controversies that resulted in heresies and eventual schisms (Burrows, 1946). In spite of this situation, which has led to various denominations in Christianity, the central doctrine as the theological foundation of the Christian faith has remained with the Christian Bible as the point of reference.

Based on the Apostles' Creed and the scripture, the Christian faith is contained in a number of beliefs and practices. As indicated earlier, the splitting of Christianity into denominations makes a comprehensive presentation of these very difficult—if at all achievable—and definitely not within the context and space of a chapter. Consequently, only the major beliefs and practices and such things that are considered to be "universal" are presented here. In addition, they are presented in the sequence of the "official Christian" Apostles' Creed.

Belief in God

The Christian belief in God is the same and derived from the Old Testament. It is the first article of the Christian creed. It is based on the monotheistic Yahwism of the Jewish Sinaitic experience (Rudolf Otto, 1928). Here, God is described as the Creator, the Owner, and the Lord of the universe. Consequently, He is the maker of history and venture. Christianity, like Judaism, credits this God with many superlative attributes. However, most important of all are God's transcendence and omnipotence. In spite of these things, He is of personal disposition. Thus, Moses could meet with him face to face (Ex. 33:11). He could enter into a covenant with the people of Israel; enter into a relationship with them; fight on their behalf, and even punish them when they disobey Him. His presence is captured in His own description of Himself as: I AM WHO I AM (Ex 3:14).

This personal disposition of God is linked to Christianity in the New Testament, as the ultimate fulfillment of God's covenant with Christians as their heavenly Father. This symbolized the extension of Jesus' relationship as son to God His Father. By being Christians, from baptism, the followers of Jesus became heirs of the same relationship with God. This is, indeed, according to Christian theology, the cornerstone of Jesus' messianic mission of salvation and right to God's heavenly kingdom (Matt. 26:26–29). Within this context, the Christians become the new Israel with a covenant reward of heaven, the house of their Father—God. However, the covenant is and can be mediated only by Jesus, who facilitates the relationship by his death on the cross.

Belief in Jesus Christ

This constitutes the sacred article in the Christian creed. It is also the point of severance between Christianity and Judaism. The article expresses the Christian belief that Jesus Christ is the expected messiah. By his death and resurrection, he made salvation available to mankind. New Testament theology regards the death and subsequent resurrection of Christ not only as the cornerstone of the Christian faith, but what sets it apart from all other religious traditions. As the expected messiah (Christ), his mission was to establish the kingdom of God in heaven. However, the Church (Christianity) stands as the foretaste of that kingdom on earth. In addition, the Christian creed designates Christ as the *logos*—the word of God—who has existed with Him from the beginning and through Whom the world was created. It is this word that is ascribed with two equal natures, the human and the divine. However, the natures are of one essence with the Father; also, the same person of Christ is both perfectly divine and human.

This belief in the dual nature of Christ as one essence has been the subject of controversy, particularly in the early era of Christian history; it actually led to a number of schisms. However, the Council of Chalcedon in 451 laid the controversies to rest with the official definition of this problem (Gutherie, 1981).

Overall, Christianity believes that the mission of Christ was accomplished with his birth, death on the cross, resurrection, and ascendance to heaven, where he is seated on the right side of the Father, as part of the Holy Trinity. He is to return at the end times to judge the whole world.

Belief in the Holy Trinity

This is another fundamental article of the Christian creed. This belief, just as the one on messianism, sets Christianity apart from other faiths, including Judaism. The belief designates that, while Christianity subscribes to a monotheistic God, He is considered to be made up of three parts, God the Father, God the Son, and God the Holy Spirit. This Christian belief is essentially derived from the religion's trimodal experience of God: God who creates as the Father; God's incarnation in Jesus Christ as the Son; and the God who enables as the Paraclete, the Holy Spirit. Through defying any logical confines, this belief has been designated as a mystery that can only be accepted by the authority of faith. The Council of Constantinople in 381 provided a resolution to the illogicality from the Christian perspective. It stated that the Holy Spirit is one in substance with the Father and the Son. Consequently, the Christian God is an undivided and simple God made up of three persons. The relationship between the three persons is located in one Godhead.

The Church

The Christian concept of the church is basically derived from the Old Testament idea of the assembly of the people of God (Bright, 1981). This term signified the current bond between Yahweh and the people of Israel, thereby emphasizing the religious dominance of Israelites' lives and the importance of the worship of Yahweh. As Judaism developed the idea of the kingdom of heaven as the abode of Yahweh and the desire of every Israelite to live within this background, it was nothing strange to the Israelites when both John the Baptist and Jesus spoke of the "kingdom of God" being at hand and calling on the people to repent so that they could attain it. Though the audience might have misconstrued the kingdom for an earthly one, in line with the Old Testament prophets, they perfectly understood the essence of the passages. The kingdom is to be a universal and everlasting one, comprising of people acknowledging Yahweh's name, by taking on a new life guaranteed under a new covenant (John 18:33–38).

As a fulfillment of this provision, the Christian Church becomes the new Israel, a new Assembly of God's people. There is a new covenant sealed by Christ the promised messiah.

Against this background, the term Church is seen as a derivation of the Greek word *ekklasia*, as a translation of the Hebrew word *gohal*.

Both religiously were understood to mean a community. In the Christian context, this translates to a community of people in covenant with God. In a way, the Christian Church is seen in the dual natures of being both a mysterious and corporal body. This mystical aspect denotes a spiritual community of both the living and the dead "saints" of God. The corporal nature of the Church establishes the earthly community as a symbol of the heavenly one. This attests to the fact that while on his earthly mission, it was indeed the intention of Jesus to establish a universal community of the people of God. In both its mystical and corporal natures, Christ remains the head of the church. This, in spite of the denominational stance of the Christian Church today, stresses the ultimate mission of the Christian universal church—one flock under one shepherd.

The Concept of Man

The Christian concept of man actually reechoed the Old Testament creation narrative. Based on this understanding, a number of claims are reinforced. These include the creation of man in God's image, the dependency of man on God, and the superiority conveyed by God, which distinguished man from all others of His creatures. Another aspect of man that again is unique is that man was created originally as good and provided with free will. The ideas of the original goodness of man and free will introduced two basic Christian postulations in the relationship between man and God, his Creator. The first is that with the free will man was given the right to choose, because God did not want to impose Himself on man. Rather, He wanted to be chosen and loved by man out of his conscious volition. The second postulation on man's original goodness addresses the eventual nature of man, which resulted from his misuse of free will. This sinful nature became the Original Sin, a consequential bane of all mankind that separates man from God. This Original Sin was brought upon man by the disobedience of the first man, Adam, and his wife, Eve. It removed the "cover" of immortality from man and substituted it with death.

The sin of Adam and Eve and man's inevitable separation and "reward" of death set the background of Christian soteriology. This is the Christian doctrine of salvation. The essence of the doctrine submits that with Original Sin, man was alienated from God and was under eternal curse (*Cur Deus Homo*, 1098). Man was therefore in need of salvation. The salvation of man is then attributed to God resolving in His infinite mercy to unilaterally reconcile with man. He therefore decided to send His son, Jesus, who, fulfilling the prophetic promises through incarnation, paid the required ransom of sacrificing himself so that man may once again be reconciled with God and attain eternal salvation. This salvific work of Christ designates him as God, who incarnate becomes the man who brought life to mankind in reverse of Adam, the first man who brought death to mankind.

Concept of Worship

More than being a religion of many beliefs and doctrines, Christianity is characterized by the act of worship practiced as a community. This constitutes the modus operandi, through which the Christian Ecclesia—the body of saints—shows allegiance to God and celebrates the fellowship as a family. The symbols of this communal act are concretized in the Christian sacraments. For Christians, the celebration of the sacraments represents the external demonstration of the inward grace showed by them as a corporate entity. They depict in symbolic ways the spiritual benefits received and shared as a community of faith. While there have been disagreements as to the number of Christian sacraments between the Roman Catholic Church, which recognizes seven, and the Protestants, who recognize only two, the sacraments of baptism and the Eucharist are universally accepted by all Christians as constituting the most important sacraments.

Baptism

The sacrament of baptism is universal to virtually all Christian denominations. This is regardless of conducting it at infancy (syspersion) as the Roman Catholics do, or at adulthood (immersion), as occurs among Protestant denominations. In both situations, the sacrament of baptism has three-dimensional functionalities. First, it functions as the initiation rite of membership in the Christian church. Second, it is symbolic of removing the Original Sin, to which all mankind has been subjected by the sin of disobedience by Adam and Eve in the Garden of Eden—by virtue of which, man was separated from God the Creator. Third, in association with the symbol of the removal of sin, baptism for the Christian is interpreted as representing a spiritual act of "dying" to the state of sin as Jesus did on the cross, and attaining a new life in line with the resurrection of Jesus. By receiving the sacrament of baptism, the Christian becomes "born again." He or she is dead to the sinful life of the past (Deming, 2005).

The Eucharist

The sacrament of the Eucharist (the Last Supper, as instituted by Christ himself) is not only regarded as being the center of Christian worship, but it is also celebrated by all Christian denominations, though in different forms and with varying significance. For example, in the Roman Catholic Church, the celebration of the Eucharist is the central and essential part of the Holy Mass (service). It is the actual reenactment of the sacrifice of Jesus Christ. In receiving the Eucharistic meal, the Catholic takes the body and blood of Jesus, represented by the Communion water and sacramental wine. This is the doctrine of Transubstantiation (Mark, 13).

On the other hand, for most Christian Pentecostal denominations, the sacrament of baptism functions as both memorial and social phenomena other than Transubstantiation. As a memorial symbol, the Eucharist is celebrated in memory of the Last Supper act of Jesus. Thus, in remembering the act, it is accepted that Christ is present. The social dimension of the Eucharist establishes the fact that all those who participate in the sacrament become a corporate part of the "body of Christ." This affords members to partake of the divine life of Christ and share it among themselves. This is why the term Communion best represents the social emphasis of the sacrament. By partaking in it, there is a celebration of fellowship depicting a sharing community. Further, the communicants are thereafter designated as brothers and sisters in one family with God as the Father (Deming, 2005).

Eschatology

The Christian doctrine on the end of the world—Eschatology—is essentially located in four backgrounds. These are the Old Testament pronouncement on the messianic expectation, Jesus' statements on the last days, Paul's teachings, and the book of Revelation. Materials from each of these formed and developed the Christian position on what would eventually happen to the world and humanity. However, the expectation of the time, process and the nature of the events that will signal the phenomenon have been diversely presented.

For example, the messianic expectation indicated the coming of an earthly kingdom of God, in which all nations would come together in peace and where Jerusalem would be the capital. All nations will recognize Yahweh and be under his domain—a messianic kingdom. Indeed, this expectation was combining faith with both John's thoughts in Revelation and synoptic narratives to describe the Christian perception of eschatology. These traditions indicated that the Second Coming of Christ was at hand. This was evidenced on the promise that Jesus as Christ has already established the expected messianic kingdom on earth. With this, the *Eschaton (Heavenly Kingdom)* has been established. The next stage has to be the *Parousia (the second coming of Christ)*, when the faithful Christians would be resurrected from death to reign with Jesus Christ for a thousand years. After this period, the world would be destroyed in a hail of catastrophes, as described in the synoptic.

It is instructive to state that even when the immediacy of this expectation has been faulted by the turn of events, the Christian doctrine of eschatology still insists on the second coming of Christ—*Parousia*—and the end of the world, but now lacking a time frame. However, at the end of the catastrophe the good will reign with Jesus forever in a heavenly kingdom, while the wicked will be consigned to hellfire under the rulership of Satan.

The Christian doctrine of eschatology is said to have been substantiated by the statements of Jesus himself. The Gospel of Mark showcases statements by Jesus painting gory pictures of what the end times would involve. It would be marked by extreme moral, civil, and natural disasters. The signs would be there for all to behold. After these events, Jesus would stage his second coming—the *Parousia*—and the elect would be gathered and reign with him forever.

In his Epistles, Paul also dwelt on the theme of the end of the world and the Second Coming of Christ. While not emphasizing the catastrophe as in the case of the synoptics, he nevertheless stresses that the expected eschatology would involve the resurrection of faithful Christians who had died and together with the living ones, would join in the Rapture.

Historical Development of Christianity

Beginning with the activities of Christ found in the synoptics which were further entrenched in the Acts of Apostles, through centuries of mixed and sometimes controversial features until contemporary times, the Christian religion has grown to be a phenomenon. Its presence in different denominations is not only visible, but significantly influential in global religious Space. The establishment, growth, and influence of the Christian tradition have occurred in phases covering different epics.

a) Early History

The historical development of Christianity in early centuries can be divided into three segments. The first was as a movement under Judaism. The second was the persecution years. The third came with the adoption of the religion by Constantine.

As a Movement within Judaism

Jesus' statements and activities during his ministry essentially indicated that even if he envisaged a distinct group of followers, it was still to function within the confines of Judaist structures. Primarily, he saw himself as a reformer rather than an originator. For example, he stated "I have not come to abolish the laws but to fulfill them" (Matt. 5:17). In addition, not only was he "schooled" in the Judaic traditions (dedication on the eighth day; visit to the temple with parents, etc.), he also frequented the Jewish synagogues and celebrated the various Jewish festivals; the last being the Last Supper before his death. Consequently, Jesus' ministry was in all respects practically a "continuum" of the Jewish religion. After the death of Jesus, his disciples and followers, after their initial fear and going underground and strengthened by the events of the Pentecost, began to operate as a movement within Judaic traditions. This was evidenced by the activities of the disciples in observing the Judaic prayer hours and worshipping in the synagogues.

However, this stance did not last. Two fundamental factors might have been responsible for the eventual separation. The first was, of course, the refusal of the Jewish authorities to recognize Jesus as the messiah and Son of God. Consequently, the reforms he preached were regarded as too radical and as anticonservative to the principles and doctrines of Judaism. Secondly, and as a fallout of the above, the conservative and strict elements within Judaism regarded as anathema the admission of non-Jews into Judaism. The "Christian group" was then not only forced out of Judaism, but also was persecuted, to the extent that many members of the group ran away from Jewish cities—particularly Jerusalem—and a number of the members, including Peter, were eventually killed.

The hostility from the Judaic authorities in a way benefited the emerging group. Those persecuted in Palestine found refuge in other lands and took with them the Christian message. However, the propagation of the Christian faith among Gentile was achieved almost exclusively by Paul, originally named Saul, who aggressively persecuted Christians all over Palestine. When he converted to Christianity, he took the name Paul. Both his missionary journeys and writings (Epistles) became the bastions for not only the conversion of Gentiles, but also the mainstream doctrines of the Church till today. However, he has been most importantly recognized for his mission among the Gentiles and has consequently been called "the Apostle to the Gentiles."

Period of Early Persecution

From the Apostolic Age and up to about the third century of its existence, the Christian religion was subjected to very crippling persecution. The introduction of Christianity into different communities, particularly through the activities of Paul's missionary journeys, met with a lot of resistance. This was a result of the very radical messages of the religion, which called for changes—usually the abandonment of people's set ways of living and the acceptance of new dictates, particularly the worship of the Christian God and the acknowledgement of Jesus as the Son of God and Savior. Indeed, in the Gentile lands, where the religion spread, it found itself in conflict and opposition with the authorities of the native gods and religions. This was also the situation in the Roman Empire, what included Palestine at the time. Consequently, Christianity faced varied and sustained persecutions from different quarters up till 313, when reprieve came its way through the conversion of Emperor Constantine, who then made Christianity the state religion and therefore a state-protected religion.

Immediate Post-Constantine Era

Unfortunately, once Christianity was freed from external persecution problems, internal crises took over. The problems were essentially associated with doctrinal issues. Various doctrines of the church, such as the divine and human natures of Christ, were interpreted differently. The orthodox interpretations often led to different heresies and schisms which the young Church struggled to contain by holding major church councils. Through the councils, attempts were made to rein in controversies by giving clearer and more precise formulations of the contended doctrines. Invariably, not much success was achieved in defeating the heresies and the schisms. Consequently, the foundation for splitting the Church in two—West and East—and then ultimately into numerous denominations, was laid during this period.

b) Christianity Splits

From a stage of diverse interpretations ending in heresies and schisms, the Christian religion degenerated to the stage of major splits. The first split in Christendom came in the 11th century with the emergence of the Roman Catholic Church in the West and the Orthodox Church in the East. Then beginning from the middle centuries, the phenomenon of the multiplicity of Christian denominations began. Both the first split into two and subsequently numerous denominations have been two majorly different but inclusive factors. These are the papacy and an attempt at doctrinal reformation.

The Papacy

The office and authority of the pope, known as the "Bishop of Rome," has a background in the charge given to the Apostle Peter by Jesus. This charge is found in two biblical passages. The first is where Jesus declared, "And I say this to you: you are Peter the Rock and on this rock I will build my church, I will give you the keys of the kingdom of Heaven, what you bind on earth I shall bind in heaven and what you loose on earth I shall loose in heaven" (Matt. 16:18–19). The second is found in John 21:15–17. Here, the risen Jesus gave Peter the responsibility of feeding his sheep. With these, Peter become the leader of the Christian community—later recognized as the first Bishop of Rome with authority over the universal Church, which he passed on to each succeeding as Bishop of Rome—the pope as head of the Christian church over the centuries. The position of the pope as the head of the papacy—the central governing institution of the Church—became very powerful, not only in religious matters, but also in the civil and political affairs of the world then. Indeed, by the fourth century, the popes (for example, Pope Gregory VII) were wielding enormous political power to the extent that they had the authority to crown and depose emperors in Europe.

Doctrinal Differences

The fallout of the pope's supremacy, particularly in civil and political matters, instigated a high level of confrontation and resentment from many quarters, both ecclesiastically and temporarily. The first casualty was the 11th-century splitting of the Christian Church in two—the Eastern Orthodox Church and the Roman Catholic Church in the West.

However, the events that led to what is today numerous Christian denominations, involved primarily doctrinal issues which other political powers, such as the German princes and the king of England, took advantage of. The Reformation (the revolt against the Roman Catholic Church) was started by Martin Luther. He was an Augustinian monk who intended to correct the various laxities he noticed in the Church, particularly on the issue of the sale of indulgences and salvation. Eventually, his confrontation with the Church led to the German princes, who had grown tired of the overbearing authority of the pope and saw Luther's revolt as a "freedom route." Not only did Luther succeed in breaking away from the Roman Catholic Church, but his actions and success led to other breakaways, such as Lutheranism, Calvinism, Anglicanism, Pentecostalism, and Presbyterians, among others. Those breakaway denominations are collectively called Protestants.

Today, though the Christian religion is perhaps the most practiced religion globally with about 1.5 billion members (Deming, 2005), it is fractured into a multiplicity of denominations and sects. However, it is noteworthy that in spite of this situation of very glaring diversity in methodology and organizational dynamics, all Christian denominations are held together by the core and universal Christian beliefs in the Trinity, the Sonship of Christ, and the salvific message of Jesus Christ.

REVIEW QUESTIONS

1. To what extent can Christianity be seen as a "continuum" of Judaism?
2. Outline the history and spread of Christianity.
3. What would you consider to be the factors that led to major schisms and finally, Denominations, in Christendom?
4. Identify the main doctrines of Christianity that have remained universal despite its denominationalism.
5. How do the beliefs in the divine and human nature of Christ and his resurrection constitute the fundamentals of the Christian faith?
6. Trace and account for the historical impact of Christianity, both negatively and positively, in global and human affairs since it was first adopted as the state religion by Emperor Constantine in the Roman Empire.
7. What fundamental differences do you think exist between Christianity and Islam, particularly regarding the concept of monotheism?

BIBLIOGRAPHY AND BOOKS FOR FURTHER READING

Barrett, David B. 1982. *World Christian Encyclopedia: A Comparative Survey of Churches and Religions in the Modern World, 1900–2000.* Nairobi: Oxford University Press.

Bright, J. 1981. *History of Israel,* 3rd ed. Philadelphia: Westminster Press.

Borg, M. J. 2003. *The Heart of Christianity.* San Francisco: Harper.

Burrows, M. 1946. *An Outline of Biblical Theology.* Philadelphia: Westminster Press.

Collins, G. O. 1987. "Jesus," in M. Eliade et al., eds. *Encyclopedia of Religion.* London: Macmillan Publishing Co.

Crossan, J. D. 1994. *Jesus: A Revolutionary Biography.* San Francisco: Harper.

Davidson, Robert. 1970. "Moses," in Robert C. Walton, ed. *A Source Book of the Bible for Teachers.* London: SCM Press.

Goetz, P. W. et al., eds. 1990. "Jesus: The Christ and Christology," in *Encyclopedia Britannica,* Vol. 22, Auckland, etc. (Encyclopedia Britannica), 5th ed.

_____. 1990. *The New Encyclopedia Britannica,* vol. 16. Chicago: Macropedia.

Guthrie, Donald. 1981. *New Testament Theology.* Leicester, IL: Inter-Varsity Press.

Gunton, C. E. 1988. *The Actuality of Atonement: A Study of Metaphor, Rationality and the Christian Tradition,* Edinburgh: T & T Clark Ltd.

Hardon, John A. 1962. *The Religions of the World,* vol. 2. New York: Image Books.

Iwe, N. S. S. 1979. *Christianity, Culture and Colonialism in Africa.* Port Harcourt: Day Star Press.

Irvin, Dale T. and Scott W. Sunquist. 2001. *History of the World Christian Movement, Vol. 1: Earliest Christianity to 1453.* New York: Orbis Books.

Jenni, E. 1962. "Messiah, Jewish," in *Interpreters' Dictionary of the Bible.* New York: K. Q.

Kung, Hans. 1950. *The Church.* New York: Sheed & Ward.

Leeming, B. B. 1981. *Principles of Sacramental Theology.* Westminster, MD: The Newman Press.

Ladd, G. E. 1969. A *Theology of the New Testament*. Grand Rapids: W. B. Eerdmans.

Marty, Martin E. 2008. *The Christian World: A Global History*. New York: Modern Library.

McKenzie, J. L. 1966. *Dictionary of the Bible*. London: Geoffrey Chapman.

Obersteiner, J. 1970. "Messianism," in J. B. Bauer, ed. *Batter Encyclopedia of Biblical Theology*. London: Oxford University Press.

Prestige, G. L. 1956. *God in Patristic Thought*. London: Society for the Promotion of Christian Knowledge.

Rad, G. 1975. *Old Testament Theology*, vol. 1. London: SCM Press.

Rawlinson, A. E. J., ed. 1926. *Essays on the Trinity and the Incarnation*. New York: Oxford University Press.

Ridderbos, Herman. 1962. *The Coming of the Kingdom*. Philadelphia: The Presbyterian & Reformed Publishing Co., 1962.

Reynolds, Stephen. 1977. *The Christian Religious Tradition*. CA: Wadsworth Pub. Co.

Vansina, F. 1974. *Philosophy of Religion: Ancient Symbols and Modern Myths*. Leuven: ACCC.

Walker, Williston. 1970. *A History of the Christian Church*, 3rd ed. New York: Charles Scribner's Sons.

Ware, Timothy. 1993. *The Orthodox Church*. Maryland: Penguin Books.

Welles, M. 1967. *The Making of Christian Doctrine: A Study of Early Doctrinal Development*. Cambridge: Cambridge University Press.

Wilson, Ian. 2000. *Jesus: The Evidence*. Washington, DC: Regnery Publishing.

CHAPTER ELEVEN

ISLAMIC TRADITION

INTRODUCTION

Islam today is a religious tradition practiced by "nearly one-fifth of the world's people" (Fisher, 2012). Based on the teaching of the Prophet Muhammad, the religion subscribes to a monotheistic belief, different not in substance, but in form from the Christian trinity based on monotheism. The totality of the Islamic beliefs and traditions are captured in the simple phrase: "There is one God and Muhammad is His messenger." From the religious reform mission of Muhammad, born around 570 ce, Islam has developed into a formidable religious institution with enormous influence in practically every aspect of global engagement. The combination of faith with practice gives the religion a unique slant, by virtue of which it has been able to combine diverse human activities. This is vividly captured by Akintola (2001), when he opines:

> Its (Islam) uniqueness is evident in its comprehensiveness as it combines *imam* (faith) with *aural* (ritual) and encapsulates *siyasah* (politics), *igtisad* (economy), *shariah* (law), *ulum* (science) and *akhlaq* (morality) in its "complete way of life."

In discussing Islam through this multifarious prism, this chapter briefly explores background, major teachings, major beliefs, and its historical developments as a "window" of having the basic information, understanding, and appreciation of the of the Islamic tradition, or what Akintola (2001) calls "Islamdom."

BACKGROUND—ORIGIN, MEANING, AND SCRIPTURE

Origin

Like its Judaic and Christian counterparts, Islam is of Abrahamic "descent." This is not only because of the tracing of the patriarchs of the religions biologically to Abraham, but also by virtue of the fact that the three of them had the same theater of origin (Middle East). Indeed, Islam, as Muhammad's religious reform mission, was targeted not only for ending idol worship, but—more importantly—to reform the messages of the prophets before him, as these were abused and not practiced in their original and perfect forms. By this, Muhammad is regarded as the last of the prophets with a final reformation mission. This significantly also accounts for not regarding Muhammad as the founder of the religion. Rather, he is seen as a reforming prophet. This also explains why the religion is not called Muhammadism after Mohammad, as in other world religions named after their founders (Christianity, Buddhism, Confucianism, etc.).

The reformative mission of Mohammad and the receipt of the Quran are usually depicted in a combination of spiritual and mystic unique experiences that were extraordinary. These experiences manifested themselves during scores of spiritual retreats undertaken by Muhammad when he turned forty. During the retreats, Muhammad experienced revelations, and these which became the foundation and tradition of the Islamic religion. He began to share his experiences with his wife, Khadija, his siblings, and friends. These people not only believed him but also encouraged him, and after he had been instructed in his revelation experiences, he began public preaching.

Meaning of Islam

The word *Islam* has been interpreted in different ways to capture the essence and proper understanding of the religion. There are Islamic scholars who have interpreted the word to mean "obedience," or "submission." This comes from the Arabic etymology of the word *Salima*. This depicts the injunction of the religion that its followers must totally submit to God and absolutely trust Him. Other Islamic scholars have stressed the derivation of Islam from the Arabic word *salaam*, meaning peace. However, as pointed out by Khurshid Ahmad (2011), the word Islam can be interpreted to mean both submission and peace. This is possible if the word Islam is taken to be derive from two root words, *salaam*, meaning peace, and the other word, *Salima*, meaning submission.

On the whole, there is a basic consensus among Islamic scholars that Islam can be defined from the perspectives of peace—signifying being at peace with Allah and all men—and submission, based on the injunction to obey Allah's laws in subordination to His will.

Scripture

The Quran is the sacred scripture of Islam. Its contents are revealed messages that came to Muhammad over a period of about twenty-three years. The significance of the Quran to Islam is first located in the form in which its contents were received and preserved. The revelations were received verbatim by Muhammad, who in turn dictated them to his companions. They in turn memorized and recited them. Second, the revelations at the beginning constituted the belief of Muhammad in the unity of Allah and the fate of those who refused to accept His message. Later on, they stipulated the form of organization and the social dynamics essential to the evolving Muslim community.

Perhaps what constitutes the singular uniqueness of the Quran is the acknowledgement of other revelations in the scriptures of Judaism and Christianity and the acceptance of the main figures in them as true prophets. However, the point of departure from the earlier scriptures is the claim that God's original messages have been adulterated, either by addition or by subtraction. For example, though Islam recognizes Jesus as a prophet, it disagrees with the Christian doctrine of the "Sonship" of Christ. Also, in citing the prediction by Jesus of the coming of Muhammad, the Quran attested to the finality of its revelations and the Prophet Muhammad as the final reformer of the teachings of all the prophets before him, including Jesus. This is why Muslims refer to him as the "last Prophet."

Major Teachings

The major teachings of Islam that constitute its uniqueness as a religious tradition are centered on two interwoven components of faith and deeds. This Islamic position vividly reflects the link envisaged between human intentions and acts. The Prophet Muhammad affirmed this position by insisting that "works shall be judged according to actions," in the same vein as the Quran, in demonstrating the veracity of the position (actually, more than sixty verses mentions the two components together).

Articles of Faith

The faith component can be itemized as articles of faith that the Muslims are enjoined to hold.

Oneness of God

Islamic belief in the oneness of God is graphically captured in the phrase, "There is no god but God and Muhammad is the messenger of God." The importance and significance of this statement to Muslims is demonstrated in the first words to be chanted traditionally into the ear of a Muslim infant. The statement also vividly expresses the Islamic belief that Allah is the creator of all things—human and nonhuman.

The oneness ascribed to Allah by Muslims is evidenced by His intention of creating humans to worship Him. It also designates the teaching that Allah cannot have partners, wives, and children. Such designation of Allah would certainly contradict the Islamic harmony and orderliness of creation and rule out any possibility of conflicts of interest and power-grabbing intrigues. Indeed, Islam's unified conception of Allah is extended to all human actions and relationships, which are to be guided by the ultimate objective of achieving unity in thoughts and in deeds. Thus, all Muslims wherever they live in and whatever status they enjoy are to regard one another as family.

Supernatural Existence

Islam's belief in the supernatural existence is characterized mainly by the belief in the existence of jinn, angels, and saints. With particular reference to angels called *al-malaikah*, Islam demonstrates the undeniable existence of the supernatural realm, quite distinct from the human realm. The angels who possess immaterial substances are considered important because they constitute the "vehicles" of revelation, through whom Allah transmits his messages to humans. Without these angels, Allah's messages would be nonexistent. This is also why there are numerous angels given specific "portfolios" by Allah. The angels are also categorized. For instance there are archangels like Gabriel, who is regarded as the messenger of revelation between Allah and the prophets. However, as important as the angels are, they are not to be worshipped, as this would be contrary to the belief in the unity of Allah.

Islam also believes in the existence of jinn. These are "immaterial beings of fire," among whom Satan originally belonged, before he was cursed and banished for his disobedience. Apart from the beliefs in angels and jinn, there is also the Islamic belief in saints. The saints are humans who have lived holy lives and have consequently become models of piety for Muslims. Usually the tombs of such saints (mystics) become venues of pilgrimages for devotees seeking blessings and holiness.

Prophets of God and Scriptures

Islam recognizes messengers of God, called prophets, who came before Muhammad. Indeed, Muhammad is seen as continuing their messages and finally perfecting them as the last of the prophets. This is because Muhammad is also referred to as the last Prophet who brought Islam's message of salvation, and he is regarded as the most successful among them. The basic belief of Islam is that prophets were sent at different periods of human existence to save religion from slipping from monotheism into polytheism. For example, Ibrahim (Abraham) in the Islamic scripture is called "a truthful man." Musa (Moses) is regarded as "pure" (19:51). Yahya (John the Baptist) is seen as "tender and dutiful to his parents" (19:12–13). Isa (Jesus) is said to be "worthy of regard" (3:44).

Another feature of Muslims concerning prophets is that as messengers of Allah, they are never regarded as divine, but as human. They may be holy and powerful, but since there is only one Divinity and that is Allah, the prophets do not enjoy that status.

Because the scriptures of various religions contain the messages of the prophets, Islam enjoins Muslims to honor them. Indeed, Islam subscribes to this belief in four scriptures: The *Taurat* (the first five books of the Old Testament), which was given to Musa, the *Injil* (New Testament), given to Isa (Jesus), the *Zabur* (Psalms of David) given to Daud (David), and the Quran, which was given to Muhammad. However, it is only the Quran that should be held as fully authentic. This authenticity is based on the claim that the Quran contains the direct, unchanged, and untranslated word of Allah.

Afterlife and Final Judgment

The Islamic beliefs on the hereafter and the final judgment are based on the teaching of the significance of the consequences of human life while on earth for life after death. This teaching is a derivation of the belief in the dual composition of humans—the material and the spiritual. Indeed, for the Muslims, as Ajijola points out, there is need for life after death as a guarantee for a spiritual sanction. To deny this belief is to make nonsense of all other beliefs and ultimately eradicate the necessary sanction of pious living. From the foregoing, believing in life after death becomes the greatest deciding factor in the life of a man, and his acceptance or rejection of it actually determines the course his life takes.

The dispensation of the reward or punishment by Allah occurs at the final judgment. Though the time of the final judgment is unknown, it will definitely happen, and will be individualistic as a form of taking responsibility for humans' earthly acts. This occurs through the process of individuals who have died spending a period of time in the grave and then bodily resurrecting to account for their deeds while on earth. After the judgment, those found virtuous will go into *al Jannah* (paradise) as reward for their good deeds on earth. On the other hand, the sinners, who did not live according to Allah's precepts, will be banished into *al-Naar* (hell). The difference between the two domains is that while those in *al Jannah* will live in perpetual joy in the company of their wives and family and attended by young boys like pearls as servants and beautiful virgins, those in *al-Naar* will forever be subjected to the torture of being burned in ever raging fires. They will be perpetually in garments on fire and always in chains.

Deeds (Practice) in Islam—The Five Pillars

The Five Pillars are the required practices for Muslims. They are to be strictly observed because they emanated as direct commandments of Allah. Being designated as pillars symbolizes their significance as the fundamentals upon which the Muslim faith is built and practiced.

Imam

As the first pillar of Islam, this demonstrates the acts of belief and witness required of a Muslim. It makes it incumbent on the Muslim not only to believe, but also to publicly profess the unity of Allah and the role of Muhammad as His messenger. It is by this injunction that the faithful Muslim derives the mission to propagate Islam and to convert people to it without forcing them, in compliance with the dictates of the Quran, which states:

> *Let there be no compulsion in religion: Truth stands out Clear from Error: whoever Rejects Evil and believes In God hath grasped the most trustworthy Hand-hold that never breaks (Sura 2:256).*

Salat (Daily Prayers)

This is the second pillar of Islam. The word *Salat* in literary terms means "supplication." However, in practical usage it designates ritual prayer. This stipulates the five obligatory prayers required from Muslims at specific times of the day. The Quran injunction to Muslims to observe the five daily prayers with ablutions is to stress the need to worship Allah as the creator of the Universe. The prayers are also seen as a means of gaining righteousness and do away with sinful lives. By observing the *Salat*, the Muslim is able to separate him- or herself from evil and unjust acts.

But observing the *Salat* should not be just a physical ritual. It must involve an inner disposition of offering the prayers form the heart and in an attitude of being in the presence of Allah. Thus, as the Muslims recite and go through the motions, spiritual meditation on Allah becomes a form of true worship, which makes the prayers efficacious.

Zakat (Almsgiving)

The third pillar of Islam, *Zakat* deals with the acts of charity or almsgiving required of Muslims. However, it is a mandatory act of charity in the form of an annual rate paid in cash or kind by a Muslim and distributed among those qualified to receive it. Viewed as a functional economic system of wealth distribution, the *Zakat* becomes a strategy for bridging the gap between rich and poor and ensuring social justice.

The importance and significance of *Zakat* in Islam are vividly demonstrated, not only in the linkage that exists between it and *Salat* but also the fact that it is mentioned about eighty-two times along with *Salat*. Thus, *Salat* is, in fact, regarded as meaningless if the charitable act is omitted. In stressing this, Muhammad gave the warning that:

> Whoever is made wealthy by Allah and does not pay the poor rate, his wealth will turn into a bald-headed poisonous male snake with two black spots over its eyes. The snake will encircle his neck and bite his cheek, saying, "I **am** your wealth, I am your treasure" (57).

Also, the importance of *Zakat* in Islam is demonstrated by the fact that not only individual Muslims are required to comply with it, but also Muslim communities, groups, and governments are required to give *Zakat* corporately. For instance, the government of Saudi Arabia devotes 15 percent of its GDP to fulfill this obligation (Fisher, 2012). This is also done in every Islamic country.

Sawm (Fasting)

The fourth pillar of Islam recommends that Muslims fast frequently. This is a form of abstinence from drinking, eating, sexual acts, and so on. The fasting takes place from sundown to sunset. To Islam, the act of fasting is to avail the Muslim of the opportunity to get rid of bodily impurities. By so doing, the body is not only made lighter to make movement easier, but more importantly, for the soul to become transcendent and capable of providing a clear mind for spiritual meditation. During the month of Ramadan, which moves from season to season according to the Muslim lunar calendar of 3,534 days, Muslims are able to suppress bodily needs as a form of sacrifice in order to concentrate on spiritual values that would draw them closer to Allah. Apart from the annual Ramadan, Muslims also fast to rectify unwanted or ungodly situations or circumstances, such as atoning for sins, marking sad events, asking Allah for favors, being remorseful and penitent, among others.

Hajj (Pilgrimage)

This fifth pillar of Islam obligates all Muslims who are physically and financially able to go on a pilgrimage to Mecca at least once in their lifetime. The pilgrimage to Mecca is regarded as the apex of all acts of faith. However, the *umrah* (lesser pilgrimage) can be performed many times. For the Muslims, the various rites that accompany the *Hajj* are designated as forms of instructions to teach salient lessons. For instance, the *ihram* dress—the only types of dress pilgrims are to wear throughout the pilgrimage—is designed as a leveler of the pilgrims. Thus, the discriminatory garment of rank, status, and all other forms of distinction are shed. The gesture enjoins humility for all the pilgrims in the realization that worldly posts are temporary and that the only lasting quality is piety, which guarantees the hereafter.

Another lesson of the pilgrimage is the discipline required of the pilgrims. Throughout the duration of the exercise, arguments, violence, and all forms of immorality are forbidden. The pilgrims are expected to imbibe the highest level of morality and discipline. In addition, the high moral standard attained by the pilgrimage is supposed to be lifelong. This is why he or she bears the title *al-haj* till death.

As part of the rites to be performed by the pilgrims, they walk around the ancient Kaaba seven times, symbolizing how the angels and all creations dance around Allah to the seventh heaven. Another part of the ritual is the visit to the field of Arafat to commemorate how Adam and Eve were taught the importance of the fact that humans were created to worship Allah exclusively. In addition, the sacrifice of an animal symbolizes the obedience to Allah of Abraham, who was ordered to sacrifice his only son, Isaac.

HISTORICAL DEVELOPMENT AND THE SPREAD OF ISLAM

Islam as a religious tradition grew out of Muhammad spreading the revelation he received. As previously mentioned, he began first with his wife, then his siblings and some followers. Muhammad and his followers were soon persecuted. As an example, Muhammad's Abyssinian slave, Bilal, was imprisoned for accepting the Prophet's message. Muhammad and his followers were thereafter banished for three years; even when they were asked to return to Mecca, the persecution grew even more intense.

The second stage was the *hijra*, when the Muslims migrated to Medina in 622 ce. It was in Medina that Muhammad fought and defeated the forces in Mecca and triumphantly returned to the city in 630. Mecca thereafter became the spiritual and political center of the Islamic faith. From this humble beginning, Islam was soon to spread to all parts of the globe, both during Muhammad's lifetime and particularly after his death. Islam spread to North Africa, Persia (Yemen, Oman, and Bahrain). After the death of Muhammad and under the Abbasids, Muslim rule and civilization attained its peak, with merchants and Islamic scholars becoming the arrowhead of Islamic propagation and intellectual landmarks.

In the seventh century Tunisia and Egypt came under the Islamic religion. Subsequently, Islam also became part of other regions in Africa through jihads, trade, and the missionary efforts of Islamic teachers and scholars. Today, Islam competes with Christianity for religious space in Africa as the two dominating religious traditions. The Islamic spread and influence in the Western hemisphere got as far as Spain, before the Christian Inquisition of the thirteenth century.

In the Eastern hemisphere, Islam also spread dramatically. It gained control of central Asia; the Turks were converted to Islam. Also, Islam spread into North India and flourished there, particularly under the Muslim Moguls, competing with Hinduism. In later years, the Islamic faith had a significant presence in Pakistan, Indonesia, China, and the former Soviet Union. These places still have large Muslim populations today, with Pakistan and Turkey dominated by Muslims.

Although Islam is not fractioned into several denominations as Christianity is, two major sects have emerged. These are the Sunnis and the Shiites. The Sunnis are said to comprise nearly 80 percent of all

Muslims globally today (Fisher, 2012). The Sunnis follow the sayings and practices of Prophet Muhammad, which were compiled under the Sunni Caliphs. In addition, the Sunnis are regarded as traditionalists who emphasize the Quran and believe that the Prophet died without appointing a successor, which therefore gave legitimacy to the caliphs elected by the *ummah* (the community) as true successors of Muhammad.

On the other hand, the Shiites hold to the conviction that Ali was the legitimate successor of Muhammad, judging by the actions of the Prophet on his deathbed. He was said to have held Ali's hand and pronounced:

> *Whoever I protect, Ali is also his protector. O God, be a friend to whoever is his friend and an enemy to whoever is his enemy.*

With this statement and the holding of Ali's hand, as far as the Shiites are concerned, Muhammad has transferred his spiritual authority to Ali to become his legitimate successor.

REVIEW QUESTIONS

1.   Give a brief historical background of the life and mission of the Prophet Muhammad.
2.   Why do Muslims prefer to be called Muslims rather than Muhammadans?
3.   Identify and briefly discuss the major teachings of Islam on faith.
4.   Briefly examine the substance and significance of the Five Pillars of Islam.
5.   In your own view, what factors aided the rapid spread of Islam in the decades after Muhammad's death?
6.   Briefly compare the concept of monotheism in Islam and Christianity.

BIBLIOGRAPHY AND FURTHER READING

Abdalati, H. n.d. *Islam in Focus*. Islamic Teaching Centre.

Ahmed, A. S. 2003. *Islam Under Siege*. Cambridge: Polity Press.

Ali, M. 1986. *The Religion of Islam*. Delhi: Taj Company.

Awolalu, J. O. 1980. "The Concept of Death and the Hereafter in Yoruba Traditional Religion," *Sierra Leone Bulletin of Religion*, vol. 1, Dec.

Brockelmann, C. 1979. *History of the Islamic Peoples*. London: R. and K. Paul.

Delong-Bas, Natana. 2004. *Wahhabi Islam: From Revival and Reform to Global Jihad*. Oxford: Oxford University Press.

Doi, A. R. I. 1981. *The Cardinal Principles of Islam*. Lagos: Islamic Publications Bureau.

Galloway, D. 1992. "Resurrection & Judgment in Qur'an," in *Muslim World*, vol. 12, no. 4, Oct.

Gibbon, E. 1870. *History of the Saracen Empire*. London: Macmillan.

Goethe, T. 1964. "Qur'an." In T. F. Hughes, *Dictionary of Islam*. Lahore: Book House.

Hirschfield, H. 1902. *New Researches into the Composition and Exercises of the Qur'an*. London: Royal Asiatic Society.

Hitti, P. K. 1984. *History of the Arabs*. London: Macmillan.

Johnson, S. 1921. *History of the Yorubas*. Lagos: CMS Publishing Company.

Lamb, D. 1987. *The Arabs*. New York: Random House.

Lane, E. 1980. *Arabic English Lexicon*. Lahore: Islamic Book Centre.

Law, R. C. C. 1977. *The Oyo Empire: 1600–1836*. Oxford: Oxford University Press.

Lawrence, Bruce. 2007. *The Qur'an: A Biography*. New York: Atlantic Monthly Press.

Moshe, G. J. O. 1990. *Who Is This Allah?* Ibadan: Fireliners International.

Muir, W. 1984. *Life of Muhammad*. London: Smith and Elder.

Musa, A. H. M. 1974. *Al-Filth ul-Islam al Muyassar*. Bukhari: Dar Ul-Fikril-Arabi.

Nasr, Seyyed Hossein. 1985. *Ideals and Realities of Islam*. London: Unwin Hyman Ltd.

O'Leary, D. L. 1923. *Islam at Crossroads*. London: SCM.

Ramakrishna Rao, K. S. 1989. *Muhammad, the Prophet of Islam*. Riyadh: World Assembly of Muslim Youth.

Rosenthal, F. 1979. "Literature." In J. Schacht and C. E. Bosworth, eds. *The Legacy of Islam*. Oxford: Oxford University Press.

Rushdie, S. 1988. *The Satanic Verses*. England: Viking Penguin Group.

Ruthven, Malise. 2006. *Islam in the World*, 3rd ed. Oxford: Oxford University Press.

Safi, Onud, ed. 2003. *Progressive Muslims: On Justice, Gender and Pluralism*. Oxford: Onward Publication.

Sajoo, Amyn, ed. 2004. *Civil Society in the Muslim World: Contemporary Perspectives*. London: I. B. Tauris.

Smith, B. 1974. *Muhammad and Muhammadanism*. Lahore: Sind Sagar Academy.

Sumrall, L. 1980. *Where Was God When Pagan Religions Began?* Nashville: Thomas Nelson.

Tritton, A. S. 1951. *Islam*. London: Macmillan.

Ul-Haqq, M. 1977. *A Short History of Islam*. Lahore: Bookland.

Wadud, Amina. 1999. *Qur'an and Women*. New York/Oxford: Oxford University Press.

Zaman, Muhammad Qasim. 2002. *The Ulama in Contemporary Islam*. Princeton, NJ: Princeton University Press.

CHAPTER TWELVE

ASIATIC TRADITIONS

INTRODUCTION

The religions whose origins in the region designated as the Asian hemisphere are usually categorized as Asian religions belonging to the Asiatic religious tradition stock. There are many of these religions that have one time or another competed as—and are even contemporarily competing—viable world religions. The focus and scope of this book understandably limits the number of such religions to be discussed. The choice of the three (Buddhism, Confucianism, and Hinduism) discussed here are by no means based on exclusive preference or authenticity over others omitted.

BUDDHISM

Background Introduction

Siddhartha Gautama is the founder of Buddhism. He is called the Buddha, an appellation he received because of his intelligence; it designates him as "the enlightened one." Siddhartha Gautama was born in 544 bc to the royal family of King Suddhodana and Queen Mayadevi, rulers of Lumbini, Nepal. Gautama was also known as Shakyamuni to signify his linkage with the Shakya clan. Three important events happened on the same day in Siddhartha Gautama's life, which remarkably changed his destiny. The three events were his birth, enlightenment, and death. They all happened on a full moon night in April or May; hence, that day is called Buddha Purnima or Buddha Jayanti.

A few days before Siddhartha was born, Queen Mayadevi, his mother, had a dream that a white elephant came down from heaven and entered her womb and told her that the child that she is conceiving was pure and powerful. The elephant told her that her child had come down from Tushita Heaven. This is the heaven for Buddhists. Later, when Queen Mayadevi gave birth to Siddhartha, she did not feel any pain. She experienced a smooth and pure vision in which she was holding a branch of a tree with her right hand, while the gods, Brahman and Indra, took the child from her. Then the gods praised the child by offering him ritual ablutions.

Five days after the baby's birth, he was named Siddhartha, meaning "wish fulfilled." After a few more days, Siddhartha's father invited a Brahim to come read the baby's future. The Brahim predicted that when Siddhartha grew up, he would venture off into the world as a sage and leave all his material objects to search for wisdom to overcome suffering and misery from the world. Despite this prophesy, King Suddhodana still raised Siddhartha in luxury.

When he was sixteen, Siddhartha was married to his cousin, Princess Yasodhara. They lived a happy and luxurious married life in the royal palace for thirteen years. But one day, Siddhartha went outside his palace and saw the grief of others when seeing an old crippled man and a corpse. This experience made him realize the sorrow and suffering of humans. Based on this incident, he left his lovely wife and son in the middle of the night in search of enlightenment and the true meaning of life, with the ultimate goal of helping others in need of assistance.

Siddhartha went all over India, unsuccessful in his search for answers. However, one day while Siddhartha was under an Ajapala banyan tree, a lady named Sujata, sitting under a Bodhi tree, randomly offered him some rich milk rice, specially made by her. After eating the meal, he fasted and meditated for seven weeks under the Bodhi tree. Finally, after seven weeks, Siddhartha attained enlightenment and became the Enlightened One. He thereafter began his mission by preaching at the deer park in Sarnath on how to live a harmonious and balanced life. From that day, Siddhartha traveled and preached. He engaged in the multiple practices of preaching in the morning, meditating in the afternoon, and talking to visitors at night. As he began to gather followers, the Brahmins became his strongest opponents because his preaching was considered unorthodox. Eventually, Siddhartha died of an illness resulting from his diet.

Development and Teachings

The historical development of Buddhism can be divided into four separate phases. These are: early Buddhism; interpretations of the teachings; the rise of Mahayana Buddhism; and Buddhist Tantra. These phases mainly developed in India. The spread of Buddhism to Asia actually witnessed its decline in India before it was reestablished and thereafter spread throughout the region and other parts of the world (Kagyu Office, 2011).

From the middle of the sixth to the middle of the fifth century bce, Buddhism was in its infancy with the teachings of the Buddha himself and the preservation of these by his followers (Kagyu Office, 2011). The roots of Buddhism lie in the religious thought of ancient India, starting with the sacrifices and rituals of Vedic Brahmanism. Buddha was a particular critic of the ritual sacrifices of Brahmanism, and claimed that the priests who memorized the Vedas really knew nothing. His thoughts on this and other teachings were passed on to his followers and with these, Buddhism began to spread.

After the death of Gautama Buddha, the first Buddhist council was held. The major objective of the council was to collect and recite all the teachings of the Buddha to ensure there were no errors in the transmission (Macmillan, 2008). After the first council, the second council was held. It was at this point that the collective followers of the Buddha began to break into separate factions, with various beliefs and interpretations of his teachings. Thereafter, several traditions emerged, which included the Dipavamsa, the Pudgalavada, the Sarvastivada, Vasumitra, and Mahasanghika. Subsequently, from the divided traditions, various schools were established based on the divided traditions beginning from the third century bce, and 100 to 200 years after the death of Buddha (*Journal of the Pali Text Society*, 2011).

Mahayana Buddhism became one of the byproducts of these different schools. Though the date of and reasons for its origin are not ascertained, most scholars have come to the conclusion that its ideals and doctrines were based on older traditions. In addition, it has been established that much of Mahayana history is located in translated Chinese texts from the second century bc, indicating its eventual spread to other parts of Asia (Nattier, 2003).

The Buddhist Tantra, or Vajrayana, is said to represent a more modern interpretation; it has been partially influenced by Hinduism. The recent nature of the tradition has accounted for its interpretation still being in its early stages and therefore faced with many challenges. Consequently, the Scriptures of Vajrayana have not been organized, thus necessitating closer examination of its doctrines and rituals.

As a religious tradition, Buddhism witnessed a gradual movement from India proper to the surrounding islands and lands. Buddhism's slow spread in India was given a boost by the Mauryan emperor Ashoka's construction of *stupas* (Buddhist religious memorials). His efforts paid off. Buddhism spread to parts of modern-day Afghanistan, Central Asia, and the island of Sri Lanka. The religion eventually spread to China (Gombrich, 2006).

With its spread into different regions, Buddhism was influenced by various ethnic groups. These included both the Persian and Greek civilizations. This became evident with the emergence of Greek-speaking Buddhist monarchs, as well as the development of the Greco-Buddhist art of Gandhara. Indeed, a Greek king, Menander, is immortalized in the Buddhist canon. Thereafter, Buddhism spread to China around the late second century bc or the first century. Ultimately, the religion made its way into Korea and Japan, and by the eighth century, Buddhism had spread from India to Tibet and Mongolia (Zurcher, 1972).

Today, Buddhism has become significantly different from when it began. Though it is quite difficult to have specifics in terms of demographics and actual numbers of devotees, its spread worldwide is estimated to be anywhere between 500 million to 1.7 billion (Tamney, 1998).

It is important to point out that Buddhism was founded in India between the seventh and fifth centuries bc. During this period, India was greatly influenced by both intellectual revolution and Hinduism, the religion being practiced in India at the time. However, there were other religions which grew out of the Hindu beliefs and practices, such as the Upanishads, whose religious practices were based specifically on the doctrine of transmigration. Buddhism also developed alongside the religion of Jainism.

As indicated earlier the name Buddha means "the Awakened One." This becomes the name by which Siddhartha Gautama is recognized by his followers, and it has been used as the name of the religion in the aspiration to reach the same level of enlightenment that Siddhartha reached.

In terms of doctrine, Buddhism is based upon the Four Noble Truths laid out by Buddha. These four noble truths actually typify a holistic system of beliefs shared by all Buddhists. These include seeing the Buddha as the only master, taking shelter in the Buddha, Dhamma, and Sangha, and also believing that the world was created or ruled by a God. In addition, Buddhists are required to live in the Buddha's example, specifically following his example of Great Compassion and Great Wisdom. In doing so, Buddhists believe that the real purpose of life—which is to gain a sense of compassion for everything, living in order to be good, obtain happiness and peace, and lastly, to gain wisdom to become closer to understanding the Ultimate

Truth—can be achieved. However, the state described above can only be attained if the four noble truths are followed. These are: Dukkha, the Arising of Dukkha, the Cessation of Dukkha, and the Path leading to the Cessation of the Dukkha.

Further, Buddhists also believe that there are Thirty-seven Qualities that are imperative in order to attain Enlightenment. These qualities may be attained in three ways by being a disciple; a Pratyeka-Buddha; and lastly, a Samyak-sam-Buddha. The last way, which is becoming a fully Enlightened Buddha, is considered the noblest and most honorable.

Although there are variants of practices in Buddhism, they can be synthesized into four basic ones, comprising Meditation, Mantras, Mudras, and Prayer Wheels. Meditation is a mental concentration that leads to enlightenment and spiritual freedom. Though meditation is found in all forms of Buddhism, there are different characteristics to the act of meditation. There are mainly two major types of meditation, those being *vipassana*, or insight, and *samatha*, or tranquillity, and also the practice of meditation while sitting. Mantras are sacred sounds believed to have supernatural powers. They are chanted during meditation and often involve mala beads, which are used for protection from evil and hardships. In addition to Mantras, sometimes Prayer Wheels are used while the chants are said, and a wheel is turned. Finally, Mudras are symbolic hand gestures in Buddhism.

Currently, though the practice of Buddhism may not be as widespread as those of Christianity and Islam, it is becoming more and more prominent across the world, with a lot of interest being generated in the religion as it competes with other religious traditions in the global religious space.

Confucianism

Background Introduction

As a religion, Confucianism developed from the famous Chinese philosopher Confucius, whose beliefs were collected and spread by his disciples across China. The unique thing about Confucianism is that it is a complex system of moral, philosophical, religious, social, and political thoughts that has become greatly influential on Chinese culture and other eastern Asian countries. Followers of Confucianism believe in strong moral and ethical codes. This is consonant with the main goal of the religion, which is the cultivation of virtue and the development of moral perfection. These are regarded vital in building relationships and harmony in the society. Thus, Confucianism is primarily an ethical system and way of life rather than a divinely oriented one.

Confucius was born in 551 bc in what is now the province of Shangdong. He was born into an aristocratic family during a period of social revolution. The Zhou Dynasty had declined significantly to the point that it was just a figurehead creating disorder and human misery (Jianying, 2006). Confucius, despite this situation, continued to maintain the concept of love, harmony, and order in the world. He spent a lifetime "in pursuit of an ideal world of national prosperity, universal peace, and happiness for the entire populace" (Jianying, 2006). He believed that social mores and ethics would create a new social order in order to accomplish this. Confucius traveled to various states promoting his doctrine in an attempt to spread his beliefs. He desired a world where "elders could spend their later years in peace and happiness, and people could trust one another as they would their close friends. Where all children would be loved, cared for, and given good education" (Jianying, 2006).

However, in all these, Confucius regarded himself as merely "a 'transmitter' and not a 'maker' or 'originator', giving the world only a powerful restatement of the fundamental principles of human morality or ethics" (Sivananda, 2010). Consequently, Confucius did not lay claim to creating a new religion. As far as he was concerned, he only reiterated the current moral and ethical codes, with the objective of creating a better society. This, of course, did not leave much time to concentrate on the divine. As a result, Confucius did not consider it essential to themes of God and life after death (Sivananda, 2010). The center of the religion then became issues associated with the needs of human society, and not divine sensibilities (Weiming, 2001).

Development and Main Beliefs

As is usual in the lives of many reformers, Confucius' ideas were not accepted during his lifetime. It was only after his death that his disciples actually created a Confucian system. This obviously occurred during the philosophically fertile period of the Hundred Schools of Thought, the great early figures of Confucianism, Mencius and Xun Zi, when Confucianism developed into an ethical and political doctrine (Hoobler, 1993). It has also been shown that Zisi, Confucius' grandson, also played a major role in creating the Confucian system (Wilson, 2002:7).

Historically, Confucianism survived its suppression during the Qin Dynasty due to the fact that a handful of Confucian classics were hidden in the walls of a scholar's house. After the Qin Dynasty, the next group in power, the Han Dynasty, was favorably disposed to the Confucian doctrine. The dynasty not only approved it, but actually sponsored Confucian scholars in its court (Wilson, 2002:7). Indeed, Emperor Wu of Han became so devoted to Confucianism's political ideas that he made Confucianism the official state philosophy.

Later on, followers of Confucius, such as Mencius and Xun Zi, expanded the scope of Confucius' teaching, thereby including issues associated with human nature. This generated a lot of controversy during their time (Wilson, 2002:8). Thereafter, temples of Confucius were established throughout the land, thus introducing the state cult of Confucius. The religion, in the form of Neo-Confucianism, soon spread to Korea during the Yi Dynasty and also to Japan, with the countries being regarded as Confucian states.

In terms of beliefs, Confucianism is devoted to the importance of harmony in humanity obtainable by acknowledging and working within the scope of a natural hierarchy, and from a respect of the cosmos and Tian, Heaven. Here, the cosmos is derived from the belief of ancient cosmology as a sacred place, and all aspects of it—people and things—are considered to be interrelated (Oldstone-Moore, 2002).

Further, a central belief of Confucianism is that people should live in harmony, both with each other and with nature. In order to achieve this important goal, the religion advocates, in line with the teaching of, a system based on "interpersonal relationships and good government" (Hoobler and Hoobler, 1993). The system depends on five human relationships, particularly those between family members: father/son, husband/wife, older brother/younger brother, friend/friend, and ruler/subject (Hoobler and Hoobler, 1993).

The Confucian emphasis on family relationships is based on the notion that families are a training ground for life in society (Oldstone, 2002). With this disposition, the family is required to be primarily responsible for teaching their children how to be a positive member of society. Thus, the child typically learns from his or her parents how to deal with the problems he or she will face later in life. However, according to Confucianism, the family dynamic is not limited to blood-related families. This is why the religion advocates that government should be set up to resemble a family structure. Within this structure, the leaders are thought of as the parents and the citizens' act out of obligation to respect and obey the leaders, just as they would the senior members of their immediate family (Oldstone, 2002:54). But for this structure to be effective—and therefore succeed—it must depict a relationship as mutual as the one existing in a family. Thus, the emperor, for example, must be virtuous and set a good example for the people (O'Donnell 2007:180). The absence of this will leave people without a good example on how to act, and a harmonious society can never be created.

Confucians belief the above could be achieved if five basic virtues are developed in all relationships. These are: courtesy, magnanimity, good faith, diligence, and kindness so as to become an ethical person (Hoobler and Hoobler, 1993). It is also important to point out that Confucians believe that one is not born into or bestowed with these virtues. Rather, they are self-cultivated, by studying and practicing appropriate behaviors (Oldstone-Moore, 2002).

Nevertheless, though Confucianism does not place a high premium on the supernatural, Tian (translated as "Heaven") is regarded to be the Supreme Being, "the source of power and order" (Oldstone-Moore, 2002). In this case, in the submission of Confucius, one must strive to know Heaven's will, with Tian being considered a moral order (Oldstone-Moore, 2002).

One other important feature of Confucianism is its subscription to a completely intertwined relationship between religion and government. Thus, there is the belief in a "Mandate of Heaven" in Confucianism (O'Donnell, 2007:183). This is why the ruler should regard his authority as given by Tian. This sacralizes the job of the ruler, in ways such as making sure the economy runs smoothly, the availability of water for irrigation, canals being operational, and roads being safe to travel. If the state of the nation starts deteriorating, then Confucians believe this is an indication that the emperor has lost his "Mandate of Heaven" (O'Donnell, 2007).

Today, over 6 million people follow the teaching of Confucianism, though there has been a rapid decline in many Eastern countries such as China, due to the rise of communism. However, there is no doubt that Confucianism has played a large role in the building and shaping of the economies and values of the people of Korea, Japan, Singapore, Taiwan, and Hong Kong. There is, of course, the ever pertinent debate as to whether Confucianism should be regarded as a religion, or just simply a moral tradition, or a political theory. Because of its insistence that moral and ethical principles guarantee an ideal society, there are many who would describe it as guidelines for a way of life and for creating a much larger entity—a government. This situation is further compounded by the fact that from the twentieth century, Confucianism has come to be characterized by "scholasticism, accompanied by extreme moralism ... intellectual, political and social failures of East Asia" (Yao, 2000:245).

There is also no doubt that the influence of Confucianism has greatly diminished with the rise of the Communist Party, which does not hide its opposition for a Confucian political approach with a commitment to eradicating it as a "political party" (Zhang, 1999).

This ethical system of Confucianism has given the modern generation the morality and guidelines to dictate day-to-day behavior, but it lacks a larger following due to the negative connotations created by communism, of its political positions. Communism is opposed to Confucianism because "economic freedom with minimum government intervention is a main feature," the opposite of Communist beliefs (Zhang, 1999:194). In the Western hemisphere, its role as a religion—as opposed to a philosophy or government—has, on the whole, been discredited, because the Confucianism versus communism battle it is not seen as similar to the Christianity versus atheism battle, but as similar to that of democracy versus socialism. Although it is still shadowed by its political undertones, Confucianism's guidelines have been credited with creating order in East Asian countries and fueling the economic boom that some have witnessed since World War II. All these notwithstanding, it is absolutely within reason to submit that the ideas and traditions of Confucianism will continue to impart the global religious space and survive into the future as it has done for centuries.

HINDUISM

Introduction

There are some who indicate that Hinduism is arguably the world's oldest religion. Unlike Christianity, Buddhism, Confucianism, and to some extent Islam, Hinduism has neither a "single founder," nor a "unified system of beliefs," and no single god or defined set of gods to worship (Flood, 1996). The religion is compared more to a tree that has grown gradually than like a building that has been erected by some great architect at a specific period (Sharma, 2003). There also are a number of scholars who submit that Hinduism is a polytheistic religion, with multiple gods and multiple paths to internal peace and understanding. This discourse attempts to briefly present Hinduism as a unique world religion through its origin, beliefs, doctrines, practices, development, spread, and current status.

Origin

Devotees of Hinduism regard the religion as eternal or timeless. Interestingly, scholars have not been able to disprove this claim. Indeed, there are no Hindu religious texts that point to a single founder or group of founders. Consequently, followers of the religion simply call the creators of the religion "great sages" or "scientists of spirit" (Johnsen, 2009). Based on this claim, the religion is said to derive from the dedication of these scientists in defining the spiritual laws of man and creating a foundation that would transcend time and space. The ancient origin of Hinduism is substantiated by the discovery of small Hindu goddess figurines that date back to the time of the Ice Age—ten thousand years ago, according to archaeologists (Johnson, 2009). In addition, efforts have been made to determine the origin of the name of the religion. Some scholars, such as Klaus Klostermaier, have presented some etymological breakthroughs in this regard (Klostermaier, 2007). For instance, Klostermaier suggests that the term *Hindu* arose in the eighth century and was used as the Muslim invaders' reference to non-Muslim Indians. The Muslims took *Hindu* from *Sindh* and *Sindhu*, the ancient Persians' references to the land and people of the Indus River Valley. By the 1830s, it was further suggested that English scholars added *–ism* to *Hindu* and created the term *Hinduism*, in order to describe the religious practices of India's natives (Klostermaier, 2007:n17). However, in spite of these submissions, many researchers have insisted that Hinduism has existed in India for a very long period of time, despite the works of Abbé Dubois, who attempted to link the origin of Hinduism to Aryan invasion. His argument submits that there had to be a Sanskrit-speaking ancestor between India and the western borders of Europe. According to him, the Aryans would be the perfect candidates to fill this role (Klostermaier, 2007:19). Unfortunately, archaeological findings in the abandoned cities of Mohenjo Daro and Harappa have not supported the Aryan invasion theory. The indication is that the residents of both cities simply left, and there was no evidence of damage or a hostile takeover (Klostermaier, 2007:19). In further disagreeing with the theory, scholars of religion have pointed out that none of "the literature of the Vedas, the Buddhotov, the Jain writings, or Tamil" present information about an Aryan invasion (Klostermaier, 2007:21). In addition, there has been no evidence found by anthropologists to suggest that a new race came into the area.

Doctrines and Development

Although no one has been able to pinpoint the factual details of Hinduism's origin, the complexity, sacred nature, and impact of the religion is undeniable. Hindus are extremely spiritual, dedicating their lives to ideals such as dharma, or fulfillment of moral, social, and religious duties; artha, or financial and worldly success; kama, or minimization of desires; and moksha, or freedom from reincarnation (Flood, 1997). The basic foundations of Hinduism are derived from the understanding that there is no right or wrong way in Hinduism. Consequently, there are many alternate versions of stories, many incarnations of gods or goddess, and many alternate universes presented in the religion. The religion preaches a cycle of life that comprises everything. People die; their souls are reborn in new bodies, and they die again. Rivers flow up, they flow down, and they flow up again. Mountains grow, shrink, and grow again. Lands surface, become the bottom of the ocean, and surface again. Universes form, cease, and form again. Therefore, Hinduism is a religion constantly involved in expansion, new interpretations, and new connections and forms of enlightenment.

For Hinduism, understanding is based on the expansion of the past, devoid of the limitations of the physical world. Apart from its abstract nature, Hinduism insists on some order and structure in society. Thus, as a social institution, the caste system is formed around Hinduism's focus on rebirth, groups of individuals based on their souls' previous levels of dharma, artha, and kama. Upon rebirth, Karma, a supernatural judge, chooses the caste system that an individual will be born into. The caste system is made up of four major castes broken down into numerous subcastes.

The major castes are the Brahmans, the Kshatriyas, the Vaishyas, and the Shudras (*Encyclopedia Britannica*, 2011: Hinduism). The highest, the Brahman, consists of individuals born with the right to teach the Vedas, the primary religious texts of Hinduism (*Encyclopedia Britannica*, 2011: Hinduism). The Kshatriyas, or nobility and warriors, are below the Brahman, and they are responsible for defending society. The Vaishyas are the common people who farm, trade, raise cattle, and care for the land and the animals of the Earth (*Encyclopedia Britannica*, 2011: Hinduism). The Shudras, the lowest caste, are the servants of society (*Encyclopedia Britannica*, 2011: Hinduism). Beyond the caste system, there is a group of forbidden individuals who are referred to as the untouchables. They live on the outskirts of civilization, and no one is allowed to interact with them.

Although there is the acknowledgement of various degrees of social rank in Hinduism, individuals are still held responsible for their actions. They are expected to respect the world around them so as not to be negatively connected to the sacred and thereby removed from the profane. Further, the four main branches of Hinduism are divided into numerous sects that encourage individuals to focus on the responsibilities of their current life and increase their chances of reincarnation into a higher caste or possible moksha.

The four primary branches of Hinduism are Vaishnavism, Shaivism, Shaktism, and Smarta. In Vaishnavism and Shaivism, the focus is on praising and connecting to the gods Vishnu "the Pervader" and Shiva, "the

Auspicious One" (*Encyclopedia Britannica*, 2011: Hinduism). In Shaktism, devotees honor Devi, the goddess of power and energy, and in Smarta. The focus is on demonstrating allegiance to Vishnu, Shiva, Devi, Ganesh, and Surya (*Encyclopedia Britannica*, 2011: Hinduism).

While these four branches are centered on different gods and goddesses, their framework is built on the same foundation—the ancient Vedas. Accepting the Vedas is the first step to being considered a Hindu. The Vedas, which comprise all the messages of the great sages of Hinduism, actually address virtually all human subjects, such as agriculture, hell, medicine, mysticism, creation, revelation, education, philosophy, chronology, ethics, prayer, purification, law, and more (*Encyclopedia Britannica*, 2011: Hinduism). The central teachings of the Vedas present followers with the existence of an ultimate reality (*Brahman*) that individual souls (*Atman*) connect to in order to reach their final liberation (*moksha*), that breaks the cycle of reincarnation (*Samsara*), and appeases or supersedes the judge (*Karma*) in rebirth (*Encyclopedia Britannica*, 2011: Hinduism).

The Vedas depict a chronological order that is broken into four main sections: the Rig Veda, the Yajurveda, the Samaveda, and the Atharvaveda. The Rig Veda, which is the oldest book of the Vedas, contains a lot of basic information about Hinduism. It presents Indra as the leader of the gods, Varuna as the protector of the universe, Agni as the sacrificial fire, and Surya as the sun. The Rig Veda also provides a framework for the caste system. Also found in it are rituals for marriage, animal sacrifice, death, and funeral cremation. The second most important book of the Vedas is the Atharvaveda; this book is divided into twenty books that are filled with hymns and prose passages on a wide variety of subjects like "spells for long life, curses, cures, love charms, kingship, Brahmanhood, marriage, funerals, magical rituals, and evil" (*Encyclopedia Britannica*, 2011: Hinduism).

Beyond the religious framework the Vedas create for Hinduism, stories about popular Hindu gods and goddesses can be found in the *Mahabharata*, the *Ramayana*, and the *Puranas*. The *Ramayana* tells the story of King Rama, an adaptation of Vishnu, and his struggle to reclaim the land that he is rightfully heir to. Also, the *Ramayana* presents great men and women who encourage and portray the high moral and ethical standards supported by Hinduism (*Encyclopedia Britannica*, 2011: Hinduism). The *Mahabharata* relays "the battle between the five sons of Pandu and the sons of Pandu's brother." The book is often referred to as the fifth Veda because of its heavy focus on dharma, "the religious and moral law of Hinduism" (*Encyclopedia Britannica*, 2011: Hinduism). The *Bhagavad Ghita* is an extremely popular epic tale in the *Mahabharata*, highlighting "the three dominant trends of [Hinduism]: dharma-based householder life; enlightenment-based renunciation; and devotion-based theism" (*Encyclopedia Britannica*, 2011: Hinduism). Dwarka and Puri are dedicated to Krishna and Krishna's family and kingdom (*Encyclopedia Britannica*, 2011: Hinduism). Rameswaram is special to both Shaivas and based on "theism" (*Encyclopedia Britannica*, 2011: Hinduism). Lastly, the Puranas function like an encyclopedia and discuss Hinduism's vast number of gods, saints, and heroes through myths, legends, and genealogies; this is frequently referred to as "the book of the common people" (*Encyclopedia Britannica*, 2011: Hinduism). While the religious texts of Hinduism lay out the framework of Hindu culture and beliefs, the various levels of enlightenment presented in the religious works were developed over a vast period of time. These popular texts will continue to stand as Hinduism's core of eternal natural law (Johnsen, 2009).

The expansion of Hinduism's core can be divided into four periods: the Vedic period; the Epic and Puranic period; the medieval period; and the modern period (Flood, 1996). The Vedic period lasted between 1500 and 500 bce and is believed to be the birth of the Vedas and the preliminary rituals and texts connected to the dharma (Flood, 1996). The Epic and Puranic period occurred between 500 bce and 500 ce and is believed to be the formation of the four major sects of Hinduism and the Mahabharata and the Ramayana (Flood, 1996). The medieval period lasted between 500 ce and 1500 ce. It is thought to be the period of the joining of Hinduism and its primary language, Sanskrit (Flood, 1996). The modern period, which dates from 1500 to the present, represents the growth of Hinduism into the major world religion that is practiced today and the further division of sects in the major branches of the religion.

Beyond the development of the sects and sacred texts of Hinduism, many sacred places have arisen over the religion's vast existence. The sacred places are associated with gods and goddesses, and these are typically places where individuals can gain close connections to supernatural beings. The central sacred locations of Hinduism are "Benares, Mathura, Dwaraka, Puri, Rameswaram, Gaya, Ujjain, and Haridwar" (*Encyclopedia Britannica*, 2011: Hinduism). Consisting of "over two thousand temples and half a million idols," Benares is arguably the most sacred city of Hinduism. In many quarters, the city is referred to as Shiva because most of the temples are devoted to Shiva and his family (*Encyclopedia Britannica*, 2011: Hinduism). Mathura is Vayishnavas, the battleground between Rama and Lanka. Gaya is located on the Ganges River, and it is a special place for funerals. The souls that are released at this point are believed to have reached deliverance. Ujjain contains temples for Ganesh, and Haridwar is considered the "gateway of Ganga" (*Encyclopedia Britannica*, 2011: Hinduism).

Each of these places is of great importance to Hindus, their practices, and their texts. Hindus travel to these sacred places in hopes of achieving high personal stages of enlightenment and in order to conduct traditional rituals and make large sacrifices to the gods.

The current Status of Hinduism in Global Religious Space credits the religion with 950 million followers and 14 percent of the world population—as such, it is considered the third largest religion of the world. However, its global spread is quite limited, with about 80 percent of Hindus living in India alone. In recent years, population explosions in India have led to the high emigration of Hindu devotees to countries like Nepal, Bali, Malaysia, Indonesia, and Bangladesh, thus enhancing the regional spread of the religion. Apart from this concentration of followers in the Asian region, Hinduism has been making inroads into other parts of the world, such as the United States, Canada, Great Britain, and even some parts of Africa (Johnson, 2009).

REVIEW QUESTIONS

1. With a background description of the birth and life of Buddha, highlight and discuss the main doctrines of Buddhism.
2. What would you consider the factors responsible for the early spread of Buddhism?
3. Highlight and discuss the main similarities and differences among the three traditions of Buddhism.
4. How much did the personal lifestyle of Confucius shape the beliefs of Confucianism?
5. Is it completely justified to regard Confucianism as just a "catalog" of moral guidance?
6. Hinduism has no specific founder. How then can we account for its origin?

7. How is the caste system justified from the perspective of the social doctrine of Hinduism?
8. Highlight and discuss elements of the Hindu central doctrine you consider spiritually revealing.

Bibliography and Further Reading

Agnivesh, Swami. 2003. *Religion, Spirituality, and Social Action: New Agenda for Humanity*. New Delhi: Hope India Publication.

Batchelor, Martine and Kerry Brown, eds. 1992. *Buddhism and Ecology*. Worldwide Fund for Nature.

Beyer, Peter. 2006. *Religions in Global Society*. US: Taylor and Francis.

Carter, John Ross and Mahinda Palihawadna (trans.). 2000. *The Dhammappada: The Sayings of Buddha*. Oxford: Oxford University Press.

Chapple, Christopher Key and Mary Evelyn Tucker, eds. 2000. *Hinduism and Ecology*. Cambridge, MA: Harvard University Press.

Coleman, James William. 2002. *The New Buddhism: The Western Transformation of an Ancient Tradition*. US: Oxford University Press.

Conze, Edward et al. (trans.). 1995. *Buddhist Texts through the Ages*. Oxford: Oneworld Publications.

Elmore, Wilber T. 2003. *Dravidian Gods in Modern Hinduism*. Whitefish: Kessinger Publishing.

Eppsteiner, Fred, ed. 1988. *The Path of Compassion: Writings on Socially Engaged Buddhism*. California: Parallax Press.

Flood, Gavin D. 1996. *An Introduction to Hinduism*. UK: Cambridge University Press.

Groner, Paul. 1993. *A History of Indian Buddhism*. Delhi: Motilal Banarsidass Publishers.

Gross, Rita M. 1993. *Buddhism after Patriarchy*. Albany: State University of New York.

Habito, Ruben. 2005. *Experiencing Buddhism: Ways of Wisdom and Compassion*. Maryknoll, NY: Orbis Books.

Johnsen, Linda. 2009. *The Complete Idiot's Guide to Hinduism*. New York: Penguin Press.

Kagyu Office of His Holiness the 17th Gyalwang Karmapa. 2011. *Buddhism*. India: Kagyu Office.

Klostermaier, Klaus K. 2007. *A Survey of Hinduism*. Albany: State University of New York Press.

Kohn, Livia. 1993. *The Taoist Experience*. Albany: State University of New York.

Macmillan. 2008. *Buddhist. Encyclopedia of Religion*. New York.

Nattier, Jan. 2003. *A Few Goodmen: The Bodhisattva Path according to the Inquiry of Ugra*. Princeton: Princeton University Press.

Hoobler, Thomas and Dorothy Hoobler. 1993. *Confucianism*. New York: Facts On File.

Lopez, Donald S. Jr., ed. 1996. *Religion of China in Practice*. Princeton, NJ: Princeton University Press.

_____. 1995. *Religions of India in Practice*. Princeton, NJ: Princeton University Press.

_____. 1995. *Buddhism in Practice*. Princeton. NJ: Princeton University Press.

Mitchell, Donald W. 2002. *Buddhism: Introducing the Buddhist Experience*. New York and Oxford: Oxford University Press.

O'Donnell, Kevin. 2007. *Inside World Religions: An Illustrated Guide*. Minneapolis: Fortress.

Oldstone-Moore, Jennifer. 2002. *Confucianism: Origins, Beliefs, Practices, Holy Texts and Sacred Places*. New York: Oxford University Press.